HOW TO TUNE & MODIFY
FORD
FUEL INJECTION

Ben Watson

Motorbooks International
Publishers & Wholesalers ®

First published in 1992 by Motorbooks International Publishers & Wholesalers, PO Box 2, 729 Prospect Avenue, Osceola, WI 54020 USA

Motorbooks International is a certified trademark, registered with the United States Patent Office

The information in this book is true and complete to the best of our knowledge. All recommendations are made without any guarantee on the part of the author or Publisher, who also disclaim any liability incurred in connection with the use of this data or specific details

We recognize that some words, model names and designations, for example, mentioned herein are the property of the trademark holder. We use them for identification purposes only. This is not an official publication

Motorbooks International books are also available at discounts in bulk quantity for industrial or sales-promotional use. For details write to Special Sales Manager at the Publisher's address

·Library of Congress Cataloging-in-Publication Data
Watson, Ben.
    How to tune and modify Ford fuel injection / Ben Watson.
        p.   cm.—(Motorbooks International powerpro series)
    Includes bibliographical references and index.
    ISBN 0-87938-621-5
    1. Ford automobile—Motors—Fuel injection systems—Maintenance and repair.   2. Ford automobile—Motors—Modification.   I. Title. II. Series.
TL214.F78W38   1992
629.25′3—dc20   92-19206
                                        CIP

On the front cover: A 1988 Mustang 5.0 Liter shows off its EEC IV-equipped engine. *Mike and Denise Mueller*

Printed and bound in the United States of America

Contents

Introduction   4

1 The History of Fuel Injection   5

2 A Brief Overview of Electronics   7

3 Tools   18

4 Tuning the Fuel-injected Engine   22

5 Automotive Emissions   30

6 EEC III   36

7 EEC IV Components and Operation   43

8 EEC IV Onboard Diagnostics   71

9 Troubleshooting by Symptom   115

10 Performance Modifications   148

11 Legalities of Engine Modification   158

Appendices

Resources   159

Glossary   159

Index   160

Introduction

Beginning in the 1960s and continuing through the 1970s, the automotive industry was faced with new, ever-complicating issues: safety, increasing labor costs, foreign competition, and government- and consumer-mandated mileage requirements and emissions. One result of this mix of demands was a series of fuel and ignition systems that did not work out well. Ford Motor Company began marketing cars with computer-based fuel and ignition control systems intended to meet mileage and emission regulations during the last half of the 1970s.

To the student of the automotive art, it appears that Ford was going off in several directions at the same time during this period. At midyear 1978, Ford introduced the Electronic Engine Control Generation I (EEC I) system on the 5.0-liter Lincoln Versailles. In 1979, they continued EEC I for forty-nine states and introduced EEC II for California. In 1980, EEC III was introduced. Up to EEC III, all the Ford engine control systems had been carbureted. Although many EEC III cars were also carbureted, the EEC III system saw the first mass production use of fuel injection for Ford. In 1984, Ford introduced the EEC IV system, mostly fuel injected and with an onboard self-diagnostic system that would please NASA. The EEC IV system ushered in a new era in engine control.

This book will cover the fuel injection versions of the EEC III and EEC IV systems: their components, their function, and their troubleshooting. The beauty of the EEC III system and especially the EEC IV system is their friendliness toward the mechanic and their lack of dependence on complicated and expensive test equipment. No other North American manufacturer has made its fuel injection and engine control system easier to understand and repair.

This book will be divided into three major sections:
Background and basics (chapters 1 to 5)
Components and operation (chapters 6 and 7)
Troubleshooting, repair, and modifications (chapters 8 to 11)
I strongly advise reading and studying the first two sections before attempting the third. Unlike troubleshooting Chevrolet or Chrysler fuel injection systems, which lend themselves to spot testing, troubleshooting the Ford systems requires a holistic understanding of the engine controls.

1

The History of Fuel Injection

The history of fuel injection dates back to the nineteenth century. Both N. A. Otto and J. J. E. Lenoir displayed internal-combustion engines at the 1867 Paris World's Fair. In 1875, Wilhelm Maybach of Deutz first converted a gas engine to run on gasoline. This engine used a carburetor that featured a wick suspended across the flow of incoming air. The ends of the wick were submerged in gasoline held in a fuel bowl below the wick. When the engine was started, the incoming air would pass across the wick, evaporate the gasoline, and carry the fuel vapors up into the engine to be burned.

By the turn of the century, Maybach, Carl Benz, and others had evolved carburetor technology to a high level. The dependable float-level-controlled spray jet carburetor had been developed.

As early as 1883, alongside those working on the carburetor, others were experimenting with crude fuel injection. Edward Butler, Deutz, and others developed crude fuel injection systems.

Gasoline fuel injection really came into its own through aviation. From the beginning, fuel injection played a major role in the development of practical aviation. In 1903, the Wright Flier used a 28 horsepower fuel-injected engine. Throughout Europe before World War I, the aviation industry saw the obvious advantages that fuel injection afforded. Carburetors on aircraft are prone to icing during altitude changes, limiting available power; fuel injection is not. Carburetor float bowls are prone to spillage and fires during anything other than normal, "level," controlled flight; fuel injection is not. World War I brought with it an emphasis on expediency and development costs, however. Carburetor development pressed on, and fuel injection was placed on a back burner.

The postwar prosperity of the 1920s saw a mild renewed interest in the development of fuel injection. In the mid-1920s, Stromberg introduced a floatless carburetor for aircraft applications that is the predecessor of today's throttle body injection systems.

The military build-up that began in pre-Nazi Germany brought Bosch into the evolution of gas-oline fuel injection for aviation. These early Bosch systems featured direct injection, which sprays the fuel under high pressure directly into the combustion chamber in the same way as a diesel injection system does. In fact, the injection pump Bosch used for these systems was a modified diesel injection pump.

During World War II, fuel injection dominated the skies in all theaters. Late in the war, Continental used a fuel injection system designed by the SU Carburetter company of England. It was built in the United States by Simmonds Aerocessories on the air-cooled engine Simmonds developed for use in the Patton tank. In 1940, Ottavio Fuscaldo became the first to incorporate an electrical solenoid for controlling fuel flow into the engine. This started the automotive industry down the path toward modern electronic fuel injection.

After World War II, fuel injection hit the ground. With the research and development monies in the aircraft industry shifted away from fuel injection and toward jet engines, wartime improvements seemed destined for oblivion. Then, in 1949, a car equipped with a fuel-injected Offenhauser was entered at the Indianapolis 500. The injection system was designed by Stuart Hilborn and featured indirect injection, with which the fuel is injected into the intake manifold just ahead of the intake valve. It was like having a throttle body injection system for each cylinder. It could also be compared to Bosch's K-Jetronic system—found in the Volkswagen (VW) Rabbit, Audi 5000, Volvo, and so on—in that the fuel was not pulsed into the intake port but rather sprayed continuously, which earned it the nickname constant-flow injection.

In 1957, Chevrolet introduced its first fuel-injected engine for mass production in the Corvette. Borrowing heavily from the Hilborn design, the Rochester Ramjet fuel injection system was used by Chevrolet in 1957 and 1958 and by Pontiac in the 1957 Bonneville. The Ramjet system used a high-pressure pump to move fuel from the tank to the injectors. The injectors sprayed fuel ahead of the intake valve continuously. A control diaphragm monitored the intake manifold pressure and engine load. This diaphragm was in turn connected to a lever that controlled the position of a plunger that operated a valve. A change in the position of the plunger-operated valve changed the amount of fuel diverted back to the pump reservoir and away from the injectors. This altered the air-fuel ratio to meet the needs of the engine.

This system suffered from a lack of understanding by those responsible for its day-to-day maintenance. As a result, both Chevrolet and Pontiac dropped it from their list of options in 1959.

Seeing development at the same time as the Ramjet system were the electronic fuel injection (EFI) systems destined for mass production. Design work began for these systems in 1952 at the Eclipse Machine Division of Bendix Corporation, and in 1961, a blanket patent was issued on the Bendix Electrojector system. Almost simultaneously with the issue of the patent, EFI was declared a dead-end project by Bendix management and was shelved.

Though the Electrojector system itself never made it into mass production, it was the predecessor of virtually all modern fuel injection systems. When Bendix put EFI aside in 1961, interest waned until 1966, when the company began to grant patent licenses to Bosch. In 1968, VW introduced the Bosch D-Jetronic system into the U.S. market on its Type 3 models.

The D-Jetronic system was used on a variety of European applications—including those of SAAB, Volvo, and Mercedes—through the early 1970s. Although those confronted with servicing the system did not fully understand how it worked, the D-Jetronic persisted and the service and diagnostic procedures of EFI were introduced to the U.S. mechanic. In spite of its extensive use on European imports, this system was largely seen by the auto repair industry as a fluke, a one-shot deal.

Cadillac introduced the first mass-produced domestic EFI system in September 1975. It was standard equipment on the 1976 model Cadillac Seville. This system was developed through a cooperative effort between Bendix, Bosch, and General Motors (GM). It bore a striking resemblance to the Bosch D-Jetronic system. By this time, systematized troubleshooting methods had been developed to aid in the servicing and repair of fuel injection.

The Cadillac-Bendix system was used until the introduction of the next technological improvement of fuel injection, the digital computer. Cadillac introduced its Digital Fuel Injection system in 1980. For simplicity, this was a two-injector throttle body injection system.

For Bendix, the idea for digital control of fuel injection dated back to patents it filed for in 1970, 1971, and 1973. The benefits of the digital computer include the more accurate control of the injectors plus the ability of the computer to control a wide variety of engine support systems. With the use of a digital computer, ignition timing, air pump operations, torque converter clutch functions, and a wide variety of emission-related items could all be controlled by a single compact control module.

In 1965, Hilborn fuel injection was fitted to the Ford four-cam V-8 engine developed for the Indy cars. A four-cylinder, sixteen-valve Lotus engine equipped with Lucas fuel injection was used in a few European Ford Escorts during the 1970 model year. It was not until 1983 that any Ford division decided to use fuel injection in a serious manner. That year, European Ford began to use the Bosch K-Jetronic system, which had been widely used by northern European manufacturers since the early 1970s.

Meanwhile, beginning in 1978, North American Ford went through three generations of electronically controlled carburetors. The EEC I, EEC II, and EEC III systems were intended to meet the ever-tightening emission standards of the late 1970s and early 1980s. From an outsider's perspective, either Ford, along with its North American competitors, had a fear of marketing fuel-injected cars or they were all holding off in order to perfect their systems.

In 1980, Ford introduced its high-pressure centralized fuel injection (CFI) on the EEC III–equipped 5.0-liter Versailles. In 1981, the usage was expanded to the LTD and Marquis. The 1983 model year saw the introduction of multipoint injection (MPI) on the 1.6-liter applications. With the introduction of the EEC IV system during the 1984 model year, carburetion became the exception rather than the rule for Ford. As we entered the 1990s, the only Fords still equipped with carburetors were special equipment packages, such as police application and towing packages.

2

A Brief Overview of Electronics

In the early 1980s, most professional technicians thought electronics would disappear if they buried their head in the sand long enough. A lot of this attitude can be blamed on members of the automotive training profession. Either they felt the need to impress their students with the mystery of electronics or they lacked the background to simplify the subject.

This chapter will not address quantum mechanics, electron flow, or unified field theory. On the contrary, it will stick to the fundamentals of automotive electronics, addressing only the topics that are necessary to understand, troubleshoot, and make repairs on modern Ford fuel injection.

To work on these systems effectively, you will need to familiarize yourself with the following:
Basic units of measurement
Ohm's law
Kirchhoff's laws
Waveforms
Monitored parameters
Controlled functions
Basic electronic devices

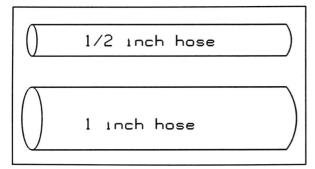

Amperage is a measurement of the flow rate of electricity. At least part of what controls this flow rate is the size and resistance of the conductor. Large current flows require large conductors. The current flowing through the electronic sensors of the injection system is extremely small, whereas the current flowing through the actuators is larger and will require larger wires.

Radio frequencies and induction
Microprocessors
Eleven types of circuits

Basic Units of Measurement

Volts

Volts are measures of electrical pressure, or voltage. Voltage is also known as electromotive force. It has often been compared to pressure in a water system. The accurate measurement of voltage is critical to troubleshooting modern electronic fuel injection. The computer gathers information about the functioning of the engine by measuring voltages and changes in voltages.

Amps

Amperes (amps) are measures of the flow rate, or amperage, of electricity. Like gallons per second in a pressurized water system, they denote the volume of electricity passing a given point.

Watts

Watts are measures of power, or wattage. Like horsepower, they indicate the amount of energy being expended by an electrical circuit. As a measurement of power, wattage is sometimes used in place of horsepower. A total of 746 watts are in 1hp. Mathematically, watts equals volts times amps.

Ohms

Ohms are not so much measures of electricity as measures of a quality of a conductor. They refer to resistance to current flow, or ohmage.

In the past, ohmage was an important consideration when a circuit did not work. We were looking for a point in the circuit we were testing where the resistance was too high. For instance, if we were dealing with a starter that had a slow cranking speed, the possibilities would include a bad starter, a weak battery, or high resistance in the power or ground cables. For circuits like this—which most car owners have been exposed to—the tiniest bit of resistance will have a major effect on circuit operation. For example, a typical cranking voltage is in the vicinity

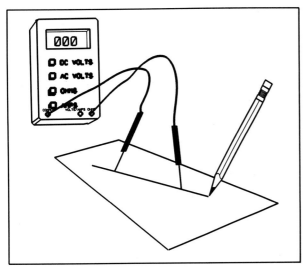

Resistance is the measurement of a substance's tendency to reduce or restrict the flow of electrical current. Resistance can be observed by drawing a pencil line on a piece of paper. Place the red lead of an ohmmeter at one end of the line. Place the black lead close to the red lead. Slowly slide the black lead along the pencil line. The resistance will increase.

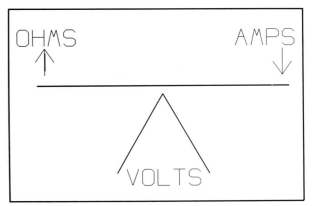

Ohm's law states that when the resistance increases in a circuit, the current flow decreases. When the resistance decreases, the current flow increases. This principle is used, among other things, to limit the amount of current that can flow out of the computer. This protects the computer.

of 10 volts. For a small V-8, a typical current flow through the starter circuit is around 200 amps. Just 0.01 ohm of resistance can cause a reduction in available voltage to the starter of 2 volts. This is a significant effect from a relatively insignificant amount of resistance. The effect is so significant because of the high current flow in the circuit.

As shown by this example, in the past, we were primarily concerned with looking for high-resistance problems in the range of hundredths of an ohm to a dozen or so ohms. Today, we might be looking for a problem in an electronic fuel injection circuit where the normal resistance is several hundred ohms to several thousand ohms. For some of these circuits, hundreds of ohms may make little or no difference in their functioning. For other circuits, such as those that measure temperature, resistance is critical.

Ohm's Law

If you ever get an opportunity to teach at a vocational school, to mechanics who have been working in the field for several years, and if you like to hear deep, heartfelt groans, bring up the subject of Ohm's law.

Ohm's law (named after Georg S. Ohm) says volts, amps, and ohms are related. The relationship is that when the resistance in a circuit changes but we keep the voltage the same at the source, then the current flow will change. Increase the resistance (ohms), and the current flow will decrease; decrease the resistance, and the current flow will increase.

Computers do not gather data or control actuators through changes in current flow. For the real

world of troubleshooting electronics in fuel-injected cars, Ohm's law is not of much use to us—except that if the resistance in the wiring harness of a circuit, particularly an actuator circuit, drops to 0, you will probably damage the electronic control assembly (ECA).

Kirchhoff's Laws

Everybody talks about ohms, but really it is Gustav Robert Kirchhoff who deserves a round of applause for helping us gather engine data and troubleshoot onboard computer systems. Kirchhoff gave us two basic laws:
1. The sum of the voltage drops in a series circuit is always equal to source voltage.
2. The algebraic sum of the current flowing toward a single point is 0.

Automotive computer diagnosticians do not have a lot of direct use for the second law, but they have a great deal of use for the first. A voltage drop occurs as a current flows through a resistance. Using the water system analogy again, when a current of water being moved by a pressure passes through a restriction, the water pressure on the downstream side of the restriction will be less than the pressure on the upstream side of the restriction. As an electrical current flows through a resistor, the voltage (pressure) on the outbound side will be less than the voltage on the inbound side.

Voltage drop measurements are not the only data on engine operating parameters gathered by the ECA, but they are a primary diagnostic tool.

Waveforms

When voltage changes in a regular or rhythmic fashion, it is called a waveform. The only way to see waveforms is with an oscilloscope. We deal with basically two types of waveform patterns in automotive electronics: sine waves and square waves.

Sine Wave

The sine wave is produced as a voltage slowly builds to a peak, then slowly decreases to a valley or trough. Components like alternators and some ignition pickup coils produce a sine wave. We seldom need to measure any part of the sine wave other than to determine that it is present.

Square Wave

The square wave is a little more complex than the sine wave. It is an on-off pulse or signal created to monitor or control. The voltage does not slowly build and decrease; it is either high or low. This waveform is created by such things as the manifold absolute

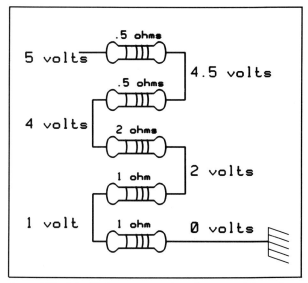

One of Kirchhoff's laws states that the sum of the voltage drops in a series circuit equals the source voltage. As a current flows through a series of resistances, the voltage drops. When the current passes the last resistance, the voltage is 0. The sum of all the voltage drops is the source voltage.

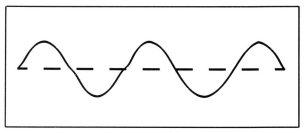

A sine wave is a voltage that slowly builds to a maximum level, reaches a peak, then slowly drops to a minimum. Although sine waves are most often associated with AC, a sine wave can be DC. Many of the fuel injection sensors produce a slowly rising and dropping voltage. Among these are the TP sensor and the EVP sensor. Although these sensors do not produce a classic sine wave, their slowly changing voltage is sinusoidal.

pressure (MAP) sensor and the Hall effect sensor, which Ford calls a profile ignition pickup (PIP) sensor. These sensors are monitored by the ECA to control the opening and closing of injectors and the switching on and off of the ignition coil.

The square wave has four characteristics that you may need to measure:
Amplitude
Frequency
Duty cycle
Pulse width
Chapter 3 provides techniques for measuring these characteristics with the simplest tools possible.

Amplitude

Amplitude is the amount of voltage change that occurs as the current flowing through a circuit is switched on and off. This is a measurement you will seldom take. Amplitude measurements cannot be accurately taken without an oscilloscope.

Frequency

Frequency is the number of complete on-off cycles that occur in a given time frame. The most common unit of measurement for frequency is hertz. A frequency of 10 hertz means ten complete ons and ten complete offs are occurring each second. Several Ford fuel injection sensors, including the crank sensors on cars equipped with a distributorless ignition system (DIS) and the MAP sensor, produce a variable frequency square wave.

Duty Cycle

Duty cycle is a difficult concept to appreciate. It is the ratio of the time current is flowing through the circuit and the time current is not flowing through the circuit, measured as a percentage. This concept is not new to the automobile engine. For decades, we have measured the relationship between the time the current is flowing through the ignition coil and the time it is not. We called this relationship dwell. Dwell is nothing more than the duty cycle of the primary ignition circuit measured in degrees of rotation.

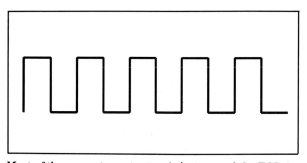

Most of the computer outputs—injectors and the EGR for instance—are controlled by controlling the characteristics of a square wave. A square wave is a voltage that suddenly rises to a peak, then just as suddenly drops to a minimum. In addition to the control of sensors, the MAP sensor also produces a square wave.

Pulse Width

Pulse width is the length of time—measured in seconds, minutes, hours, or days—that an actuator is energized. The measurement of pulse width is almost exclusively reserved for injector on-time, for which the unit of measurement is milliseconds.

Monitored Parameters

Monitored parameters is a blanket term for computer inputs. On late-model Ford fuel injection, these would include the following:
Revolutions per minute (rpm)
Coolant temperature
Air temperature (not on all applications)
Mass airflow
Manifold pressure (not on all applications)
Barometric pressure (not on all applications)
Exhaust oxygen
Exhaust gas recirculation (EGR) function
Throttle position
Others, depending on the application

The monitoring of the various functions around the car usually happens at 5 volts, which is used as a reference voltage (VREF). When the ECA sees 5 volts from one of its sensors, it interprets that to mean whatever is being monitored by that circuit is happening to its fullest.

Controlled Functions

Functions and operations around the car are controlled by the computer with solenoid-operated valves. These valves can control vacuum, fuel, EGR, or airflow. Two types of solenoid-operated valves are used to control these functions: normally open valves and normally closed valves.

Normally open valves allow vacuum—or whatever is being controlled—to flow through them when current is not flowing through the solenoid. Typically, a normally open valve is used either where the device needs to receive vacuum—or whatever is being sup-

plied—during most of the time of vehicle operation or when the limp-home mode requires vacuum to be applied.

A normally closed valve does not allow vacuum—or fuel or air or EGR—to flow when current is not flowing through the solenoid. The best example of this is the injector itself. When the solenoid does not have current flowing through it, the valve is closed, keeping fuel from flowing through the injector. The normally closed valve is used when the normal state for a system during driving is not to receive vacuum—or fuel or whatever. As odd as it may sound, the fuel injector is not usually open when driving. The duty cycle of the injector varies between 1 percent and 20 percent, depending on driving conditions. This means that although the valve is opening and closing continuously while driving, it spends most of its time closed. The normally closed valve is also used where the limp-home mode for a given function should not allow the flow of vacuum—or fuel or EGR or air.

Solenoid-operated valves are not the only means for controlling functions. The ECA will control the ignition system and other electrical devices directly.

The following functions are among those controlled by the ECA. Note that not all of these functions will be controlled by the ECA in the car you are working on.
Canister purge (CANP) solenoid
Air management (AM) (air pump) system
EGR operation
EGR position control
Lockup torque converter
Check engine (service engine soon) lamp
Fuel pump relay
Injectors

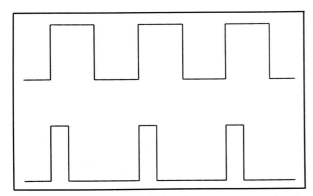

One important characteristic of a square wave in the control of computer outputs is duty cycle. If we were to observe a changing duty cycle on an oscilloscope, it would appear as a shift in the relationship of the high voltage and the low.

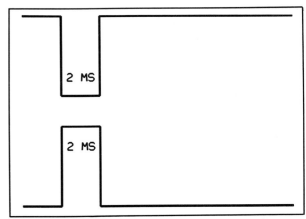

The length of time the injectors are open is called pulse width. The pulse width of the injectors is measured in milliseconds (thousandths of a second). If the computer provides a ground for the injectors, the waveform that will be seen on the oscilloscope will look like the top one. If the computer provides a voltage to the injectors to open them, the waveform will look like the bottom one.

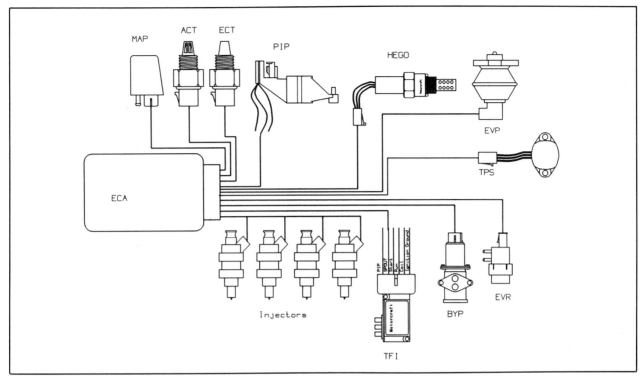

This drawing shows the monitoring devices on top. The monitored devices common to almost all the Ford fuel-injected cars are the MAP, ACT, ECT, PIP, EGO, and EVP sensors. The controlled systems common to almost all Ford fuel-injected cars are the injector or injectors, ignition module, idle speed, and EGR system.

Air conditioner (A/C) compressor clutch (ACC)
Ignition timing
Others

Basic Electronic Devices

It will be helpful as you progress through this book to become familiar with the electronic basis for many of the sensing devices that are used. Since this book is not intended to be a course in electronics, each item will be covered only with respect to the job it performs in a fuel injection system.

Resistor

A resistor is an electronic device used to limit current flow and reduce voltage within a series circuit. Two types are in common automotive use today. The first is the wire-wound resistor, which is commonly found in high-current uses such as that of the ballast resistor in the old point-condenser ignition system. The other type is the carbon resistor, which is used in low-current-flow circuits such as the ECA.

One important use of the resistor in the ECA is to limit current flow into and through the ECA. Most of the output or driver circuits of the ECA have a resistor in series with the output to prevent the driver circuit from overloading. Should the wire from the ECA to the actuator become grounded or shorted-to-voltage, it could damage the ECA.

Thermistor

The thermistor is a resistor used to monitor temperature. The type that Ford uses is called a negative temperature coefficient thermistor. As the temperature of what is being measured increases, the resistance drops. At −40 degrees Fahrenheit, this device will have 248,000 ohms; as the temperature it is being exposed to increases, the resistance slowly drops to about 1,800 ohms at 210 degrees Fahrenheit.

Thermistors are used to measure the temperature of the coolant and intake air on most Ford fuel injection applications. The mass airflow (MAF) sensor uses a thermistor to measure the temperature of the air passing through it to help measure the air mass.

Potentiometer

A potentiometer is a resistor that utilizes a metal wiper that moves back and forth across a carbon element. It is used to sense or detect the physical location of a moving device. A potentiometer has three connectors: one connected to the 5-volt reference, the second connected to ground through the ECA, and the third connected to the input section of the ECA to detect the position of what is being measured as a varying voltage.

Potentiometers are used to measure throttle position and in some cases EGR position.

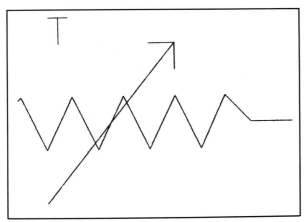

The thermistor is a resistor that changes resistance as the temperature changes. Although all resistors do this, the thermistor is designed for very large changes to be caused by small changes in temperature. The two types of thermistors are the positive temperature coefficient (PTC) and the negative temperature coefficient (NTC). With the PTC thermistor, resistance increases as the temperature increases. With the NTC thermistor, resistance decreases as the temperature increases. The thermistor used by Ford in its fuel injection systems is the NTC.

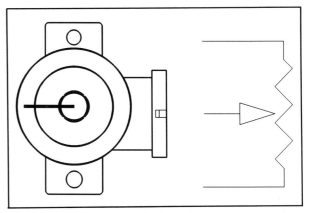

The potentiometer is used when the computer needs to know the precise position of a device. Ford uses two types. The rotary potentiometer is used to indicate the position of components that rotate, such as the throttle shaft. The linear potentiometer is used to indicate the position of a component that moves back and forth, such as an EGR valve diaphragm.

Strain Gauge

The strain gauge is the principal component in Ford's pressure feedback EGR (PFE) sensor. A strain gauge consists of a silicone chip approximately 3 millimeters (mm) square and 250 microns thick (1 micron equals 1 millionth of a meter). The center of the square is only about 25 microns thick to form a diaphragm. The edges of the chip are sealed to a Pyrex plate with a vacuum between the chip and the plate. A set of four resistors around the edges of the plate forms a Wheatstone Bridge. These resistors are sensitive to being stretched by the flexing of the silicone chip. As pressure on one side of the chip works against the vacuum on the other side of the chip, the resistors are stretched and contracted, causing their resistance to change. The strain gauge in the PFE has a 5-volt reference, a ground, and a wire that carries pressure information as a variable voltage to the ECA.

Diode

Two important types of diodes are used in automotive electronics: the light-emitting diode (LED) and the photodiode. In automotive electronics, when we speak of diodes, we normally think of the devices in the alternator that convert alternating current (AC) voltage into direct current (DC). We call them one-way electronic valves. For our purposes, it might be more appropriate to think of these diodes as a light bulb and a light-sensitive switch, respectively.

The LED we will most often refer to in this book produces infrared (invisible) light when current is flowing through it. Pairing this with an infrared

A strain gauge is a device that electronically measures pressure. Although this device is commonly used by other manufacturers, its use is limited on Ford products. This PFE sensor is used to detect the amount of EGR opening on many late-model EEC IV injection systems.

photodiode, which allows current to flow through it when infrared light falls on it, forms a sensor capable of detecting the presence of an opaque object between the two diodes. Such a sensor can be used to detect the rotation of a shaft or cable. Ford uses a sensor like this in some of its digital instrument panels to detect vehicle speed.

Transistor

Dealing with automotive fuel injection systems, we do not have to be concerned with the functioning or testing of transistors, which could be called electronic relays. Transistors are used as output, or controlled device, drivers by the ECA.

Transistors have three connectors: the base, the collector, and the emitter. Voltage applied to the base can be compared to voltage applied to the pull-down winding of a standard electromechanical relay. The collector and emitter form the connections for the switch, which connects power to the controlled device.

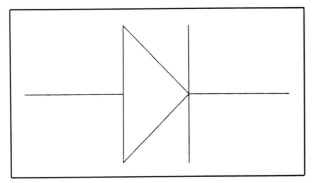

The diode is often called a one-way electronic valve. It is used in electronic systems to control the direction of current flow, to reduce voltage spikes created by the collapse of magnetic fields, and to convert AC voltage into DC voltage. Special diodes, called LED's, are also used in many electronic systems.

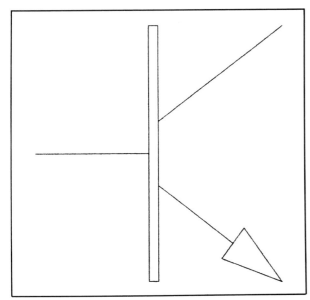

Transistors play a crucial role in today's electronic systems. Our most direct contact with them in fuel injection systems is when they are used as relays to control the activation of the computer outputs. In this role, they are called drivers. The transistor shown here is an NPN. The arrow represents the terminal of the transistor known as the emitter. The line forming a V with the emitter is called the collector. The broader line they each touch is called the base. When a voltage is applied to the base terminal of the NPN transistor, it connects the collector to the emitter and a current can flow.

Two types of driver transistors are used in automotive electronic systems. The first is called the NPN transistor. The NPN transistor will have the collector connected to the ground side of the controlled device; the other side of the controlled device will be connected to power. The emitter of the transistor is then connected to ground. When a high voltage—such as 5 volts—is applied to the base of the NPN transistor, the collector becomes connected to the emitter, grounding the controlled device.

The PNP transistor will have the plus side of the controlled device connected to the collector, with the emitter connected to power. The controlled device will be grounded to the engine block or to the back of the battery. When the base is grounded, the PNP transistor connects power from the emitter to the collector, which then applies power to the controlled device.

For most controlled devices in Ford's EFI system, the NPN transistor is used. Ford's preferred method of controlling the actuators of the engine is by grounding them through the ECA. This makes the NPN transistor the natural choice as a controlling device.

Radio Frequencies and Induction

The spark ignition is a hostile environment for transistor-based systems to operate around. Radio frequencies are generated anywhere a spark jumps an air gap. In an automobile, sparks jump in the distributor cap and across the spark plugs. These sparks can interfere with the proper operation of transistors.

Automobiles also have sources of induced voltages, such as secondary ignition and the alternator. These induced voltages can activate a controlled device at the wrong time. The NPN transistor circuit is chosen to drive most actuators because it has the

Inside the computer—this is the EEC IV ECA—are many integrated circuits and microprocessors. Each of the larger chips seen here may contain thousands of transistors, resistors, and diodes.

actuators powered all the time and grounded by the ECA. It is impossible for a ground to be induced in a circuit that is continuously powered; therefore, it is unlikely that the controlled device will be falsely energized.

Microprocessors

The heart of the ECA is three microprocessors used for memory storage and decision making: read-only memory (ROM), programmable read-only memory (PROM), and random-access memory (RAM).

Read-Only Memory

The ROM contains the basic program of the ECA. It is the part that says, "When I see this happen, I have to make that happen." The ROM features a nonvolatile memory; this means that when power is taken away from the ROM, it retains its programming and memory.

Programmable Read-Only Memory

The PROM, also known as a calibration unit, is the fine-tuning microprocessor. Like the ROM, it is also nonvolatile. This chip contains information about the specific car in which the ECA is installed, like the following:

Size
Weight class
Wind drag
Rolling resistance
Engine size
Final drive ratio
Transmission type
Camshaft design
Emission control devices

Information from the PROM is used by the ROM to help it make decisions. When engine modifications are made on a late-model fuel-injected Ford, the PROM should be replaced.

Random-Access Memory

The RAM is used by the ECA for the temporary storage of information or to perform mathematical computations. In addition, the ECA stores information about the air-fuel ratio history of the engine and faults that have been detected in the sensor and actuator circuits of the fuel injection system.

Eleven Types of Circuits

The good news about electronic fuel injection and engine control systems is that only eleven types of electronic circuits are used. Each of the sensor and actuator circuits will fit into one of these categories. Nine are sensor circuits; two are actuator circuits. Become familiar with these eleven circuits, and you will be familiar with automotive electronics.

Sensor Circuits

Switch-to-Voltage Circuit

The switch-to-voltage circuit is used where the ECA needs to sense when an event occurs. As an example, let's say that the ECA needs to know when the driver is sitting in the driver's seat. We put a switch in the seat, with one side always connected to power and the other connected to the computer. When the driver sits in the seat, the switch closes, allowing 12 volts to be connected to the computer. The computer knows that the event has occurred.

This circuit assumes that the switch used is a normally open switch. Another circuit that works the same way might use a normally closed switch. If a normally closed switch is used, then voltage will be applied to the computer until the event occurs. At that time, the switch will open, causing the voltage at the computer to drop low (to 0 volts), and the computer is made aware that the event has occurred. This type of circuit, though used extensively by some manufacturers, is seldom used by Ford.

Switch-to-Pull-Low Circuit

In the switch-to-pull-low circuit, the ECA applies a reference voltage—usually 5 volts—to one side of a switch through a current-limiting resistor. The other side of the switch is connected to ground. The computer monitors voltage on the circuit at the outbound side of the resistor. When the event occurs, the switch closes, grounding the outbound side of the current-limiting resistor and causing the voltage seen by the computer to drop to 0. The computer knows that the event has occurred.

As described, this circuit uses a normally open switch. It could also use a normally closed switch, so that when the event occurs, the voltage seen by the computer will rise.

Example: Brake pedal application sensor

Variable-Resistance-to-Pull-Low Circuit

The variable-resistance-to-pull-low circuit oper-

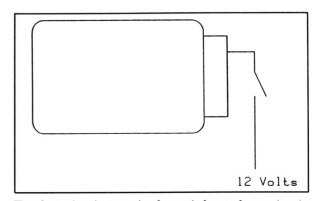

The first circuit type is the switch-to-voltage circuit. Twelve volts is connected to one terminal of a switch. This switch can be used to monitor events such as the application of vacuum to an EGR valve. The other terminal of the switch is connected to the computer (ECA). When the event being monitored by the switch occurs, the voltage at the ECA terminal rises. When the computer sees the voltage rise, it knows the event has occurred. The use of this type of circuit is rare.

ates much like the switch-to-pull-low circuit. In this circuit, however, the switch is replaced with a variable resistor, usually a thermistor. As an event occurs, such as an increase in engine temperature, the resistance in the resistor decreases, causing the voltage on the outbound side of the current-limiting resistor to decrease. The computer knows that the event is occurring.

Examples: Engine coolant temperature (ECT) sensor and air charge temperature (ACT) sensor

Variable-Resistance-to-Push-Up Circuit

The only difference between the variable-resistance-to-push-up circuit and the variable-resistance-to-pull-low circuit is that when the event occurs in the former, the resistance of the resistor increases, causing the voltage seen by the computer at the outbound side of the current-limiting resistor to increase. The computer then knows that the event is occurring.

Example: Knock sensor (KS)

Three-wire Variable Voltage Circuit

The three-wire variable voltage circuit has the computer supplying a reference voltage—usually 5 volts—and a ground to the sensor. A third wire carries information about the changing condition or position of something from the sensor to the computer.

Examples: Throttle position (TP) sensor, MAF sensor, and EGR valve position (EVP) sensor

DC Frequency Pulse Generator Circuit

The DC frequency pulse generator is usually an integrated circuit that is used to monitor the condition of something. Power—either 5 volts or battery voltage (VBAT)—and ground are fed into the sensor to power its circuitry. The sensor creates a square wave, the frequency of which varies as the condition being monitored varies. The voltage source to form the square wave can be the computer. This means that the sensor grounds and ungrounds the computer to create the pulse. The source can be the sensor, which means that the computer turns the voltage on and off to create the signal.

Example: MAP sensor

AC Rotational Pulse Generator Circuit

For those familiar with electronic ignition systems, the AC rotational pulse generator is an old friend. Commonly called a pickup coil, its more scientific name is variable reluctance transducer. This sensor consists of a permanent magnet, a coil of wire, and a rotating cog wheel. As one of the teeth of the rotating cog enters the magnetic field of the permanent magnet, it causes the field to distort across the coil of wire. This results in the induction of a voltage. As the tooth of the cog swings past the coil-magnet assembly, the magnetic field is distorted in the other direction. This causes a voltage to be induced in the opposite direction. The result of all of this is an AC voltage being generated as each of the cog teeth passes through the magnetic field.

The computer, being a digital device, has a little trouble dealing with this AC signal. As a result, before this signal can be put to use, the computer must convert it to a DC pulse.

This type of sensor is used to sense rotational speed.

Examples: EEC III distributor pickup coil and some vehicle speed sensors (VSS)

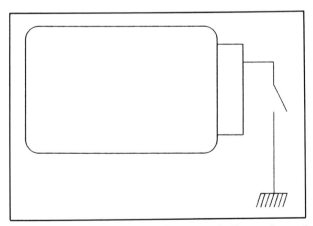

The switch-to-pull-low circuit has uses similar to those of the switch-to-voltage circuit. In this circuit, a low-voltage regulator—9 volts on the EEC III system and 5 volts on the EEC IV system—supplies a VREF through an internal resistor. When the switch is open, the voltage on one terminal of the switch will be the full VREF. The other terminal of the switch is connected to ground. When the switch closes, the VREF is grounded out. The computer sees 0 volts.

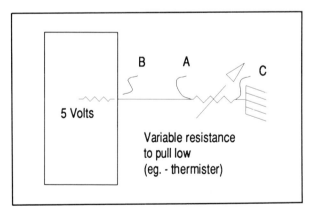

The variable resistance circuit is used to monitor events that change gradually. The most common of these is temperature. A resistor inside the computer causes a voltage drop on the wire between the computer and the sensor. As the resistance of the sensor changes, the voltage on the wire between the computer and the sensor changes. The circuit can be used either as described in this drawing, where the resistance decreases as the event occurs, or where the resistance increases with the event.

DC Rotational Pulse Generator Circuit

Two types of DC rotational pulse generators are used by Ford: the optical pulse generator and the Hall effect switch. Like the AC rotational pulse generators, they are used to monitor the rotational speed of some devices.

The optical pulse generator is used as a VSS on applications that have a speedometer cable. It uses an LED, whose light shines on a rotating shiny metal and reflects to a photodiode. The shiny metal has a notch, so that as it rotates, it will cause the photodiode to create a pulse that is directly proportional to the rotational speed of what is being monitored. This pulse is then sent to the computer.

The Hall effect switch consists of a permanent magnet that sits opposite a transistor. This transistor is extremely sensitive to magnetic fields. A set of ferrous metal blades rotates through the gap between the magnet and the transistor, causing the magnetic field to be alternately interrupted and not interrupted. The result is a pulse directly proportional to the speed of rotation.

Example: DIS crankshaft position sensor

Both the optical and Hall effect pulse generators use three wires. Two wires are used to supply either 5 volts or VBAT and a ground. The third wire carries the pulse to the computer.

Voltage Generator Circuit

The oxygen sensor is the only sensor that creates its own voltage. This device consists of a ceramic element made of zirconium dioxide, which will become conductive for oxygen ions when heated to about 600 degrees Fahrenheit. This element is shaped like a thimble. On both the outer and inner

surfaces of the thimble is a thin, gas permeable layer of platinum. A channel down the center of the sensor allows outside air, with a constant 21 percent oxygen content, to contact the layer of platinum on the inside of the thimble. The layer of platinum on the outside of the thimble is exposed to the exhaust gases. As the air-fuel ratio delivered to the engine varies, the oxygen content of the exhaust gases varies. A difference in oxygen content on the two sides of the ceramic thimble will cause a voltage to be generated.

The exhaust gas oxygen (EGO) sensor might be described as a chemical generator. When it is heated to a minimum of 600 degrees Fahrenheit, it will begin to produce a voltage ranging from 100 to 900 millivolts. Once the operational temperature is reached, the sensor will begin to respond to changes in the content of exhaust oxygen. When the oxygen content

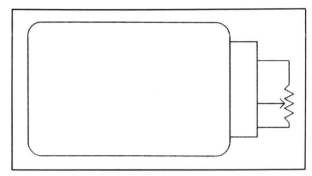

The three-wire variable voltage circuit has one wire that carries 5 volts to the sensor, a second wire that provides a ground, and a third wire that carries a variable voltage signal back to the computer. This type of circuit is typically used with a potentiometer. The signal wire will tell the computer about the position of an EGR valve or the amount of rotation on a throttle shaft. Similar circuits are used to indicate airflow or EGR flow.

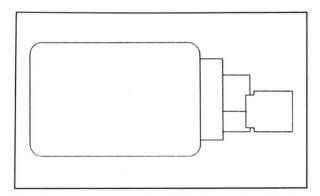

The frequency generator circuit has three wires. The best examples of this circuit on Ford applications are the MAP and BP sensors. One wire carries the power supply to the sensor; Ford uses a 5-volt power supply originating in the computer, whereas other manufacturers use a 12-volt power supply. The second wire provides a ground for the sensor. The third wire carries a square pulse with a variable frequency back to the computer. As the sensor detects changes, the frequency of the pulse changes. The frequency of the Ford MAP sensor varies from over 160 hertz KOEO to about 90 hertz on deceleration.

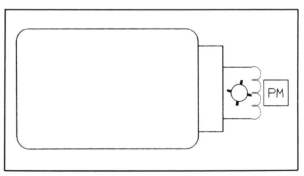

This sensor is the AC rotational pulse generator. This type of device dates from the earliest days of automobile electronics. Its purpose is to detect the rotational speed of a shaft, such as a distributor shaft. More familiar as the pickup coil, it has been used as the distributor reference sensor on many ignition systems, including the one used with the EEC III system. In the EEC IV system, it is used as a VSS.

of the exhaust is high, the ECA assumes that the engine is running lean. The design of the EGO sensor is such that it will produce a low voltage when the exhaust oxygen content is high. Oxygen content in the exhaust gases resulting from a lean combustion will result in a voltage of less than 450 millivolts being delivered to the ECA. When the exhaust gases result from a rich combustion, the EGO sensor voltage to the ECA will be greater than 450 millivolts. When the EGO sensor voltage is indicating a lean condition, the ECA will respond by enriching the mixture. When the EGO sensor voltage is high, the ECA will respond by leaning out the mixture. In this manner, the ECA adjusts for minor errors and variations from the rest of the input sensors and controls the air-fuel ratio at 14.7:1.

Actuator Circuits

Normally Grounded Circuit

In the normally grounded circuit, the negative side of the actuator is always connected to ground and the computer switches voltage to the device on and off to control it. Ford seldom uses this type of circuit.

With this circuit, it is possible for a voltage to be induced into the feed wire to the actuator from the computer. This could cause the actuator to energize when it should not. Furthermore, it is impossible for the computer to monitor for damage to the circuit when it is supplying the voltage. All the ECA knows for sure is that it sent voltage out; it has no idea if the voltage was received. Finally, if the computer sends voltage out along a wire and that wire becomes grounded, the computer driver circuit could be overloaded and damaged.

Normally Powered Circuit

The normally powered circuit is Ford's method of energizing its actuators. The actuator is connected

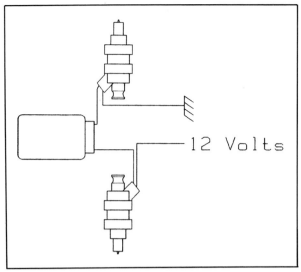

The computer can energize an actuator in two ways. In the normally grounded circuit, the actuator is connected to a chassis ground and the computer energizes the actuator by supplying power. In the normally powered circuit, the actuator is connected to a switched ignition voltage and the computer energizes the actuator by supplying ground.

to either battery power or switched ignition voltage all the time. The computer supplies the ground.

With this circuit, since the computer is not supplying power, a grounded wire might blow a fuse or melt a wire, but it will not destroy the computer. In addition, the computer is able to monitor the presence of 12 volts to the actuator, since it is supplying the ground; should anything happen to the actuator's power supply, the computer would know immediately. Finally, the actuator virtually could not be improperly activated, since it is impossible to induce a ground.

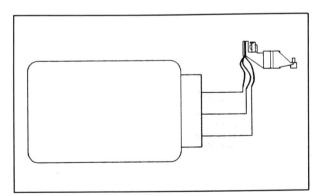

Ford introduced the Hall effect sensor with the EEC IV system. This sensor, like the AC pulse generator, can be used to detect rotational speed. The output signal is a DC pulse—a square wave. Ford calls the Hall effect sensor in the distributor-type systems and the crankshaft position sensor of the distributorless systems the PIP sensor.

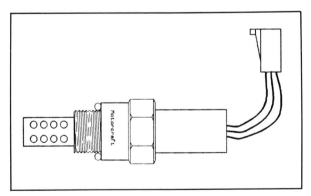

The only example of the voltage generator is the EGO sensor. This sensor begins to produce a voltage as the oxygen content of the exhaust decreases. The voltage ranges from a low of about 0.1 volt when a lot of oxygen is in the exhaust to a high of 0.9 volt when little oxygen is in the exhaust.

3

Tools

We will limit our look at tools in this chapter to those that may be new to the Saturday afternoon mechanic, the enthusiast, or the professional mechanic. We will also look at new ways of using old tools. An effort has been made throughout this book to emphasize the simplest, most available tools to perform each diagnostic task.

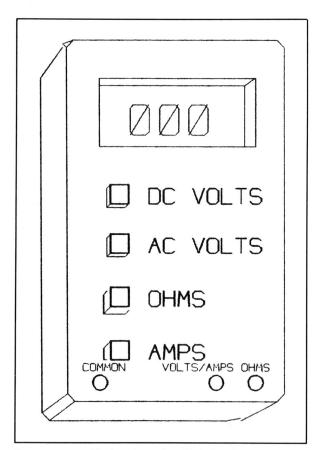

For most troubleshooting, the digital voltmeter is the recommended type of meter. One reason for this is its ease of use. Another reason is its high internal resistance, which increases the accuracy of the readings.

We will look at the various uses of the following:
Digital voltmeter
Analog voltmeter
Test light
Ohmmeter
Tachometer (new uses)
Dwell meter (new uses)
Hand-held vacuum pump
Fuel pressure gauge
Vacuum gauge
Low-voltage oscilloscope
Road shock simulator
Scanner

Digital Voltmeter

The most important tool in working with and troubleshooting modern Ford fuel injection systems is one of the least expensive and easiest to acquire. Digital voltmeters that are adequate to do the job range in price from about $25 to more than $500. Some of the more expensive meters have an advantage: they combine into one package many of the functions using tachometers and dwell meters that will be described later in this book.

The digital voltmeter boasts a high-impedance input—10 million ohms or more. This allows it to be connected to circuits with a very small current flow without affecting the voltage reading. Voltmeters with a low input impedance rob power from the circuit being tested, which causes the voltage readings to be lower than the voltages really are. For this reason, the digital meter should be used any time that precise voltage readings are required.

The use of digital voltmeters has a disadvantage. Since the meters are digital, they merely sample voltage and display the sample readings. Major gaps occur between these samples. Transient fluctuations are completely missed. Devices such as the throttle position sensor potentiometer create a steadily increasing voltage as the throttle is opened. As the TP sensor wears, the wiper may no longer contact the carbon film strip in places, resulting in a sudden drop in voltage. If the digital voltmeter's sampling did not match up with the voltage fluctuation, the cause of a major drivability problem could be missed. For this reason, the analog voltmeter is a better tool for measuring variations in voltage.

Analog Voltmeter

Where the digital voltmeter displays its reading as digits, the analog voltmeter uses a needle moving across a scale to display its readings. The benefits of the analog voltmeter have been ignored since the introduction of the EEC systems at the end of the 1970s. This is because most inexpensive analog meters have a low input impedance, which can distort readings. Nevertheless, rumors about technicians ruining ECAs and other components by using analog meters to take measurements are largely exaggerated.

The analog meter will detect fluctuations in voltage much better than the digital voltmeter will. When a transient voltage change occurs, it will show up in the analog meter as a fluctuation in the needle.

Use the analog meter when you are looking for fluctuations in voltage. Use the digital meter when you are looking for precise readings.

Note: Because of the extremely low current output of the oxygen sensor, most analog voltmeters will ground out the EGO reading; the meter will display 0 volts. Always use a digital voltmeter or an analog meter with a 10-megohm input impedance when taking EGO readings.

Test Light

It may seem odd to include such a low-tech testing device as a test light in a book about sophisticated fuel injection systems. The fact is that

it still has a purpose. Many of the diagnostic flow charts in the Ford fuel injection service manuals suggest the use of test lights to diagnose wiring harness grounds.

Ohmmeter

Ohmmeters are used to measure the resistance in electrical and electronic devices. You may wonder if it is okay to use a low-impedance ohmmeter on a given circuit. Actually, the concept of high impedance and low impedance does not apply to ohmmeters at all. An ohmmeter should always be connected to a component of a given circuit with the power removed from that component. Connecting an ohmmeter to a powered circuit can damage both the tester and the circuit.

Special Warning: Connecting an ohmmeter to an EGO sensor will destroy the EGO sensor.

Tachometer

Still handy for checking engine speeds, a digital tachometer also has other uses. One new diagnostic instrument needed on fuel-injected cars is a frequency counter. Since even most professional fuel injection technicians do not own a frequency counter, consider the use of a digital tachometer.

The tachometer measures the number of primary ignition pulses per minute and mathematically converts them into crankshaft rotations per minute. With some simple computations, we can reverse the mathematics to get a frequency reading in cycles per second, or hertz.

Switch the tachometer to the four-cylinder scale. It does not matter whether the engine you are working on is a four-cylinder, six-cylinder, or eight-cylinder (remember, we are counting pulses per second, not crankshaft revolutions per minute); always use the four-cylinder scale. This technique will work equally well on the six- or eight-cylinder scale, but the math is more complex.

Connect your tachometer to the wire you want to test—usually the ground side of an actuator circuit or the output of an appropriate sensor—and a good ground. Observe the reading on the tachometer and divide by 30. That will be the reading in hertz.

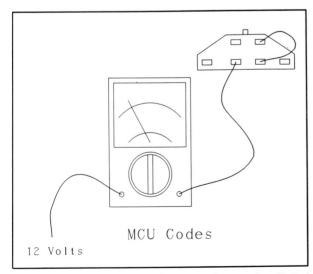

The analog voltmeter is often superior to the digital voltmeter when testing pulsing and varying voltages. This drawing shows the hookup for testing one of Ford's older carbureted systems.

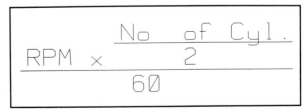

This formula can be used to convert a tachometer reading into a frequency. A simpler version of the formula is to place the tachometer on the four-cylinder scale and divide the reading by 30. This formula is necessary to test the response of the MAP sensor.

Example: $$\frac{4\text{cyl rpm}}{30}$$

or

$$\frac{4800}{30} = 160 \text{ hertz}$$

An analog tachometer is not recommended for this purpose, as this requires a precision that is not found in most analog units.

Dwell Meter

Since the advent of electronic and high energy ignition, the dwell meter has been gathering dust. No longer do we adjust points during a tune-up. Just as the tachometer was actually measuring the frequency of the primary ignition system, however, the dwell meter was measuring its duty cycle. Therefore, when duty cycle needs to be measured, the dwell meter becomes a handy tool again.

Remember that the duty cycle is a measure of the relationship of the on-time and the off-time. Place

Dwell × 1.1 = Duty Cycle

This formula converts a dwell reading (only if taken on the four-cylinder scale) into a duty cycle reading. Although the formula is necessary when accuracy is desired, seldom does automotive electronics require a high level of accuracy. Simply using the dwell readings as duty cycle readings is usually adequate.

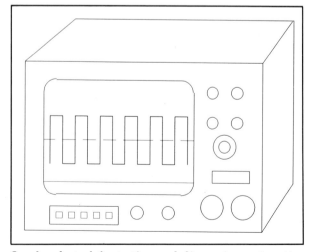

One handy tool for testing and diagnosing automotive electronics is the oscilloscope. This device is used to read changing voltages over time. It is especially valuable when trying to detect intermittent failures.

the dwell meter on the four-cylinder scale; again, do not be concerned with how many cylinders the engine that you are working on has. Connect your dwell meter to the wire on which you want to read the duty cycle, and observe the reading. Multiply the reading by 1.1.

Note: In reality, the degree of precision attained by multiplying the observed result by 1.1 will almost never be required in automotive troubleshooting. Simply using the observed reading will usually suffice.

Hand-held Vacuum Pump

The hand-held vacuum pump can be an invaluable addition to your toolbox. Not only will it come in handy in testing MAP sensors, EGRs, and vacuum-controlled actuators, but it is also handy for testing low-tech items such as vacuum advance units.

Fuel Pressure Gauge

If you do not have a fuel pressure gauge, you might as well forget about troubleshooting fuel injection systems. All good troubleshooting begins with a fuel pressure test. The fuel pressure gauge that is combined with your vacuum gauge will no longer be adequate. You will need a gauge capable of accurate readings of up to 75 pounds per square inch (psi). A variety of fittings and adapters will also be necessary. Shop around a little; the prices on these gauges with fittings can run anywhere from $100 to $1,000. A little ingenuity and a trip to a local hydraulics or air conditioning supply store could probably yield an adequate gauge and a savings of dozens of dollars.

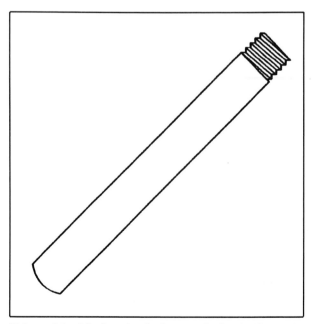

If the tool in this drawing looks amazingly similar to the handle of a plumber's friend, it's because that is exactly what it is. For automotive testing purposes, it is a road shock simulator.

Vacuum Gauge

An ancient workhorse, the vacuum gauge is still as valuable as it ever was for detecting mechanical problems with the engine and troubleshooting misrouted and damaged vacuum circuits.

Low-Voltage Oscilloscope

The low-voltage oscilloscope, also a valuable tool, is new to the arsenal of automotive diagnostic weaponry. Its predecessor, the engine analyzer scope, has been used for decades to troubleshoot primary and secondary ignition systems. The manufacturers of the analyzers early in the 1980s saw the need to test patterns and waveforms at much lower voltages than are found in the ignition system. They began to incorporate low-voltage functions in their professional-quality engine analyzer scopes.

For much less than the thousands of dollars a shop has to invest in one of these testers, however, a low-voltage oscilloscope can be purchased. When found used, these scopes can cost as little as $100. Even new, through an electronics hobby store, they cost as little as $500.

Keep in mind, though, that this type of scope cannot be used to analyze either primary or secondary ignition.

Road Shock Simulator

A fun, though severely misused test tool, is the road shock simulator. It consists of a piece of wood approximately 18 inches (in) long and ³⁄₄in in diameter. The weight of this tool falling on a device—with no muscular assistance—can help identify intermittent open circuits in various sensors and actuators.

Scanner

Scanners come in all sizes, price ranges, and degrees of user friendliness. They are incorporated into engine analyzers costing tens of thousands of dollars, as well as into hand-held units such as those marketed by Snap-on, OTC, and others at between $400 and $1,400.

Although scanners are necessary when troubleshooting GM or Chrysler products, they are of little value on the Ford systems.

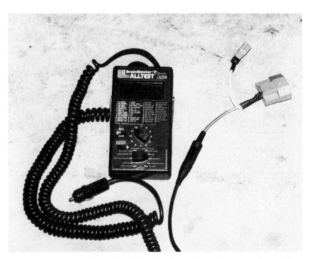

The scanner makes the job of extracting the service codes simple. Most late-model scanners prompt the technician through the steps required to get accurate codes. For Ford products, however, the scanner is a luxury, not a necessity.

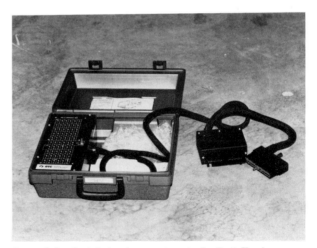

One of the fuel injection system tools that Ford recommends for its dealers is the breakout box. This installs between the ECA (computer) and the ECA wiring harness. The breakout box provides the technician with a convenient place to test voltages and signals being sent to the ECA. Although a technician working daily on Ford fuel injection must have a breakout box to be efficient, it is a luxury for the general mechanic or do-it-yourselfer.

Although not absolutely necessary, a good engine analyzer can save a lot of time and guesswork. An engine analyzer, regardless of the type, is only as good as the skill of the operator.

4

Tuning the Fuel-injected Engine

Fuel injection, computerized engine controls, tough emission standards, and extended service intervals have not eliminated the need for regular maintenance and routine tune-ups. Many cars of the late 1980s and early 1990s boast of spark plug replacement at intervals of 50,000 miles or more. Some air filters and fuel filters have similar service intervals. These service intervals may be fine for typical consumers who use their cars to go to and from work, with an annual trip to Yellowstone or Disneyland. Owners who expect a little more out of their cars—a little more performance, a little more economy, or a little more reliability—should consider the following tune-up maintenance schedule:

Every 12,000 Miles
Replace spark plugs
Replace fuel filter
Replace air filter
Check vacuum hoses and intake air tubes
Check for codes

An amazing number of drivability problems are ultimately traced to the ignition system. My earliest experiences with fuel injection in the early 1970s proved this to me. Often, my colleagues and I would change many of the fuel injection parts, only to find the problem was a cracked distributor cap.

Every 24,000 Miles
Replace spark plugs
Replace fuel filter
Replace distributor cap
Replace rotor
Replace plug wires
Check vacuum hoses and intake air tubes

Spark Plugs
Replacing the spark plugs is one of those tasks that gives a Saturday afternoon mechanic a feeling of pride. Yet many subtle details are involved in spark plug replacement and what the old spark plugs can tell you. Let's begin with some of the basics of what the spark plug does.

The spark plug ignites the air-fuel charge in the combustion chamber. It accomplishes this by means by a high-voltage spark across its electrodes. The source of the spark is the ignition coil, and the spark is conducted to the spark plugs through the secondary ignition cables. This spark lasts for about 1.5 to 2 milliseconds at around 1,000 volts. For the first 30 microseconds, however, the voltage of the spark is considerably higher: somewhere between 5,000 and 30,000 volts. This higher voltage is necessary to initiate, or begin, the spark across the gap of the plug. Since the ignition coil is basically a transformer, the amount of energy available to the plugs is limited to the number of watts passing through the primary. If too much of the available energy is used to initiate the spark, then the amount of energy left to maintain the spark will be reduced. Today's leaner-running engines extinguish the fire in the cylinder when the spark goes out. Therefore, anything that affects the duration of the spark affects power and drivability a lot more than it did in the 1960s. Anything that affects the voltage required to initiate the spark will affect the duration of the spark.

Spark Initiation Voltage
The following will affect the spark initiation voltage:
Spark plug heat range

Compression
Air-fuel ratio
Plug wear
Condition of the distributor cap, the rotor, and the
    plug wires

Spark Plug Heat Range

Unless you have a highly modified engine, stick with the heat range recommended by Ford or by the spark plug manufacturer. If the selected heat range is too cold, the plug can greatly increase the spark initiation voltage, robbing power from the engine. Another difficulty with a cold plug is that it can result in misfiring and fouling. Using spark plugs with a heat range that is too hot can result in preignition or pinging.

Compression

The effect of compression on the power from an engine is like a two-edged sword. On the one hand, increased compression greatly increases the power potential of the engine; on the other hand, increased compression also increases spark initiation voltage. The increase in spark initiation voltage means that high-performance, high-compression engines may require an ignition coil with greater potential energy. In a stock engine, however, as compression in each cylinder drops, the voltage required to initiate the spark across the electrodes decreases—but so does engine power.

Air-Fuel Ratio

The air-fuel ratio is a critical variable affecting drivability. If the air-fuel ratio is too rich, the spark initiation voltage will be quite low and the burn in the combustion chamber will be slow and incomplete. A lean air-fuel ratio makes it difficult for the spark to start jumping the spark plug gap. A great deal of energy will be used during the first 30 microseconds, leaving little energy to maintain a burn in the combustion chamber. The result is reduced power, stumbling, hesitation, and misfiring.

Plug Wear

If you have ever removed an old spark plug, you may have noticed that the gap is much wider than when it was installed. This is because, like many other components in the engine, spark plugs wear as they are used. The wider the gap, the higher the voltage required to start the spark jumping the gap. This means less energy is available to accomplish the burn in the combustion chamber. This has a direct effect on combustion, decreasing power, increasing toxic emissions, and causing poor drivability.

Condition of the Distributor Cap, the Rotor, and the Plug Wires

Within the high-voltage side of the ignition system are several other items that wear as they work. The distributor cap, on cars equipped with a distributor, is used along with the rotor to transfer the high-voltage spark from the ignition coil to the spark plug wires. High voltage arrives at the center of the distributor cap through the coil wire from the ignition coil. This voltage is conducted to the rotor by means of a carbon nib. The current then travels through either a solid metal conductor or a resistive element in the rotor. As the rotor swings past each of the plug wire electrodes, a spark jumps from the rotor.

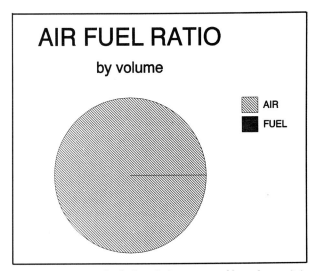

When the proper air-fuel ratio is measured by volume, it is 10,000 parts of air to 1 part of fuel. A good illustration compares this ratio to that of a man holding a jigger of gasoline inside the passenger compartment of a VW Rabbit.

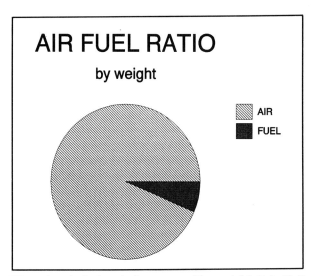

When the air-fuel ratio is measured by weight, it is 14.7 parts of air to 1 part of fuel. This ratio is called the stoichiometric point. When a combustible mixture is at the stoichiometric ratio, all the air and all the fuel will be mutually consumed. An imbalance in the ratio causes excessive oxygen, carbon monoxide, hydrocarbons, or oxides of nitrogen to be present in the exhaust gases.

Wear on the carbon nib or an excessive gap between the rotor and the distributor cap electrodes will increase the amount of energy consumed on its way to the spark plugs. This decreases the amount of energy available to fire the cylinder. Distributorless ignition systems are one method Ford is using to reduce the number of places where wear can affect secondary ignition energy, thereby increasing tune-up service intervals.

As plug wires age, their resistance increases. As their resistance increases, a greater portion of the potential spark energy heading toward the spark plugs is consumed.

Spark Plug Replacement

Removal

With the engine cold, unscrew the spark plugs two or three turns. Using compressed air or a solvent-soaked brush, clean the area around each plug to remove any dirt or foreign objects that might fall into the cylinder when the spark plug is removed. Should you find the spark plug difficult to unscrew, it might be that the plug has dirt or grit on the threads. If this is the case, put a couple of drops of oil on the exposed threads and allow it to soak in for a few minutes. Screw the plug back in, then out several times, a little more each time, until the plug is removed.

Inspection of the removed spark plugs can tell you a lot about the running condition of the engine. Carbon deposits, ash formations, oil fouling, sooting, and other conditions can indicate engine or injection system problems.

Installation

Before installing the new spark plugs, check the gap. Although some spark plug manufacturers make an effort to pregap their plugs, these plugs can be accidentally regapped in shipping.

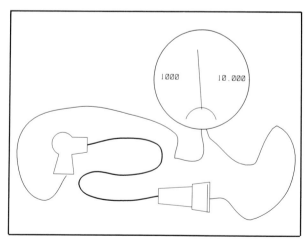

To test a spark plug wire, connect the terminals of an ohmmeter to the ends of the wire. The resistance through the wire should be between 1,000 and 10,000 ohms per foot.

Inspect the threads in the cylinder head to ensure that they are clean and undamaged. Also check the mating surface where the plug contacts the head; it should be clean and free of burrs. Start the new spark plug and screw it in a few turns by hand. Continue to screw the plug in either by hand or with a socket and ratchet until it contacts the mating surface firmly. To avoid overtightening, use a torque wrench and tighten a tapered-seat plug to 26 pounds-feet (lb-ft) in a cast-iron head or 21 lb-ft in an aluminum head.

Note: In the real world, a torque wrench is seldom used when installing spark plugs, so use this rule of thumb: Tighten plugs to firm contact plus 15 degrees of rotation.

Spark Plug Wire Testing and Replacement

Spark plug wires are tested in two ways: the first is with an engine analyzer oscilloscope; the second is with an ohmmeter. If you are using the latter, remove each plug wire and with your ohmmeter on the X1,000-ohm scale, measure its resistance end to end. A good plug wire will have less than 10,000 ohms per foot but more than 1,000 ohms per foot.

Remember a couple of important things when replacing secondary ignition wires. First, if the plug wires are installed in the incorrect order, a backfire may occur, resulting in damage to the MAF sensor or the rubber tube that connects it to the throttle assembly. The original equipment plug wires have numbers on them indicating which cylinder they should be connected to. Aftermarket or replacement plug wires may not have these numbers; 3M and other companies make adhesive numbers that can be attached to ensure proper reinstallation.

Distributor Cap Replacement

Distributor cap replacement consists of simply releasing the attachment screws or clips and making sure that the plug wires are reinstalled in the correct order.

It is a good idea to replace the distributor cap and rotor together and use the same brand. Pairing caps and rotors of two different manufacturers is not a good idea, as this can result in an incorrect rotor air gap. Excessive rotor air gap can cause excessively high spark initiation voltage and can result in incomplete combustion.

Air Filter Replacement

The real value of the air filter is significantly underestimated. This component is the engine's only defense against sand, grit, and other hard-particle contaminants. When these substances enter the combustion chamber, they can act like grinding compound on the cylinder walls, piston rings, and valves. Replace the air filter at least once a year or every 24,000 miles. In areas where sand blows around a lot, like West Texas or Arizona, the air filter should be replaced much more often.

On most carbureted cars, a restricted air filter will cause the engine to run rich. This is because the restriction causes a reduction of pressure in the venturis of the carburetor while the pressure in the fuel bowl remains constant at atmospheric. This increased pressure differential increases the flow of fuel into the venturis, and the mixture enriches.

On some multipoint injected engines, the ECA uses the MAF sensor to measure the actual volume of air entering the engine. The ECA injects the correct amount of fuel for the measured amount of air. If you restrict the flow of incoming air, less air will be measured and therefore less fuel will be metered into the engine. Although engines equipped with a MAP sensor use a different air measurement technology, this sensor does much the same thing as the MAF sensor. CFI air measurement is a little less precise and therefore may run a little rich as a result of a restricted air filter. Even on CFI cars, the oxygen sensor should compensate for any air-fuel ratio errors that might exist once closed-loop operation begins.

Fuel Filter Replacement

The fuel filter is the most important service item among the fuel components of the fuel injection system. Technicians replace many original filters on fuel-injected cars that are more than ten years old. This lack of routine maintenance is just begging for trouble.

After removing the fuel filter, find a white ceramic container, such as an old coffee cup, and drain the contents of the filter through the inlet fitting. Inspect the gasoline in the cup for evidence of sand, rust, or other hard-particle contaminants. Now pour the gas into a clear container, such as an old glass, and allow it to sit for about 30 minutes. If the fuel has a high water content, the mixture will separate while sitting and the fuel will float on top of the water. If the tank contains excessive water or hard-particle contaminants, it may have to be removed and professionally cleaned. For minor water contamination problems, a number of additives can be purchased at your local auto parts store.

Should the fuel filter become excessively clogged, the following symptom might develop: You start the car in the morning, and it runs fine. As you drive several miles down the road, the car may begin to buck a little or lose a little power. Suddenly, the engine quits, almost as though someone had shut it off with the key. After sitting on the side of the road for several minutes, the car can be restarted and driven for a couple of miles before the symptom recurs.

This problem could be caused by a severely restricted fuel filter. The car runs good initially because the bulk of what is causing the restriction has fallen to the bottom of the fuel filter as sediment. When the engine is started and the fuel begins to flow through the injection system, this sediment gets stirred up and pressed against the paper elements of the fuel filter. As it does, fuel volume to the injectors is decreased and the engine begins to run lean. Sooner or later, the engine leans out so much that it dies.

The bad news is that often when the fuel filter becomes that restricted, some of the contaminants have forced their way through the filter and may contaminate the rest of the components in the fuel system.

Alcohol Contamination

Alcohol contamination can damage many fuel injection components. Use of gasohol can be one source of alcohol. If you suspect that excessive alcohol content has caused the failure of system components, then you might want to test a fuel sample for alcohol content.

A simple test has been recommended by Ford and others in their literature. Pour 200 milliliters of the sample fuel into a glass or clear plastic container, along with 100 milliliters of water. Immediately after putting the two liquids in the container, the dividing line will be at the 100-milliliter mark. Wait about 30 minutes. If the dividing line rises by more than 10 percent of the volume of the contents of the container, then excessive alcohol is present in the fuel. Drain the fuel from the tank and replace it with good fuel.

Many fuel additives on the market contain alcohol. These additives come in cans that are so small compared with the size of the typical fuel tank that they pose no threat to the fuel system. Nevertheless, use caution. Ask around a little bit and be selective when purchasing these products; some are much better than others.

Ignition Timing Checking

On EEC IV fuel-injected Fords, the ignition timing is controlled by the fuel injection computer, which is the ECA. Two wires are involved in the control of ignition timing; both run from the ignition module to the ECA. A blue wire sends a tach signal from the ignition module to the ECA. This signal is called the PIP signal. The ECA then modifies the signal by changing its duty cycle and returns it to the ignition module through a yellow wire with a green stripe. In the ignition module, this signal is used to control ignition timing. This is called the SPOUT signal.

Located along the yellow and green wire, a few inches from the ignition module, is the SPOUT connector. This will be disconnected to check or set the initial timing. To check the ignition timing, follow the instructions on the EPA decal found under the hood of the vehicle.

After preparing to check initial timing, use a timing light in the normal fashion to check the timing. Adjustment of the timing is still done through loosening and rotating the distributor. When you are done, reconnect the SPOUT connector.

If you are working on a car equipped with a DIS, then you will not find an initial timing specification or adjustment procedure. As discussed later in this book, the timing is controlled entirely by the computer on these.

Electronic Spark Timing System Testing

With the car in park and the parking brake set, rev the engine while monitoring the timing with a timing light. The timing should advance considerably. At this point, do not be concerned with how much it advances; just be sure that it does in fact advance. You can test DISs for timing advance by making your own marks on the harmonic balancer and the timing chain cover. Though you cannot adjust for initial timing, proper advance of timing is still essential for good acceleration and power.

SPOUT Timing Wire Testing

The yellow and green wire referred to as the SPOUT connector is used by the ECA to control the switching of the thick film integrated (TFI) ignition module to control timing. A pulse should be found on this wire. If the signal is present at the ignition module but no timing advance occurs, then the ignition module is defective.

If the SPOUT signal is not present, refer to the code 18 diagnostics later in chapter 8 of this book.

EGO Sensor Testing

The EGO sensor is used by the ECA to monitor the air-fuel ratio. In spite of what you might hear from different professionals, testing the EGO sensor is simple. Connect a high-impedance voltmeter to the EGO sensor at the point where the wire from the ECA connects to the sensor. Leave the EGO sensor connected and start the engine. Allow the engine to run at 2000rpm for 2 minutes. With the engine idling, watch the voltage reading on the voltmeter. The voltage should be constantly changing back and forth from between 100 and 400 millivolts to between 600 and 900 millivolts.

If the EGO sensor voltage does not change as described, then further testing of the oxygen feedback system is necessary; refer to chapter 9.

Minimum Airflow Adjustment

In the past, one final touch of any good tune-up was to adjust the curb idle speed. On today's fuel-

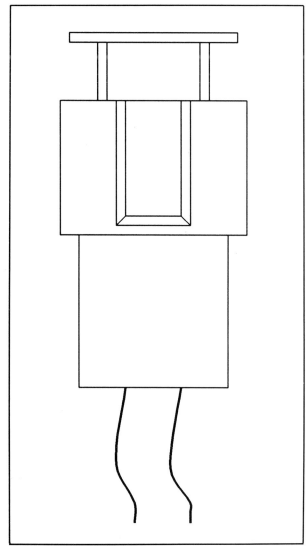

The SPOUT connector plugs into a terminal that holds two yellow and green wires. These wires carry the timing control signal (SPOUT) from the ECA to the TFI module. When the SPOUT is removed, this signal is interrupted and the timing will drop back to initial.

When checking the initial timing, it is necessary to disconnect the SPOUT connector. The SPOUT connector is located within a few inches of the ignition module. On the 460 engine, the ignition module, and therefore the SPOUT connector, is located next to the left hood hinge.

injected Ford cars, the idle speed is controlled by the ECA and is not adjustable. An important adjustment that is similar to it can be made, however. This adjustment is known as minimum airflow. It determines the amount of air allowed to pass across the throttle plates when they are closed. Incorrectly adjusted minimum airflow can result in tip-in hesitation, stumbling, and stalling on deceleration.

To begin the minimum airflow adjustment, it is necessary to check for throttle body coking. When a multipoint engine is shut off, hot crankcase vapors rise through the positive crankcase ventilation (PCV) system into the air intake system. As they rise, they carry oil and soot, which rests in the intake system, coating the connector tube between the MAF sensor and the throttle plates. When the engine is started, incoming air picks up this oil and soot and deposits it at the first low-pressure area it comes to—just behind the throttle plates. Evidence of coking is a ridge of soot that is built up behind the throttle plates and can be felt with the tip of the index finger.

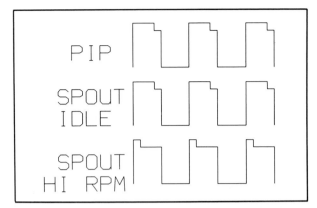

The SPOUT signal controls the ignition timing by changing the shape of a pulse being sent to the TFI module. The top waveform here is what the PIP (Profile Ignition Pickup) signal looks like on an oscilloscope. At idle, the SPOUT signal is virtually identical to the PIP signal. As the engine speed increases and the timing needs to advance, the SPOUT waveform changes. The change in the waveform causes the TFI module to advance the timing.

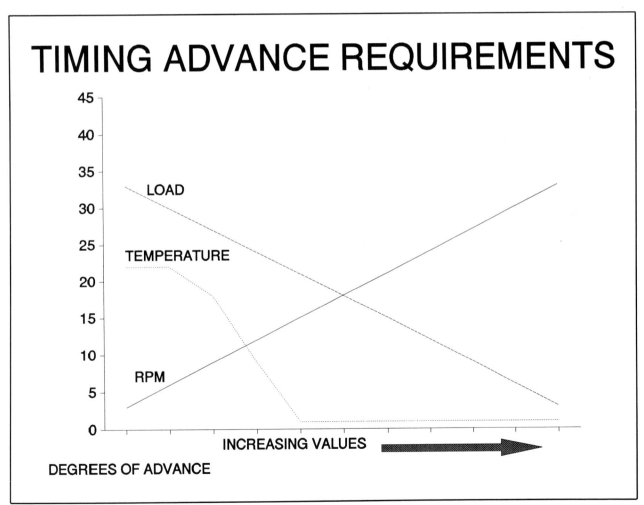

The ECA will gather information about engine load, temperature, and speed. As the engine speed increases, the need for timing advance increases. As the temperature increases, the need for timing advance decreases. As the rpm increase, the need for timing advance increases.

Located in the exhaust system, usually very close to or in the exhaust manifold, is the EGO sensor. This sensor detects the oxygen content of the exhaust system. A high oxygen content means the engine is running lean. A low oxygen content means the engine is running rich. When a low oxygen content is in the exhaust system, the output voltage of the EGO sensor will be low—less than 0.45 volt. When a high oxygen content is in the exhaust, the output voltage of the EGO sensor will be high—greater than 0.45 volt.

Coking behind the throttle plates forms a seal that reduces the amount of air passing across the plates. Minimum airflow is affected, causing hesitation and stalling. The idle air control passage can also become coked up, causing erratic idle speed control problems.

Throttle Bore Coking Cleanup

The best way to clean throttle bore coking is to remove the throttle assembly from the intake manifold. Using solvent and an old toothbrush, scrub the area in front of and behind the throttle plates. Remove and clean the throttle air bypass (BYP) air control valve from the throttle assembly. Dip a rag in solvent, and clean the pintle of the BYP valve. With a small toothbrush or several pipe cleaners twisted together, scrub out the BYP valve passage. Reassemble the throttle assembly and install it back onto the intake manifold.

Minimum airflow is the amount of air passing across the throttle plates when the throttle is closed. For multipoint Ford applications, disconnect the BYP valve. The engine should slowly die.

Multipoint Injector Cleaning

The cleaning of multipoint injectors is done chemically, and no disassembly is required. Kits for cleaning MPI systems are available from most national parts and auto mechanic tool distributors. The

To check the engine adjustments for the proper minimum idle speed, disconnect the ISC motor (also called the BYP). When the signal being sent from the ECA to the BYP is taken away, the BYP valve goes to the closed position. When the BYP closes, the engine should slowly idle to a stop.

directions for the use of these kits depend more on the brand of kit than on the car. Read the instructions for the kit you purchase.

"Dead-Hole" Testing

Distributor-Type Ignition

When a late-model fuel-injected engine has a cylinder with a misfire, the effects can go far beyond a mere rough idle or loss of power. A cylinder that is still pulling in air but not burning that air will be pumping unburned oxygen past the oxygen sensor. This confuses the ECA, making it believe that the engine is running lean. The ECA responds by enriching the mixture, and the gas mileage deteriorates dramatically.

Several effective methods can be used to isolate a dead cylinder. All of these measure the power produced in each cylinder by killing the cylinders one at a time with the engine running a little above curb idle.

Back in the good old days, we used to take a test light, ground the alligator clip, and pierce through the insulation boot at the distributor cap end of the plug wire. This would ground out the spark for one cylinder, and an rpm drop would be noted. The greater the rpm drop, the more power that cylinder was contributing to the operation of the engine. Actually, this is a valid testing procedure; however, piercing the insulation boot is only asking for more problems than you started with.

Another "good old days" method of performing a cylinder balance was to isolate the dead hole by pulling off one plug wire at a time and noting the rpm drops. The problem with this method is that you run the risk of damaging yourself, the PIP sensor, or the ignition module with a high-voltage spark.

So, let's explore some alternatives:

Cylinder inhibit tester: Several tool companies produce a cylinder-shorting tach-dwell meter. This device electronically disables one cylinder at a time while displaying rpm. Engine speed drops can be noted. Unfortunately, these testers can cost $500 or more, and most will not do a cylinder balance on a distributorless engine.

Shoestring technique: Another valid method does the old test light technique one better. Cut a piece of 1/8in vacuum hose into four, six, or eight 1in sections. With the engine shut off, and one at a time so as not to confuse the firing order, remove the plug wires from the distributor cap, insert a segment into the plug wire tower of the cap, and set the plug wire back on top of the hose. When you have installed all the segments, start the engine. Touching the vacuum hose conductors with a grounded test light will kill the cylinders so that you can note rpm drop. Again, the cylinder with the smallest drop in rpm is the weakest cylinder.

Whichever method you use, follow this procedure for the best results:

1. Adjust the engine speed to 1200rpm to 1400rpm by blocking the throttle open. Do not attempt to hold the throttle by hand; you just will not be steady enough.

2. Electrically disconnect the BYP valve to prevent its affecting the idle speed.

3. Disconnect the EGO sensor to prevent it from altering the air-fuel ratio to compensate for the dead cylinder.

4. Perform the cylinder kill test. Rpm drops should be fairly equal between cylinders. Any cylinder that has a considerably lower rpm drop than the rest is weak.

5. Introduce a little propane into the intake—just enough to provide the highest rpm. Repeat the cylinder kill test. If the rpm drop from the weak cylinder tends to equalize with the rest, then you have a vacuum leak to track down.

6. Open the throttle until the engine speed is about 1800rpm to 2000rpm. Repeat the cylinder kill test, adding propane. If the rpm drops are now equal, then the most likely problem is that the EGR valve is allowing too much exhaust gas to enter the intake at low engine speeds. If the rpm drop on the cylinder in question remains low, then the problem is most likely mechanical.

7. Perform both a wet compression test and a dry compression test. If you have low dry compression and low wet compression, then the problem is a bad valve or valve seat. If the dry compression is bad but the wet compression is good, then the problem is the piston rings. If the compression is good both dry and wet, then the problem is in the valvetrain, such as in the camshaft, lifters, or pushrods.

8. After testing is completed, reconnect anything that was disconnected or removed for testing.

Distributorless Ignition

The shoestring technique described for the distributor-type ignition will work nicely for the distributorless ignition.

Be sure to disconnect the BYP valve and the EGO sensor and to stabilize the rpm at 1200 to 1400 for the first balance test. The rest of the testing procedure is exactly what it was for the distributor-type ignition.

Before making any adjustments to the throttle stop screw to reset the minimum air, open the throttle plates and inspect for coking. Throttle body coking is a build-up of soot and oil behind the throttle plates. This build-up can affect the minimum idle speed of the engine and contribute to rough idle and hesitation. Clean the build-up with a rag soaked in solvent. Caution: Spraying carburetor cleaner and similar substances into the intake with the engine running can damage the TP sensor.

5

Automotive Emissions

The act of combining air and fuel in the combustion chamber, raising the temperature of that charge through compression, and igniting it with a spark plug is a dirty and relatively inefficient way to move an automobile down the road. A plethora of both toxic and nontoxic chemicals are created and find their way into the atmosphere and the groundwater. An understanding of the production and nature of these chemicals can assist in the understanding and troubleshooting of electronic fuel injection systems.

Fuel

Gasoline is a complex hydrocarbon made up of approximately 86 percent carbon and 14 percent hydrogen by weight. Trace impurities contribute to the noxious cloud from the tailpipe. Sulfur can combine with oxygen during the combustion process, producing sulfuric acid and sulfur dioxide. Also, a wide range of additives are used.

Until recent years, tetraethyl lead or tetramethyl lead was used as a knock inhibitor. When these oxidized in the combustion chamber, they not only produced an acid but also contributed to the background lead contamination of the environment. New legislation as well as the incompatibility of these chemicals with catalytic converters and oxygen sensors has led to their disuse. Chemicals like methyl tertiary butyl ether are now used as knock inhibitors. Other additives such as antiaging chemicals, detergents, anti-icing substances, and anticorrosives also make up the soup you pour in your gas tank.

Air

The air itself is a prime defiler of the atmosphere. Seventy-eight percent of the air we breathe is nitrogen. When this nitrogen is combined with oxygen during the combustion process, it can produce both nitrogen monoxide (NO) and nitrogen dioxide (NO_2).

Air is made up of 78 percent nitrogen and 21 percent oxygen. The remaining 1 percent consists of various trace gases such as xenon, neon, and argon.

Combustion

Complete

When air and gasoline are mixed in the combus-

tion chamber, heated, and then ignited, combustion occurs. Combustion is the act of combining the oxygen in the atmosphere with the hydrogen and carbon elements of the gasoline. If we have combined the air and fuel in the proper ratio (known as a stoichiometric ratio), applied just enough but not too much heat, and ignited the mixture with a sufficient spark, then the perfect burn takes place. The carbon element of the gasoline combines with the oxygen of the air to form carbon dioxide (CO_2). The hydrogen element of the gasoline combines with the oxygen element of the air to form water (H_2O). The result of a scientifically mixed combustion of air and fuel at precisely the right burn temperature is, therefore, CO_2 and H_2O.

Incomplete

Incomplete combustion will occur any time one of the four elements of complete combustion—air, fuel, heat, or spark—gets out of balance. Some of the toxic and unpleasant by-products of incomplete combustion or of complete combustion that occurred at too high a temperature are various paraffins, olefins, aromatic hydrocarbons (HCs), aldehydes, keytones, carboxylic acids, polycyclic HCs, carbon monoxide (CO), acetylene, ethylene, hydrogen, soot, NO, NO_2, organic peroxides, ozone, peroxyacetyl nitrates, sulfur oxides, and from the additives, lead oxides and lead halogenides. (It's a bit like finding out what they really put in sausage, isn't it?) This book will address, define, and discuss only the ones either for which a current EPA mandate exists or that can assist in fault diagnosis.

Carbon Dioxide

CO_2 emissions are of rising concern to the automobile industry. Since CO_2 is listed as a result of complete combustion, the goal of most of the pollution control devices on today's spark ignition gasoline engines is to increase the output of CO_2. Yet CO_2 is not harmless. Increasing levels of atmospheric CO_2 have been linked to the greenhouse effect. It is theorized that the burning of fossil fuels, as well as the depletion of worldwide vegetation, is causing CO_2

levels to rise to the point where solar heat will be trapped in the earth's atmosphere, increasing average temperatures worldwide. The automotive industry has not yet been mandated to lower CO_2 emissions, however.

CO_2 levels at the tailpipe are a valuable diagnostic tool. A reading of between 10 and 15 percent indicates that the quality of combustion is good and the exhaust system has no leaks. The closer the reading to 15 percent, the better the overall quality of combustion.

Low CO_2 levels can result from poor ignition quality (bad plugs, cap, rotor, plug wires); low compression (leaking head gasket, valves, rings); exhaust leaks (diluted sample); incorrect air-fuel ratio (too rich or too lean); and vacuum leaks.

Carbon Monoxide

CO is an odorless, colorless, tasteless gas that is highly toxic and very dangerous. A 30-minute exposure to a CO concentration of only 0.3 percent by volume can be fatal. This percentage is well below even the California-mandated tailpipe reading. Working on even an emission-controlled vehicle with the engine running in a closed shop can be very dangerous. In addition, your red blood cells have an affinity

for CO that is fifteen times greater than their affinity for oxygen. As a result, long-term exposure to even low levels of CO can be health threatening.

CO is produced whenever the flame front runs out of oxygen as it travels through the combustion chamber. This oxygen deficiency can occur as a result of a lack of oxygen in the combustion chamber or an excess of fuel. If the supply of oxygen is sufficient, then the carbon element of the fuel will pick up two parts oxygen and complete its transition to CO_2. When the supply of oxygen is inadequate, the carbon can combine with only one part oxygen, stopping short at CO.

Causes of high CO levels are a dirty air filter, high fuel pressure, leaking injectors (including cold-start), dirty oil, and a tricked EGO sensor.

Hydrocarbon

HC is a blanket term for a wide range of toxic and carcinogenic chemicals produced during the combustion of gasoline. Many of these chemicals in the presence of nitrogen oxide and sunlight produce photochemical smog. This is the element of smog that burns the eyes and nose and irritates the mucous membranes. Although to the environmentally conscious, HC emissions amount to a veritable soup of numerous foul substances, we will treat them as a single substance.

Allowable CO levels are relatively high, at one to two parts per hundred, or 1 to 2 percent, even for late-model cars. In most jurisdictions, the allowable concentration of various HC emissions is extremely low, at only about one hundred to three hundred parts per million, or 0.01 to 0.03 percent.

Excessive HC content in the exhaust can be caused by poor secondary ignition quality, vacuum leaks, an engine that is running too rich, a lean misfire (an engine that is running too lean), and low compression.

Oxides of Nitrogen

Oxides of nitrogen include both nitrogen monoxide (NO) and nitrogen dioxide (NO_2). Usually these two chemicals are grouped together and called NOx. NO is an odorless, colorless, tasteless gas that is basically harmless to the environment. Created along with the NO, however, is NO_2—and to further complicate matters, NO itself combines with atmospheric oxygen to become NO_2. NO_2 is a reddish brown poisonous gas that destroys lung tissue.

NOx is created when combustion temperatures exceed 2,500 degrees Fahrenheit. At these temperatures, the nitrogen combines chemically with oxygen; in other words, it burns. Although NOx is not measured for diagnostic purposes, it is the principal emission responsible for oxygen sensor–controlled fuel injection systems. The allowable level of NOx since 1982 for new cars delivered in the United States has been 1 gram per mile.

Since we have no economical way to measure NOx, it is of no diagnostic value. NOx levels will

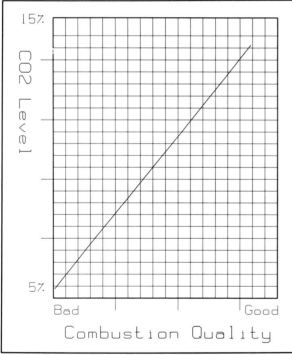

CO_2 is a normal and desired result of combustion. The percentage of CO_2 in the exhaust gases is a clue to the quality of combustion in the engine. As it approaches 15 percent, it indicates that the quality of combustion is good. When it drops below 10 percent, it indicates a problem with the combustion quality. This problem may be the result of ignition, compression, or air-fuel ratio difficulties.

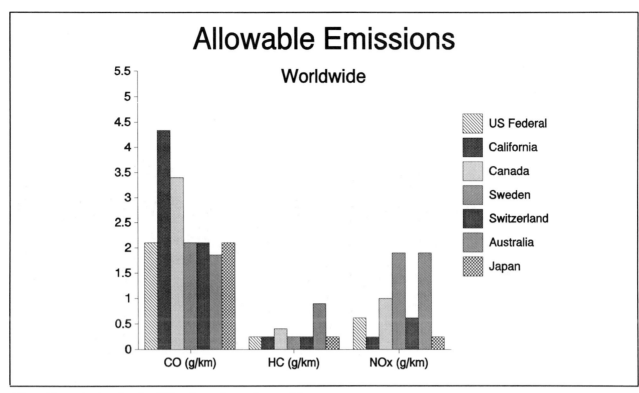

Allowable emission levels differ throughout the world. Although the United States is strict, other countries are stricter.

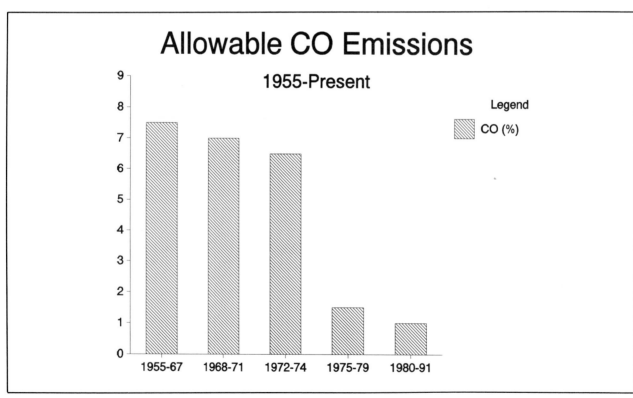

Allowable CO levels have been steadily decreasing over the years.

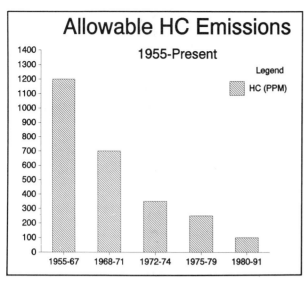

Allowable HC Emissions
1955-Present

Legend: HC (PPM)

Allowable HC levels have been decreasing since the 1950s. Today, the allowable level is less than 0.00001 percent. This compares with an allowable level of CO exceeding 1 percent.

increase, however, when the combustion temperatures increase as a result of incorrect initial timing, a lean air-fuel ratio, high compression (such as that caused by carbon build-up on the pistons), and a vacuum leak.

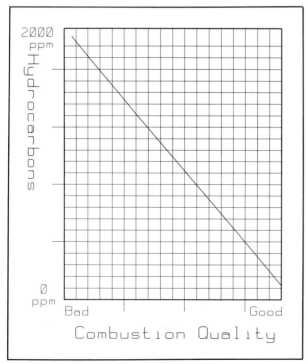

High HC emissions indicate poor combustion quality. Vacuum leaks, air-fuel ratio, compression, and ignition problems can all decrease the combustion quality and increase the HC emissions.

Emission Control Techniques and Devices

Engine Modifications

Compression

By dropping the compression ratios in the mid-1970s, the manufacturers were able to lower combustion temperatures and thereby lower the production of NOx. This caused fuel economy to plummet and destroyed the potential for performance.

Valve Overlap

Increased valve overlap allows for some of the exhaust gases to be drawn back in during the beginning of the intake stroke. These exhaust gases are inert (chemically inactive); the fuel and the oxygen were burned out of them during the previous combustion cycle. As the next combustion cycle begins, these inert gases act as a heat sink to lower the combustion temperature and decrease the production of NOx.

EGR Valve

The EGR valve is used to reduce the production of oxides of nitrogen. As the engine rpm rises above idle, either vacuum applied to a diaphragm or a solenoid lifts the pintle of the EGR valve. This allows exhaust gases into the combustion chamber. Approximately 7 percent of the combustion chamber volume will lower the burn temperature by about 500 degrees Fahrenheit. This lower temperature reduces the production of NOx.

PCV System

The PCV system draws crankcase vapors through a metered check valve known as the PCV valve into the intake manifold. These gases, the result of combustion chamber blow-by, are given a second chance to be burned. The PCV system is designed to reduce the amount of HC allowed to escape to the atmosphere from the crankcase.

Fuel Evaporation

Since the 1970s, cars have been equipped with an evaporative control system. This system consists of a canister filled with activated charcoal and connected to the fuel tank—and on carbureted cars, to the carburetor fuel bowl—by hoses. As gasoline, containing HC, evaporates from the fuel in the tank, the fumes are stored in the activated charcoal. A device known as the canister purge valve opens when the engine can accept the extra fuel, and manifold vacuum sucks the fuel into the engine to be burned.

Air Pump

The air pump has two purposes. First, air is pumped into the exhaust manifold while the engine is cold. Since a rich mixture is present in the combustion chamber at this time, the resulting exhaust gases will be laden with CO and HC. The air pump injects air into the exhaust manifold. When the oxygen in the air comes in contact with the CO and HC, the temper-

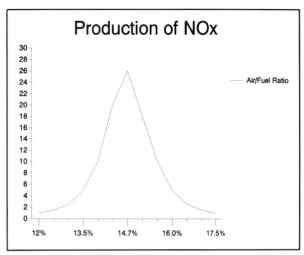

At a 14.7:1 air-fuel ratio, when HC and CO_2 emissions are at their lowest, the production of NO and NO_2 is at its highest. A shorthand used to describe oxides of nitrogen is NOx (pronounced "noks").

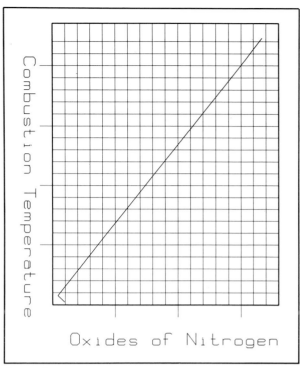

As combustion temperature increases, the production of NOx also increases.

ature of these gases increases dramatically and afterburning takes place. The afterburn consumes much of the residual CO and HC.

Second, as a side benefit from this afterburning, a great deal of heat is generated. That heat is used to help bring the catalytic converter and the oxygen sensor to their proper operating temperature.

Before the ECA goes into its closed-loop mode, the air being pumped must be diverted either to the atmosphere or downstream of the oxygen sensor.

Catalytic Converter

When the oxidizing catalytic converter was introduced in 1975, it spelled the beginning of the end for leaded gasoline. It consisted of a platinum-palladium coating over an aluminum oxide substrate. The platinum was not compatible with tetraethyl lead, which meant that tetraethyl lead could not be present in the fuel used in catalyst-equipped vehicles.

The job of the catalyst is to provide an environment where enough heat can be generated to allow further combustion of the HC and CO to occur. The converter is heated by a chemical reaction between the platinum and the exhaust gases. The minimum operating, or light-off, temperature of the converter is 600 degrees Fahrenheit, and the optimum operating temperature is about 1,200 to 1,400 degrees Fahrenheit. At a temperature of approximately 1,800 degrees Fahrenheit, the substrate will begin to melt. This and other excessive temperatures can be reached when the engine runs too rich or is misfiring.

At a meeting of the Society of Automotive Engineers (SAE), a representative of a company that built oxidizing converter substrates stated that a 25 percent misfire (one cylinder on a four-cylinder engine) for 15 minutes was enough to begin an

irreversible self-destruction process in the converter. This type of catalytic converter requires plenty of oxygen to do its job. This means that the exhaust gases passing through it must be the result of an air-fuel ratio of 14.7:1 or leaner.

Between 1978 and 1982, we saw the gradual introduction of the dual-bed converter. This converter adds a second rhodium catalyst, known as the reducing section, ahead of the oxidizing section. The rhodium coats an aluminum oxide substrate and reacts with the NOx passing through it. When heated to more than 600 degrees Fahrenheit, the nitrogen and oxygen elements of the NOx passing through it will be stripped apart. Although only about 70 to 80 percent efficient when coupled with the EGR, this converter does a dramatic job of reducing NOx. Since the task of the reducing catalyst is to strip oxygen away from nitrogen, it works best when the exhaust gases passing through it are the result of an oxygen-poor air-fuel ratio of 14.7:1 or richer.

The only air-fuel ratio that will permit both sections of the converter to operate efficiently is 14.7:1. The job of the oxygen-feedback fuel injection systems being used today is to control the air-fuel ratio at 14.7:1 as often as possible.

Note: On many applications, the air from the air pump, after preheating the catalytic converter, will be directed between the front reducing section and the rear oxidizing section of the converter. This is to supply extra oxygen to improve the efficiency of the oxidizer.

From the early 1970s, the EGR valve has been used to reduce the production of NOx. The EGR channels some of the inert exhaust gases, which have no oxygen or fuel, back into the combustion chamber. In the combustion chamber, they act as a heat sink to pull some of the heat from the combustion process. The lower combustion temperature results in a lower production of NOx.

The evaporative canister—the "tomato soup can" to the far left here—has been used since the early 1970s to trap evaporating HCs (gasoline) escaping from the fuel tank. Inside the can is activated charcoal. The charcoal traps the HCs and holds them until engine conditions are right to let them be burned.

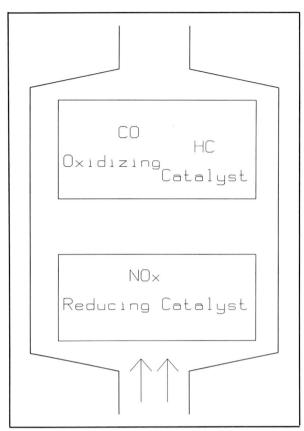

The catalytic converter was introduced in 1975 as a method of controlling HC and CO. As the exhaust gases passed through the converter, heat was generated. The heat caused the HC and CO to combine with residual oxygen forming H_2O and CO_2. This type of catalytic converter was called an oxidizing converter. In the late 1970s and early 1980s, a second section was added to the converter, in front of the first section. This section, called a reducing section, strips oxygen away from the NOx, resulting in nitrogen and oxygen out the tailpipe.

6

EEC III

There are cars which professional mechanics call "runaway cars." This term describes a model of car that is so difficult to work on that it inspires all the mechanics to "runaway" to lunch when it rolls in the door. A P1800 Volvo, for many mechanics, would be on that list.

For some mechanics any car equipped with the EEC III system falls into this category. Actually the EEC III system is simpler than its successor, the EEC IV system. Its reputation for difficulty comes from the limited onboard diagnostic capability of the system. The simplicity of the EEC III system makes the limited diagnostic capabilities excusable.

Study this section of the book well and hang up a shingle over your door saying "EEC III Expert." You will be about the only one in town.

Sensors

Engine Coolant Temperature Sensor

The ECT sensor is a negative temperature coefficient thermistor. Located in the water jacket near the thermostat housing, it measures the temperature of the engine. It is a variable resistor whose resistance decreases as the temperature of the engine increases. The ECA uses this reading to adjust the air-fuel ratio and ignition timing based on the temperature of the engine. A cold engine will accept, and requires, a richer mixture and additional timing advance.

How It Works

The ECT sensor is supplied with a 9-volt reference from the ECA. This VREF passes through an internal resistor before proceeding out of the ECA to the sensor. When the engine is cold, the voltage on the wire between the sensor and the ECA is high—about 5 volts at 68 degrees Fahrenheit. When the engine is started, and as the temperature of the engine increases, the resistance of the ECT sensor drops. As the resistance drops, the voltage on the reference wire to the ECT sensor also drops. When the engine is thoroughly warmed up, the voltage on the reference wire is around 1 volt. The ECA measures this voltage to determine the temperature of the engine.

Common Failures

The most common failure of the ECT sensor is an intermittent open in the sensor. In most cases, a

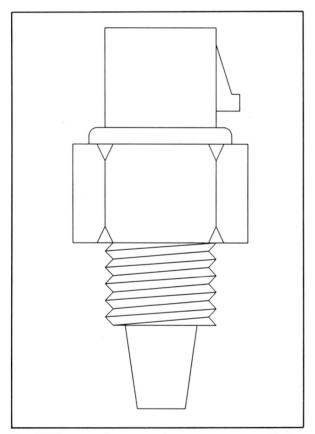

The ECT sensor is a negative temperature coefficient thermistor. This means it is a variable resistor whose resistance increases as the temperature decreases. When the temperature of the engine is −40 degrees Fahrenheit, the resistance of the coolant sensor thermistor is greater than 240,000 ohms. As the temperature increases, the resistance slowly drops. At 212 degrees Fahrenheit, the resistance is less than 2,000 ohms.

failure of the ECT circuit is a result of a problem in one of the wires or connections in the circuit.

Throttle Position Sensor

The TP sensor is a potentiometer. The ECA sends a 9-volt reference signal to the TP sensor. A second wire provides a current path back to the ECA; this is a ground wire called the signal return. A third wire is called the TP signal wire. As the throttle is opened, the voltage from the sensor to the ECA increases from its closed-throttle voltage of about 0.8 volt to its wide-open-throttle voltage of over 4 volts. The TP sensor signals the ECA about what the driver is demanding from the engine. When the TP voltage rises, the ECA enriches the mixture, providing the same function as the accelerator pump in a carburetor.

How It Works

The TP sensor consists of a carbon film painted on a backing. Nine volts is fed into one end of the sensor. The other end of the carbon film is connected to ground. A metal wiper slides back and forth across the carbon film. As the wiper slides back and forth, the voltage to the ECA changes and the computer knows the position of the throttle.

Common Failures

The most common failure is wear of the carbon film. This usually manifests itself as an improper voltage to the ECA and an error in the quantity of fuel injected. At the point where the worn area is encountered in the movement of the throttle, a stumble or hesitation will occur.

EGR Valve Position Sensor

The EVP is a potentiometer located on the top of the EGR valve. As the EGR valve opens and closes, the voltage back to the ECA changes, keeping the ECA constantly abreast of the position of the EGR valve. On most EEC III applications, the amount of vacuum delivered to the EGR valve is controlled by the computer, which can instantly correct for errors in the position of the EGR valve. The advantage of this is better control of emissions and improved drivability.

How It Works

Three wires connect the EVP sensor to the ECA. One wire carries the 9-volt reference to the sensor. The second wire provides a ground for the sensor. The third wire carries the information about EGR valve position to the ECA as a varying voltage. When the EGR valve is closed, the voltage from the EVP sensor to the ECA should be about 0.8 volt. As the ECA allows the amount of vacuum going to the EGR valve to increase, the EGR valve opens. As the EGR valve opens, the output of the EVP sensor increases.

Common Failures

As with the TP sensor, the most common failure of the EVP sensor relates to the potentiometer. As the metal wiper runs back and forth across the carbon

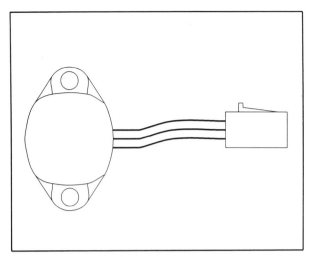

The TP sensor is a potentiometer mounted on the throttle shafts. Its job is to report the movement of the throttle to the ECA. This is the driver's most direct input to the computer. Three wires lead to the TP sensor. The first wire carries 9 volts (VREF) to the sensor. The second wire supplies a ground from the sensor to the ECA. The third wire is the ground. When the throttle is closed, the output voltage of the sensor is less than 1 volt. As the throttle is opened, the voltage steadily increases to a maximum exceeding 7 volts.

The EVP sensor is located on top of the EGR valve. This sensor has the responsibility of reporting the position of the EGR valve to the ECA. If the reported position is different from the position the EVP sensor attempted to achieve, the ECA will alter the amount of vacuum it is allowing to pass through the EGRV solenoid, which will change the position of the EGR valve diaphragm.

The EVP sensor is a linear potentiometer. As the diaphragm of the EGR valve rises and falls with changing vacuum, the plunger of the EVP sensor riding on the EGR diaphragm moves in and out. As the plunger moves in and out, the voltage to the ECA changes. One of the three wires running between the EVP sensor and the ECA carries the 9-volt reference. The second wire provides a ground between the EVP sensor and the ECA. The third wire provides a variable voltage signal to the ECA. As the EGR opens, the EVP output voltage increases.

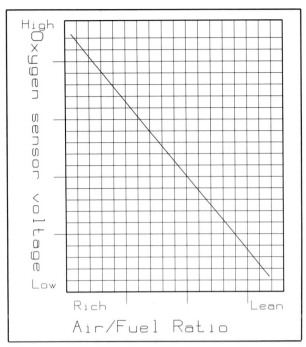

The EGO sensor measures the amount of oxygen in the exhaust system. As the amount of oxygen in the exhaust decreases (the engine is running rich), the oxygen sensor output voltage increases. As the amount of oxygen in the exhaust increases (the engine is running lean), the oxygen sensor output voltage decreases.

film, the carbon film wears. The wear in the carbon film creates spots where the EVP output signal drops to 0. These flat spots in the EVP output signal can cause the ECA to make improper decisions, which can in turn result in drivability problems.

Exhaust Gas Oxygen Sensor

The EGO sensor is used to detect the oxygen content of the exhaust system. The three primary components of the combustion process are air, fuel, and heat. The air is drawn in during the intake stroke, as the intake valve is opened and the piston starts its downward stroke. It consists of a mixture of 78 percent nitrogen, 21 percent oxygen, and 1 percent miscellaneous gases. Only the oxygen is part of the normal combustion process. If too much air enters the combustion chamber in proportion to the amount of fuel, the mixture in the combustion chamber will be lean. The resulting combustion will result in a high oxygen content in the exhaust. When the EGO sensor detects this high oxygen concentration in the exhaust, it signals the EEC computer, which responds by enriching the mixture.

The EGO sensor will also respond to vacuum leaks. Since a vacuum leak will cause at least one cylinder to run lean, the EGO sensor and the ECA will enrich the mixture to all cylinders. This will result in the entire engine running rich. It may seem odd that a vacuum leak can make the engine run rich and dras-

tically affect fuel economy, but such is the world of modern electronics.

Although the EGO sensor is designed to correct for errors in the air-fuel ratio, it will also respond to problems with the production of heat in the combustion chamber. The combustion chamber contains two major sources of heat: compression and spark. The heat of compression occurs as the piston travels upward on its compression stroke. When any gas, such as air, is compressed, heat is generated. This heat is an essential part of the combustion process. If mechanical conditions in the engine lower compression and therefore the amount of heat generated, this can seriously affect the quality of combustion. Anything that affects the quality of combustion will affect the amount of oxygen in the exhaust. As a result, bad rings, valves, or pistons can cause a high oxygen content in the exhaust. The EGO sensor will respond to this increase in oxygen by enriching the mixture.

Problems in the ignition system can also affect the quality of combustion. Since the ignition system is the most critical element of the heat portion of the combustion equation, a problem in it can severely affect the amount of oxygen in the exhaust system.

How It Works

The EGO sensor is an electrochemical device consisting of two layers of platinum separated by a

The EGO sensor becomes operative when its temperature reaches 600 degrees Fahrenheit. It detects the content of oxygen in the exhaust system, sending a variable voltage signal to the ECA. When the EGO sensor reports a lean-running engine, the ECA responds by increasing the injector on-time. When the EGO sensor reports a rich-running engine, the ECA responds by decreasing the injector on-time.

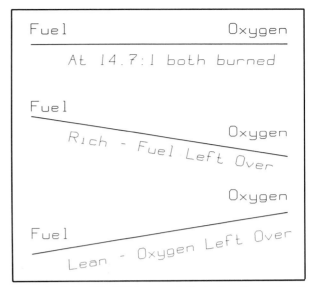

The principle of the EGO sensor is that when the engine is running rich, the oxygen is consumed before the fuel is all burned. The content of oxygen in the exhaust, therefore, is very low. When the engine is running at a perfect air-fuel ratio, both the fuel and the oxygen are totally consumed. When the engine is running lean, the fuel is consumed before the oxygen. Therefore, the oxygen content of the exhaust will be high.

layer of zirconium oxide. One plate is exposed to ambient oxygen, and the other is exposed to the oxygen content of the exhaust system. Although an electronics engineer would probably disagree, this is a lot like plates in a battery separated by an insulator.

The EGO sensor is installed in the exhaust system, usually close to the manifold. When the engine is started, the hot exhaust gases passing through the manifold begin to heat the EGO sensor. When the temperature of the EGO sensor reaches 600 degrees Fahrenheit, the EGO sensor becomes conductive for oxygen ions. In the same way that the plates of a battery begin to attract electrons from the electrolyte to create a voltage, the warm EGO sensor attracts oxygen electrons. If the number of oxygen electrons on the exhaust side is equal to the number on the ambient air side, then the electrons equalize and no voltage is produced. As the oxygen content of the exhaust decreases, an imbalance occurs and the EGO sensor begins to produce a voltage.

Normal operating voltages for the EGO sensor range from a low of 100 millivolts to a high of 900 millivolts. The voltage produced can occasionally be higher or lower than this range. About halfway between these voltages is 450 millivolts. This voltage is known as the crossover point. Any voltage less than 450 millivolts is interpreted by the computer as indicating a lean exhaust condition; any voltage greater than 450 millivolts is interpreted by the computer as indicating a rich exhaust condition. Anything that affects the content of oxygen in the exhaust will affect the EGO sensor signal.

To summarize: A cold EGO sensor will produce no signal; as the sensor warms up, it will begin to produce a voltage. A lean exhaust condition—one with a high oxygen content—will produce a voltage less than 450 millivolts, and a rich exhaust condition will produce a voltage greater than 450 millivolts.

Common Failures

The EGO sensor itself is a dependable unit. Occasionally, it will fail with an internal open circuit. The most common problem that occurs with EGO sensors is contamination. Three common sources of contamination for the oxygen sensor are RTV silicone, tetraethyl lead, and soot.

RTV silicone is a commonly used sealer and adhesive. The fumes from this adhesive can coat the EGO sensor, slowing its ability to respond to changes in the oxygen content of the exhaust. When the EGO sensor becomes contaminated with silicone, it delivers a lean signal to the EEC computer.

When the EGO sensor becomes contaminated by leaded fuel, the output voltage will be stuck above the crossover point, indicating a rich exhaust. Although this rarely occurs by accident, check the contents of any fuel additives being used to ensure that they do not contain tetraethyl lead.

The two primary sources for soot are oil and fuel. Oil soot is a result of a mechanical engine condition such as worn rings or valve guides. Fuel soot is the result of either an engine running rich or a misfire. Either form of soot impedes the operation of the EGO sensor. The output voltage remains constant at around 0.5 volt.

EEC III Quick Test

To perform this EEC III test, turn the ignition switch on. Disconnect the air pump control solenoids; these can be located by tracing the vacuum lines from the air pump control valves located on the air pump. Check for voltage on each of the wires; one of the two wires on each solenoid should have 12 volts. Reconnect the wires and connect a test light to one of the wires that did not have 12 volts.

Connect a hand-held vacuum pump to the vent side of the B/MAP (Barometric/Manifold Absolute Pressure) sensor. Start the engine. Apply 20in of vacuum to the B/MAP sensor. Hold the vacuum for 10 seconds. Release the vacuum. After about 30 seconds, the test light will blink out two-digit codes. The code 11 means that no problem was found during the test.

EEC III Two-Digit Codes

Code 21

The code 21 relates to the ECT sensor. If the temperature of the engine during the key-on, engine-off (KOEO) test is less than 50 degrees Fahrenheit or greater than 250 degrees Fahrenheit, the code 21 will be received. This code will be received during the key-on, engine-running (KOER) test if the temperature of the engine is less than 180 degrees Fahrenheit or greater than 250 degrees Fahrenheit. When performing the quick test to extract the trouble codes, be sure that the engine temperature is within these guidelines.

If the code 21 is received during either the KOEO test or the KOER test, ensure that the temperature of the engine is within the specs. If necessary, disconnect the jumper from the test connector and run the engine until the operating temperature is reached. Repeat the test. If the code 21 is still received, verify that the 9-volt VREF regulator of the ECA is working. To preclude the possibility of a bad ECT wire causing a deceptive reading, check the VREF at the TP sensor. If 9 volts is present at the TP connector, check the resistance of the ECT sensor. The resistance of the sensor should be as shown in the following chart:

Temperature of the Engine (Degrees Fahrenheit)	Resistance (Ohms)
50	58,750
68	37,300
86	24,270
104	16,150
122	10,970
140	7,700
158	5,370
176	3,840
194	2,800
212	2,070
230	1,550
248	1,180

The exact temperature of the engine coolant at the point where the ECT sensor is located is impossible to determine accurately, and the sensors may vary slightly. Therefore, do not expect the resistance reading to be exactly as indicated in the above chart.

Note: A rule of thumb is that the ECT sensors seldom become slightly defective. As a result, if the sensor reading falls anywhere on or near the chart, the sensor is probably good. It is usually sufficient to estimate the temperature of the engine as simply cold, warm, or hot.

If the resistance is good, leave the ECT sensor disconnected. Connect a digital voltmeter to the ECT signal wire. It should read 9 volts. If it does not, repair the defective wire or connection at the ECA. If the wire is not damaged, replace the ECA.

If the voltmeter does read 9 volts, leave it connected and connect a jumper wire between the ECT signal wire and the signal return wire at the ECT connector. The voltage displayed on the meter should drop to 0. If it does not, repair the signal return wire. If it does, replace the ECA.

Code 22

If the code 22 is received during the test, it means that the voltage from the B/MAP sensor is either missing or out of the expected range. Check the voltage on each of the four wires of the B/MAP sensor connector. Turn the ignition switch on. Two of the wires should read 8 volts. When the engine is started,

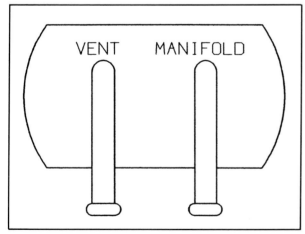

The B/MAP sensor measures the pressure in the atmosphere, detected through the vent port, and the pressure in the intake manifold. It then sends a signal to the ECA for each of these measurements. At sea level, the voltage on the four wires should be 9 volts, 8.1 volts, 8.1 volts, and 0 volts (ground).

the voltage on one of these wires should drop. If it does not, check the other two wires. One wire (usually orange) should have 9 volts. If it does not, repair as necessary. The other wire should be a ground. Repair as necessary.

If the wires test good, replace the B/MAP sensor. *Note:* If the code 22 is received during the engine-running test, make sure the EGR valve is closing and seating properly. If the EGR valve is not seating properly, this can cause erratic manifold pressures, which can result in erratic readings from the B/MAP sensor. Erratic readings from the B/MAP sensor can set the code 22.

Code 23

The code 23 indicates a problem with the TP sensor. This code will be received when the ECA sees a voltage from the TP sensor that is outside the expected parameters during the test. The low-end spec for this voltage is between 0.2 and 0.39 volt, depending on the application. The high-end spec is 8.84 volts.

Begin troubleshooting the code 23 by checking the voltage on the TP signal wire with the throttle closed. It should be within the specs listed above. If the voltage is lower than the specified minimum voltage, disconnect the harness from the TP sensor. The voltage on the orange wire, which is the VREF, should be approximately 9 volts. If it is not, disconnect the connector from the ECA. Inspect the connection. If this connection is good, check the resistance between the orange VREF wire and the signal return (TP ground) wire, which is usually black. The resistance should be infinity. If the resistance is less than infinity, repair the short between the VREF wire and the signal return wire.

If the resistance between the VREF and signal return wires is okay, connect an ohmmeter between the VREF and signal return terminals of the TP sensor. Move the throttle back and forth. If the resistance changes, replace the ECA. If the resistance does not change, replace the TP sensor.

If when the TP signal voltage was checked, the voltage was more than 8.84 volts, check for a short between the VREF wire and the TP signal wire. Also check for a short between the TP signal wire and any other voltage source. If all of these wires and connections check out okay, replace the TP sensor.

Code 31

The code 31 indicates that the EGR position-sensing device is transmitting a voltage lower than the ECA expected to see during the test.

The EEC III system uses the EVP sensor to sense EGR position. This is a potentiometer similar to the TP sensor and is located on top of the EGR. When the EGR valve is closed, the EVP sensor should be sending approximately 0.8 volt to the ECA. As the EGR valve opens, the voltage rises until it reaches just under 8.8 volts. Through this means, the ECA knows

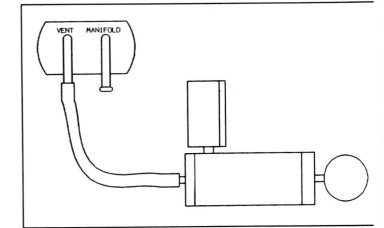

To extract the codes from the EEC III system, connect a hand-held vacuum pump to the vent port on the B/MAP sensor. Connect a test light or analog voltmeter to the ground side of either of the air pump control solenoids. Start the engine and allow it to idle until operating temperature is reached. Apply 20in of vacuum to the vent port. Hold that vacuum for 10 seconds and release it. After several seconds, the test light or voltmeter will flash out the codes.

at all times if the EGR control system is responding to the signals it is being sent.

Code 32

For EVP applications, if the code 32 is received during the test, disconnect the EVP harness connector and inspect for loose or damaged connections. Install a hand-held vacuum pump on the EGR valve. Apply and release the vacuum several times. Reconnect the EGR and run the test. If the code 32 does not return, the problem was a binding EGR valve. If the code 32 does return, replace the EVP sensor. Repeat the self-test. If the code 32 is still present, replace the EGR valve.

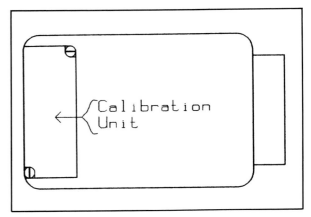

The EEC III ECA features a replaceable calibration unit. This unit is used to fine-tune the operation of the computer for a specific application.

These are the air pump control valves. Connect a test light to the ground side of one of the solenoids to receive the trouble codes on the EEC III system.

Code 41

If the code 41 is received during the test, it indicates the EGO sensor output voltage was stuck low for an extended time during the last forty operations of the engine and remained low throughout the test.

Begin troubleshooting the code 41 by connecting a high-impedance voltmeter in parallel to the EGO sensor. Leave the EGO sensor connected. Start the engine and run it at 2000rpm for 2 minutes. At the end of the 2 minutes, observe the voltmeter. The voltage should be switching from below 0.45 volt to above 0.45 volt several times during each 5-second interval. If the voltage remains low, disconnect the hoses between the air cleaner and the throttle assembly. Place the end of an unlit propane torch in the intake and open the propane control valve. If the voltage does not increase to above the 0.45 voltage threshold, check the following:

Distributor cap
Distributor rotor
Spark plug wires
Ignition coil
Spark plugs
EGR system
Fuel pressure (this should be 30psi to 40psi)

Intake leaks (these are also called vacuum leaks)
If you find no problems with any of the above, replace the EGO sensor.

Code 42

If the code 42 is received during the test, it indicates the EGO or sensor output voltage was stuck high for an extended time during the last forty operations of the engine and remained high throughout the test.

Begin troubleshooting the code 42 by connecting a high-impedance voltmeter in parallel to the EGO sensor. Leave the EGO sensor connected. Start the engine and run it at 2000rpm for 2 minutes. At the end of the 2 minutes, observe the voltmeter. The voltage should be switching from above 0.45 volt to below 0.45 volt several times during each 5-second interval. If the voltage remains high, disconnect the hoses between the air cleaner and the throttle assembly. Create a vacuum leak. If the voltage does not decrease to below the 0.45 voltage threshold, check for the following:

A saturated evaporative canister
A defective CANP valve
A defective PCV valve
Contaminated engine oil
High fuel pressure (fuel pressure should be 30psi to 40psi)

Code 43

The code 43 means the engine is running lean at wide-open throttle. This code can be caused by low fuel pressure at wide-open throttle or by clogged injectors. Connect a fuel pressure gauge to the inbound line of the fuel rail, and testdrive the car. If the fuel pressure drops at wide-open throttle, check the fuel lines for crimps and restrictions. If the fuel lines are in good condition, replace the fuel filter.

If the fuel pressure was within the specifications at wide-open throttle, have the injectors cleaned or replace them.

Code 44

When the code 44 is received during the test, it indicates the thermactor air system is not working. Possible causes include these:

Blocked, leaking, or kinked vacuum lines
Defective air pump
Defective diverter valve
Defective or blocked AM solenoids

7

EEC IV Components and Operation

The EEC IV fuel injection system combines electronic and mechanical devices to control the delivery and metering of fuel. Many of these devices are also used to control ignition timing and emission control equipment. They are divided into five categories: sensors, actuators, fuel delivery components, electrical components, and air induction components. This chapter will look at each component, its common failures, and how to troubleshoot it. It will also look at the EEC IV system function, closed-loop systems, and ECA modes of operation.

Sensors

Exhaust Gas Oxygen Sensor

The EGO sensor is used to detect the oxygen content of the exhaust system. The three primary

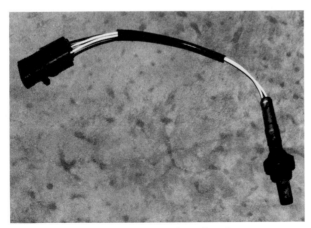

The EGO sensor becomes operative when its temperature reaches 600 degrees Fahrenheit. This sensor detects the content of oxygen in the exhaust system, sending a variable voltage along the black wire to the ECA. When the EGO sensor reports a lean-running engine, the ECA responds by increasing the injector on-time. When the EGO sensor reports a rich-running engine, the ECA responds by decreasing the injector on-time. The white wire provides a current to heat the EGO sensor. This HEGO sensor is used on most Ford EEC IV systems.

components of the combustion process are air, fuel, and heat. The air is drawn in during the intake stroke, as the intake valve is opened and the piston starts its downward stroke. It consists of a mixture of 78 percent nitrogen, 21 percent oxygen, and 1 percent miscellaneous gases. Only the oxygen is part of the normal combustion process. If too much air enters the combustion chamber in proportion to the amount of fuel, the mixture in the combustion chamber will be lean. The resulting combustion will result in a high oxygen content in the exhaust. When the EGO sensor detects this high concentration, it signals the EEC computer, which responds by enriching the mixture.

The EGO sensor will also respond to vacuum leaks. Since a vacuum leak will cause at least one cylinder to run lean, the EGO sensor and the ECA will enrich the mixture to all cylinders. This will result in the entire engine running rich. It may seem odd that a vacuum leak can make the engine run rich and drastically affect fuel economy, but such is the world of modern electronics.

Although the EGO sensor is designed to correct for errors in the air-fuel ratio, it will also respond to problems with the production of heat in the combustion chamber. The combustion chamber contains two major sources of heat: compression and spark. The heat of compression occurs as the piston travels upward on its compression stroke. When any gas, such as air, is compressed, heat is generated. This heat is an essential part of the combustion process. If mechanical conditions in the engine lower compression, and therefore the amount of heat generated, this can seriously affect the quality of combustion. Anything that affects the quality of combustion will affect the amount of oxygen in the exhaust. As a result, bad rings, valves, or pistons can cause a high oxygen content in the exhaust. The EGO sensor will respond to this increase in oxygen by enriching the mixture.

Problems in the ignition system can also affect the quality of combustion. Since the ignition system is the most critical element of the heat portion of the combustion equation, a problem in it can severely affect the amount of oxygen in the exhaust system.

How It Works

The EGO sensor is an electrochemical device consisting of two layers of platinum separated by a layer of zirconium oxide. One plate is exposed to ambient oxygen, while the other is exposed to the oxygen content of the exhaust system. Although an electronics engineer would probably disagree, these layers are a lot like plates in a battery separated by an insulator.

The EGO sensor is installed in the exhaust system, usually close to the manifold. When the engine is started, the hot exhaust gases passing through the manifold begin to heat the EGO sensor. When the temperature of the EGO sensor reaches 600 degrees Fahrenheit, the EGO sensor becomes conductive for oxygen ions. In the same way that the plates of a battery begin to attract electrons from the electrolyte to create a voltage, the warm EGO sensor attracts oxygen electrons. If the number of oxygen electrons on the exhaust side is equal to the number on the ambient air side, then the electrons equalize and no voltage is produced. As the oxygen content of the exhaust decreases, an imbalance occurs and the EGO sensor begins to produce a voltage.

Normal operating voltages for the EGO sensor range from a low of 100 millivolts to a high of 900 millivolts. The voltage produced can occasionally be higher or lower than this range. About halfway between these voltages is 450 millivolts. This voltage is known as the crossover point. Any voltage less than 450 millivolts is interpreted by the computer as indicating a lean exhaust condition; any voltage greater than 450 millivolts is interpreted by the computer as indicating a rich exhaust condition. Anything that affects the content of oxygen in the exhaust will affect the EGO sensor signal.

To summarize: A cold EGO sensor will produce no signal; as the sensor warms up, it will begin to produce a voltage. A lean exhaust condition—one with a high oxygen content—will produce a voltage less than 450 millivolts, and a rich exhaust condition will produce a voltage greater than 450 millivolts.

Common Failures

The EGO sensor itself is a dependable unit. Similar sensors installed on import applications during the late 1970s were still in good shape in the early 1990s. Occasionally, the EGO sensor will fail with an internal open circuit. The most common problem that occurs with EGO sensors is contamination. Three common sources of contamination for the oxygen sensor are RTV silicone, tetraethyl lead, and soot.

RTV silicone is a commonly used sealer and adhesive. The fumes from this adhesive can coat the EGO sensor, slowing its ability to respond to changes in the oxygen content of the exhaust. When the EGO sensor becomes contaminated with silicone, it delivers a lean signal to the EEC computer.

When the EGO sensor becomes contaminated by leaded fuel, the output voltage will be stuck above the crossover point, indicating a rich exhaust. Although this rarely occurs by accident, check the contents of any fuel additives being used to ensure that they do not include tetraethyl lead.

The two primary sources for soot are oil and fuel. Oil soot is a result of a mechanical engine condition such as worn rings or valve guides. Fuel soot is the result of either an engine running rich or a misfire. Either form of soot impedes the operation of the EGO sensor. The output voltages remains constant at around 0.5 volt.

Heated Exhaust Gas Oxygen Sensor

The heated exhaust gas oxygen (HEGO) sensor was introduced in 1986. When the EGO sensor cools down owing to a lack of exhaust volume, such as it will at idle, the output voltage drops to 0. For the brief time between the cooling of the oxygen sensor and the switching of the EEC computer to open loop, the fuel injection system will run extremely rich.

The HEGO sensor contains a heater to reduce the possibility of this occurring. The heater draws about 1 amp and can keep the sensor heated regardless of the exhaust gas volume. Other than this feature, the function of the HEGO sensor is exactly the same as that of the EGO sensor.

Manifold Absolute Pressure Sensor

The MAP sensor monitors the pressure in the intake manifold. Manifold pressure readings are used to estimate the mass of the air entering the engine. These estimates are used by the computer to determine the amount of fuel required for proper combustion. As the pressure in the manifold increases, the EEC computer assumes the air mass entering the engine is increasing. In addition, as the manifold pressure increases, the EEC computer assumes that the load on the engine is increasing. Its engine load figures are used in calculating enrichment and ignition timing.

As the ignition key is rotated through the on position heading toward start, the ECA takes a sample from the MAP sensor. At this point, the pistons are not moving up and down; the pressure in the intake manifold is atmospheric. The ECA stores this sample in memory and uses it as a base line to compare against all the engine-running MAP sensor readings.

How It Works

The EEC IV MAP sensor produces a square wave with a frequency that ranges from about 90 to 170 hertz. With the ignition key on and the engine off, the pressure in the intake manifold is atmospheric. At atmospheric pressure, the MAP sensor output frequency is around 160 hertz (this reading may differ a little, depending on altitude and weather conditions). When the engine is started, the intake manifold pressure drops, and so does the MAP output fre-

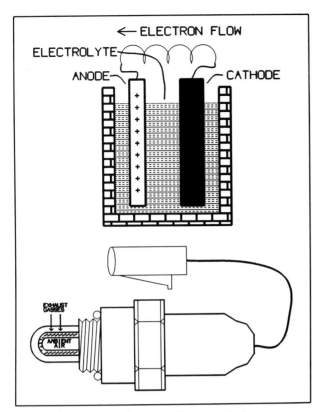

The EGO sensor produces a voltage much the same as a battery. The maximum output voltage of the sensor is about 1 volt. The minimum output voltage, when the EGO sensor is hot and operating, is about 0.1 volt. Voltages higher than 0.45 volt are interpreted by the ECA to indicate a rich operating condition. Voltages lower than 0.45 volt are interpreted by the computer to indicate a lean running condition.

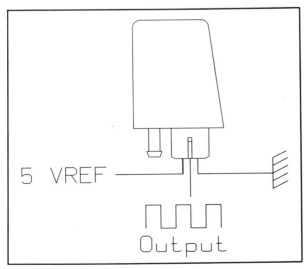

The MAP sensor has three wires. The orange wire carries a 5-volt power supply to the sensor. The middle wire carries a variable frequency square wave to the ECA. This frequency ranges from 90 hertz on hard deceleration to over 160 hertz KOEO. The last wire is a ground.

The MAP sensor is used by the computer on most older EEC IV applications to detect the load on the engine and the amount of air entering the engine. Shown here are the old-style MAP sensor, right, and the new-style MAP sensor, left.

quency. At idle, the output frequency is usually between 110 and 120 hertz. On deceleration, the frequency drops into the 90s.

Common Failures

When the MAP sensor fails, it usually ceases to produce a signal. Occasionally, an intermittent failure can cause the MAP signal to be interrupted for a very short time. A stumble or hesitation would result should the intermittent failure occur while the driver were trying to accelerate.

When in doubt about the condition of the MAP sensor, connect a frequency counter or tachometer to the middle terminal of the sensor with the sensor plugged in and the ignition turned on. At sea level, the frequency counter should read about 160 hertz. If a tachometer is being used, it should be on the four-cylinder scale and the reading should be about 4800 rpm. Connect a hand-held vacuum pump to the vacuum port of the sensor. The frequency should change inversely and proportionally to the vacuum.

Barometric Absolute Pressure Sensor

The barometric absolute pressure (BAP or BP) sensor is identical to the MAP sensor in operation. For practical purposes, if a BP sensor and a MAP sensor were placed side by side and exposed to exactly the same pressures, the output signals would be identical.

How It Works

The BP sensor is used only on applications that do not use a MAP sensor. These include turbocharged and supercharged applications as well as late-model applications that use a mass air flow sensor.

The purpose of the BP sensor is to monitor altitude by means of barometric pressure. When the vehicle changes altitude, subtle changes in air-fuel enrichment and ignition timing are required. The BP sensor monitors altitude so that the EEC computer can make these changes.

45

Common Failures

When the BP sensor fails, it usually ceases to produce a signal. Occasionally, an intermittent failure can cause the BP signal to be interrupted for a very short time. A minor stumble or hesitation would

The BP sensor is identical to the MAP sensor except for the adapter on the pressure port that prevents a vacuum hose from being attached. The BP sensor is used only on applications that use the VAF sensor.

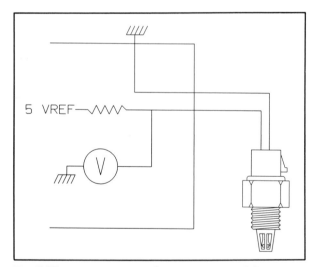

The ECT sensor measures the temperature of the engine. Two wires lead to this sensor. One wire is the signal return, or ground. The other wire carries a 5-volt reference from the ECA to the ECT sensor. A resistor in the ECA creates a voltage drop between the ECA and the ECT sensor. As the temperature of the engine rises, the resistance in the ECT sensor drops. As the ECT resistance drops, the voltage on the wire from the ECA to the ECT sensor drops. When the ECA sees a decreasing voltage, it knows the temperature is rising.

result should the intermittent failure occur while the driver were trying to accelerate.

Engine Coolant Temperature Sensor

The ECT sensor is a negative temperature coefficient thermistor. Located in the water jacket near the thermostat housing, it measures the temperature of the engine. It is a variable resistor whose resistance decreases as the temperature of the engine increases. The ECA uses this reading to adjust the air-fuel ratio and ignition timing based on the temperature of the engine. A cold engine will accept, and requires, a richer mixture and additional timing advance.

How It Works

The ECT sensor is supplied with a 5-volt reference from the ECA. This VREF passes through an internal resistor before proceeding out of the ECA to the sensor. When the engine is cold, the voltage on the wire between the sensor and the ECA is high—about 3 volts at 68 degrees Fahrenheit. When the engine is started, and as the temperature of the engine increases, the resistance of the ECT sensor drops. As the resistance drops, the voltage on the reference wire to the ECT sensor also drops. When the engine is thoroughly warmed up, the voltage on the reference wire is around 0.5 volt. The ECA measures this voltage to determine the temperature of the engine.

Common Failures

The most common failure of the ECT sensor is an intermittent open in the sensor. In most cases, a failure of the ECT circuit is a result of a problem in one of the wires or connections in the circuit.

Air Charge Temperature Sensor

The ACT sensor is a negative temperature coefficient thermistor, like the ECT sensor. It measures the temperature of the air in the intake system. Cold air is denser air. The colder the air is, the more fuel is required to provide the right air-fuel mixture for a given volume of air entering the engine. The ACT sensor trims the injector on-time to adjust for intake air temperature.

How It Works

The ACT sensor is supplied with a 5-volt reference from the ECA. This VREF passes through an internal resistor before proceeding out of the ECA to the sensor. When the air is cold, the voltage on the wire between the sensor and the ECA is high—about 3 volts at 68 degrees Fahrenheit. When the engine is started, and as the temperature of the engine increases, the resistance of the ACT sensor drops. As the resistance drops, the voltage on the reference wire to the ACT sensor also drops. When the engine is thoroughly warmed up, the voltage on the reference wire is around 0.5 volt. The ECA measures this voltage to determine the temperature of the engine. In general, the ACT sensor works exactly like the ECT sensor.

Common Failures

The most common failure of the ACT sensor is an intermittent open in the sensor. In most cases, a failure of the ACT circuit is a result of a problem in one of the wires or connections in the circuit.

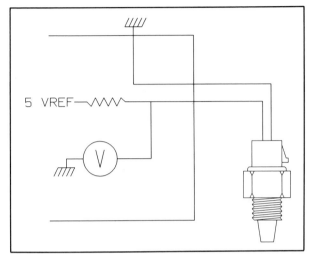

The ACT sensor measures the temperature of the air entering the intake. Two wires lead to this sensor. One wire is the signal return, or ground. The other wire carries a 5-volt reference from the ECA to the ACT sensor. A resistor in the ECA creates a voltage drop between the ECA and the ACT sensor. As the temperature of the engine rises, the resistance in the ACT sensor drops. As the ACT resistance drops, the voltage on the wire from the ECA to the ACT sensor drops. When the ECA sees a decreasing voltage, it knows the temperature is rising.

Throttle Position Sensor

The TP sensor is a potentiometer. The ECA sends a 5-volt reference signal to the TP sensor. A second wire provides a current path back to the ECA; this is a ground wire called the signal return. A third wire is called the TP signal wire. As the throttle is opened, the voltage from the sensor to the ECA increases from its closed-throttle voltage of about 0.8 volt to its wide-open throttle voltage of over 4 volts. The TP sensor signals the ECA about what the driver is demanding from the engine. When the TP voltage rises, the ECA enriches the mixture, providing the same function as the accelerator pump in a carburetor.

How It Works

The TP sensor consists of a carbon film painted on a backing. Five volts is fed into one end of the

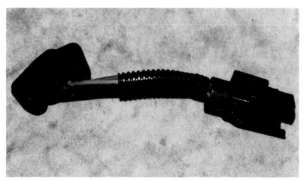

The throttle position (TP) sensor mounts on the throttle shaft.

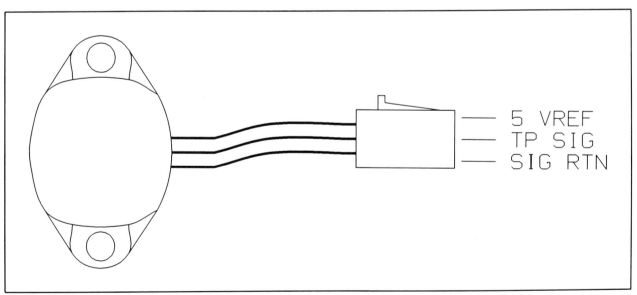

The TP sensor has three wires connecting it to the ECA. One wire carries a 5-volt reference to the sensor. The second wire provides a ground. The third wire carries a variable voltage signal to the ECA. When the throttle is closed, the TP sensor is delivering about 0.8 volt to the ECA. As the throttle is opened, the voltage to the ECA slowly rises to over 4 volts.

sensor. The other end of the carbon film is connected to ground. A metal wiper slides back and forth across the carbon film. As the wiper slides back and forth, the voltage to the ECA changes and the computer knows the position of the throttle.

Common Failures

The most common failure is wear of the carbon film. This usually manifests itself as an improper voltage to the ECA and an error in the quantity of fuel injected. At the point where the worn area is encountered in the movement of the throttle, a stumble or hesitation will occur.

Profile Ignition Pickup Sensor

The PIP sensor is located in the distributor on most engines and on the crankshaft on distributorless engines. Three wires go to the PIP: one carries VBAT to the sensor, another is the ground, and the third sends the signal to the TFI ignition module. The PIP signal then splits and goes to the coil current control section of the TFI module and to the ECA. The ECA uses the PIP signal to synchronize the injectors. The signal is also used as the tach signal to the computer.

How It Works

The PIP sensor is a Hall effect device, which is a semiconductor that responds to the presence of a magnetic field. A current passes through the semiconductor from the positive lead to the negative lead. The semiconductor is positioned opposite a permanent magnet. A windowed armature made of a ferrous metal rotates between the permanent magnet and the semiconductor. When the window is open, the output voltage of the sensor is low. When the armature rotates and the window closes, the output voltage of the sensor drops low. The result of this is that as the crankshaft rotates, a square wave is generated, the frequency of which is directly proportional to the speed of crankshaft rotation.

The PIP (Profile Ignition Pickup) is located in the distributor. As the distributor rotates, the armature blades—on the floor in front of the distributor—swing through the gap of the PIP sensor, creating a square wave. The frequency of the square wave is directly proportional to the speed of the engine. The PIP sensor provides the ECA with information about rpm for timing control and with the injector synchronizing signal.

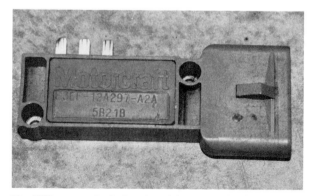

The PIP sensor feeds its signal into the TFI (Thick Film Integrated) ignition module through the three terminals on the top. The module allows the PIP signal to pass through to the ECA.

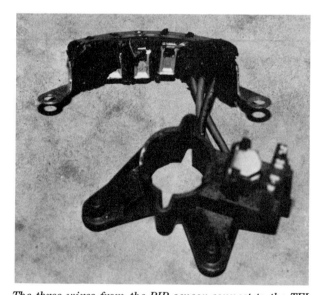

The three wires from the PIP sensor connect to the TFI module through a rubber or plastic connector block. Here, the rubber connector has been partially removed to expose the terminals.

Common Failures

The PIP sensor has an insulating connector block that connects the three terminals to the TFI module. In the early versions of the PIP sensor, this insulator block was rubber. Oil vapor would travel up the distributor shaft and deposit on the insulator block. These oil deposits would soften the insulator, making it conductive. Symptoms would include intermittent hesitation, stalling, and no start.

Vane Airflow Sensor

The vane airflow (VAF) sensor is an alternative to the MAP sensor for measuring airflow into the engine. It was developed by Bosch during the early 1970s for use on the L-Jetronic fuel injection system. Ford uses

The early, and troublesome, PIP sensor with the black connector is on the left. The PIP sensor on the right, with the light-colored connector, is the new-style and dependable version.

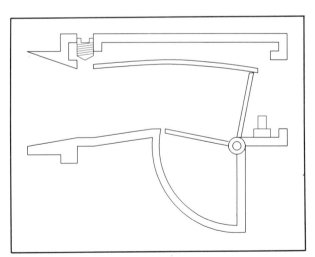

Two engines use the VAF (Vane Air Flow) sensor: the 1.9-liter and the 2.3-liter Turbo. This sensor consists of a movable flap attached to a potentiometer. When the engine starts, the flap moves, which moves the potentiometer. As the airflow increases, the voltage signal from the VAF sensor also increases.

the VAF sensor on the 1.9-liter and turbocharged 2.3-liter engines. The sensor consists of an L-shaped flap mounted on a rotating shaft connected to a potentiometer. As the volume of air flowing into the engine changes, the sensor's output voltage to the ECA changes. At idle, the output voltage of the VAF sensor is about 0.8 volt.

Incorporated within the VAF sensor is the vane air temperature (VAT) sensor. On applications using the VAF sensor, the VAT sensor signal replaces the ACT sensor.

How It Works

Four wires run between the VAF sensor and the ECA. A 5-volt VREF is sent from the ECA to the VAF sensor. A second wire between the VAF sensor and the ECA provides a ground. A third wire carries the airflow signal to the ECA. The voltage on this wire ranges from about 0.8 volt when the engine is idling to more than 4 volts when the key is on, the engine is off, and the flap is held open by hand. A fourth wire carries 5 volts to the VAT sensor. When the air temperature is cold, the voltage on this wire is relatively high—about 3 volts at 68 degrees Fahrenheit. As the temperature of the air increases, the VAT voltage to the ECA drops. At 100 degrees Fahrenheit, the voltage is about 2.2 volts.

Common Failures

As with the TP sensor, the most common failure of the VAF sensor relates to the potentiometer. As the metal wiper runs back and forth across the carbon film, the carbon film wears. This creates spots where the VAF output signal drops to 0. The symptoms related to this problem are a stumble or flat spot on acceleration.

The most common failure related to the VAT sensor is an intermittent open in the sensor. In most

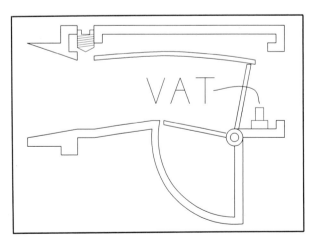

Contained within the VAF sensor is the VAT sensor. The purpose of this sensor is to measure the density of the air. Cold air is denser and requires additional fuel for a given airflow volume. Warm air is less dense and requires less fuel to be mixed with it for a given volume.

cases, a failure of the VAT circuit is a result of a problem in one of the wires or connections in the circuit.

Mass Airflow Sensor

Many later applications have replaced the MAP sensor with an MAF sensor. The MAF sensor consists of a large, hollow metal tube and a smaller parallel tube. The smaller tube contains a thermistor to measure the temperature of the incoming air. Next to the thermistor is a wire that is heated to a specified temperature above that of the incoming air. When the engine is started and air begins to flow into it, part of the airflow is diverted through the smaller tube. The heated wire is cooled. The MAF sensor's computer increases the current flow through the heated wire and sends a variable voltage signal to the ECA that is directly proportional to the amount of current used to maintain the temperature of the heated wire.

At idle, the voltage sent by the MAF sensor to the ECA is 0.8 volt. As the engine speed increases, the output voltage increases. At 60 miles per hour (mph), the output voltage is around 1.8 to 2.5 volts. The exact voltage at a given speed will vary depending on engine load and the size of the engine.

Knock Sensor

The knock sensor is used on many engines to signal the ECA when a detonation (pinging) is occurring. Since the ECA controls ignition timing while the engine is running, it will respond to a detonation by retarding the timing.

How It Works

The knock sensor is a pressure sensitive resistor. The ECA sends a reference voltage to the knock sensor the same way it does to the ECT sensor or the ACT sensor. When a detonation occurs, sound travels through the metal of the block. The result is a fluctuating change in resistance within the knock sensor, and this causes a fluctuation in the VREF from the ECA. When the voltage on the knock sensor wire fluctuates, the ECA responds by retarding the timing. When the timing retards enough, the detonation stops.

Common Failures

The knock sensor itself has an extremely low failure rate. Most failures in this circuit relate to wiring and connection problems.

Vehicle Speed Sensor

Many applications are equipped with a VSS. This sensor signals the ECA regarding the speed of the vehicle. Vehicle speed information is used to control the lockup function of the torque converter clutch on many automatic transmission applications. Some cars also use the signal as the speed reference for the cruise control and for controlling the two-speed electric radiator fan. Vehicles equipped with this fan operate it on the lower speed when at freeway speeds.

How It Works

The VSS is a pulse generator. As the car is driven, a gear in the transmission rotates the sensor. This

The VSS slips into the output shaft housing of the transmission. The two wires connected to it produce an alternating current sine wave, the frequency of which is directly proportional to the speed of the vehicle. Use an AC voltmeter to test it. Lift the drive wheels of the vehicle off the ground. Drop the transmission into drive (or second on a manual) and allow the drive wheels to idle. The sensor should put out 0.5 volt AC or more.

The MAF sensor used by Ford mounts on a tube located between the air cleaner and the throttle assembly. It delivers a variable voltage signal to the ECA. When the engine is idling, the voltage is low—around 1 volt. When the engine is at full speed, the voltage is high—around 4 volts.

The EVP sensor is a potentiometer mounted on the top of the EGR valve. Three wires are attached to it. One wire carries a 5-volt reference to the sensor. The second wire provides a ground. The third wire carries a variable voltage signal to the ECA. When the EGR valve is closed, the TP sensor is delivering about 0.8 volt to the ECA. As the EGR valve is opened, the voltage to the ECA slowly rises to over 4 volts.

creates a pulse that is directly proportional to the speed of the vehicle.

Common Failures

Like that of many of the sensors in the EEC IV system, the most common failure of the VSS is related to wires and connections.

EGR Valve Position Sensor

The EVP sensor is a potentiometer located on the top of the EGR valve. As the EGR valve opens and closes, the voltage back to the ECA changes, keeping the ECA constantly abreast of the position of the EGR valve. On most EEC IV applications, the amount of vacuum delivered to the EGR valve is controlled by the computer, which can instantly correct for errors in the position of the EGR valve. The advantage of this is better control of emissions and improved drivability.

How It Works

Three wires connect the EVP sensor to the ECA. One wire carries the 5-volt reference to the sensor. The second wire provides a ground for the sensor. The third wire carries the information about EGR valve position to the ECA as a varying voltage. When the EGR valve is closed, the voltage from the EVP sensor to the ECA should be about 0.5 volt. As the ECA allows the amount of vacuum going to the EGR valve to increase, the EGR valve opens. As the EGR valve opens, the output of the EVP sensor increases.

The EVP sensor has a plunger protruding through its bottom and resting on the EGR diaphragm. As the EGR valve diaphragm is lifted, the plunger is lifted. As the plunger is lifted, the EVP sensor output voltage increases.

The PFE sensor is used on many applications instead of the EVP sensor. This sensor measures the pressure in the tube that runs from the exhaust system to the EGR valve. When the pressure in this tube is high, it indicates the EGR valve is closed. As the pressure drops, the PFE sensor assumes that it is because the EGR valve is opening. When the EGR valve opens, it exposes the EGR tube to manifold vacuum and the pressure in the tube drops.

Common Failures

As with the TP sensor, the most common failure of the EVP sensor relates to the potentiometer. As the metal wiper runs back and forth across the carbon film, the carbon film wears. The wear in the carbon film creates spots where the EVP output signal drops to 0. These flat spots in the EVP output signal can cause the ECA to make improper decisions, which can in turn result in drivability problems.

Pressure Feedback EGR Sensor

The PFE sensor is an alternative to the EVP sensor. It detects back pressure in the exhaust system and reports the readings to the ECA. The ECA uses these readings to make decisions concerning how much to open the EGR valve. The basic theory is that the greater the pressure in the exhaust system, the greater the speed and load on the engine. The greater the speed and load on the engine, the more the EGR valve needs to be open to control oxides of nitrogen, and the more it can be open without affecting drivability.

How It Works

The PFE sensor behaves like a potentiometer: it changes pressures into voltage readings. Three wires are connected to the sensor: one wire sends the 5-volt reference to the sensor, the second provides a ground, and the third carries the exhaust pressure readings back to the ECA. As the pressure in the exhaust system increases, the output voltage of the sensor increases. At idle, the output voltage of the sensor should be between 3 and 3.5 volts.

Common Failures

The PFE sensor itself suffers from occasional failures because of proximity and exposure to exhaust gases. The most common failures in this circuit, however, are still related to the connections and wires.

Brake On-Off Switch

The brake on-off (BOO) switch signals the computer when the brakes have been applied by the driver. This information is used by the ECA to help control the operation of the torque converter clutch. Upon application of the brake, the torque converter clutch is disengaged to prevent stalling in the event of a panic stop.

Power Steering Pressure Switch

The power steering pressure switch (PSPS) signals the ECA when a load is put on the power steering system. When the power steering pump is loaded, an additional load is placed on the engine, causing a potential reduction in idle speed. When the PSPS senses a rise in power steering pump pressure, the ECA raises the idle speed to reduce the possibility of a stall. This feature is particularly important when the driver is parallel parking.

Neutral Gear Switch

The neutral gear switch (NGS) signals the computer when the manual transmission is placed in gear. This warns the computer that a new load may soon come on the engine as the clutch is released. The ECA is thereby prepared to increase the idle speed of the engine to help the driver pull away from a stop without stalling the engine.

Neutral Drive Switch

The neutral drive switch (NDS) detects when the transmission is placed in neutral. When the transmission is placed in gear, the torque converter and transmission become an additional load on the engine. This load can cause the idle speed to drop. When the ECA senses that the transmission is placed in gear, it increases the airflow into the engine by means of the idle control device. This increase in airflow prevents a dip in rpm as the transmission engages into drive or reverse.

Idle Tracking Switch

The idle tracking switch (ITS) is a component within the throttle-linkage-mounted idle speed control (ISC) motor. When the throttle comes to rest on the end of the motor, the plunger is depressed, closing the ITS. When the ITS closes, the ECA knows to begin controlling the idle speed with the idle speed control motor.

Clutch Engage Switch

The clutch engage switch (CES) is located on and activated by the clutch pedal on manual-transmission-equipped applications. When the clutch is engaged, the switch closes. The ECA adjusts the idle speed to compensate for any additional load that the engagement of the clutch places on the engine.

Clutch Interlock Switch

The clutch interlock switch prevents the engine from starting unless the clutch is depressed. This switch is incorporated in the CES.

This is the ISC motor. The unit mounts on the side of the throttle assembly of many CFI systems. Four wires are on the ISC motor. Two control the energizing and direction of the motor. The other two are for the ITS, which informs the ECA when the throttle has come to rest on the plunger.

Transmission Gear Switches

Automatic transmissions have switches in them to signal the ECA concerning when the transmission is in gear and which gear it is in.

Actuators

Fuel Control Assembly

Ford uses two different types of fuel control assemblies: centralized fuel injection (CFI) and multipoint injection (MPI). CFI uses one or two injectors to fuel the entire engine. The CFI system used on V-6 and V-8 applications is a high-pressure system operating at about 35psi. The CFI system used on four-cylinder engines is a low-pressure system operating at about 14psi.

The MPI system uses one injector for each cylinder. The injector is mounted in the intake manifold just above the intake valve. The typical fuel pressure at idle is about 35psi.

Injectors

Two types of injectors are used by Ford: side feed and top feed.

The low-pressure CFI system uses a side-feed injector. The fuel enters the injector at the bottom, just above where it is sprayed out. The injector is supplied with positive voltage from the EEC power relay. The ECA provides a ground for the injectors. Normally, the circuit through the ECA to ground is open. A ground is provided when needed to open the injectors. When the engine is idling, the injector pulse width is around 1 to 1.5 milliseconds.

The high-pressure CFI and MPI systems use a top-feed injector. Fuel enters this injector from the top, passes through the injector, and is sprayed out through the bottom. The injector is supplied with positive voltage from the EEC power relay. The ECA provides a ground for the injectors. Normally, the circuit through the ECA to ground is open. A ground is provided when needed to open the injectors.

The CFI applications that use top-feed injectors are V-8 and V-6 engines. These use two injectors to fuel the entire engine. The ECA alternates the opening of these injectors when the engine is running. When the engine is being started, the injectors are pulsed together to enrich the mixture for starting.

The CFI system used on the V-6s and V-8s was a high-pressure system. Fuel pressure on these systems was about 35psi. Later V-engines use the MPI system.

The fuel pressure regulator mounts on the fuel rail of the MPI system. Note the Schraeder valve next to the fuel pressure regulator. Note also that the pressure regulator has a vacuum port on its top side. When the throttle is opened and the manifold pressure increases, the vacuum port causes the fuel pressure to rise 5psi to 10psi. This causes a slight enrichment of the air-fuel ratio for acceleration.

A low-pressure injector is used on late-model CFI systems.

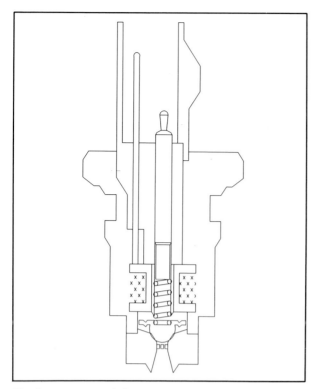

The low-pressure injector consists of a spring-loaded solenoid-operated valve. This ball-shaped valve is lifted from its seat when the solenoid is energized. As the valve is lifted, fuel is sprayed into the throttle body above the intake manifold.

MPI engines use a top-feed, high-pressure injector. These injectors are similar in design to injectors that have been used on some European cars since the late 1960s. The fuel with this type of injector enters from the top, passes through the injector, and is sprayed out the tip in a cone-shaped pattern.

Two categories of MPI systems are used: EFI and sequential electronic fuel injection (SEFI). On EFI systems, the injectors are pulsed in groups. Each injector is opened on each crankshaft revolution. When the engine is idling, each time the injectors open, they stay open for 1.5 to 2.5 milliseconds.

SEFI systems open the injectors one at a time. Each injector opens one time for every two crankshaft revolutions. When the engine is idling, each time an injector opens, it stays open for 2 to 4 milliseconds.

The most common problem that occurs with injectors is restriction. Two forms of restriction are found: internal and external. Internal restrictions are the result of contamination, usually originating in the

The low-pressure injector has six orifices through which the fuel is sprayed. As a result, it sprays a fine, cone-shaped mist into the throttle bore.

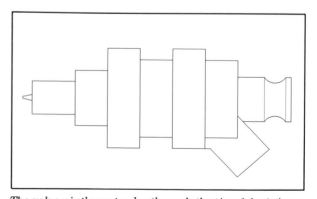

The valve pintle protrudes through the tip of the injector on the multipoint systems. This design allows sediment to build up on the tip of the injector. This sediment forms a restriction that can affect the fuel flow into the intake manifold.

fuel tank. External restrictions are unique to the multipoint engines. Waxy substances in the fuel adhere to the tip of the injector. As fine particles of dirt and carbon pass through the intake, they stick to this waxy substance. The result is a restriction to the flow of fuel through the tip of the injector. The cylinder or cylinders serviced by these injectors will run lean.

Throttle Air Bypass Valve

The throttle air BYP valve is a solenoid-operated air control valve used on the EFI and SEFI models. The ECA controls the BYP ground by switching it on and off at a frequency of about 60 hertz. The frequency is so high that the valve does not have time to seat in either the open or closed position; therefore, the valve dithers between the open and closed positions. As the ECA alters the duty cycle of the pulse, the point at which the valve dithers changes. This changes the airflow through the air bypass, which changes the idle speed.

Should the BYP valve fail, the engine will not idle—assuming that the engine idle speed has been adjusted properly.

DC Idle Speed Control Motor

The throttle body applications use a DC motor on the throttle linkage to control the idle speed. When the throttle comes to rest on the end of the ISC motor, the idle tracking switch closes. This signals the ECA to control the idle speed. By applying and reversing current through the ISC motor, the ECA can control the position of the throttle, thereby controlling the idle speed of the engine.

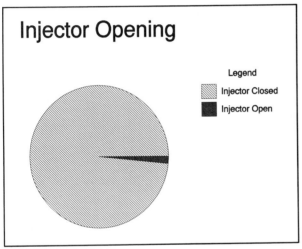

When the injector is energized by the ECA, it is open only a few milliseconds.

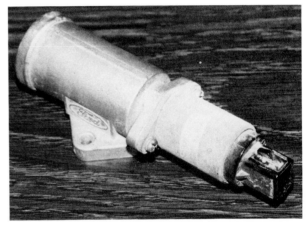

The idle speed on the MPI systems is controlled by the BYP air control valve. The ECA sends a high-frequency pulse to the BYP valve. As the duty cycle is varied, the BYP valve changes position and the idle speed changes.

As the valve opens and closes, air from in front of the throttle plates passes through the valve to behind the throttle plates. As the duty cycle to the valve changes, the amount of air passing from in front of the throttle plates to behind the throttle plates changes. As the air volume changes, the idle speed changes.

The valve controlling the idle speed airflow is activated by a solenoid. Although this solenoid is removable, it is not replaceable as a separate component.

EGR Vacuum Regulator

The EGR vacuum regulator (EVR) is a solenoid-operated vacuum control valve. The EVR is fed 12 volts of switched ignition voltage. The ECA grounds the EVR to energize the solenoid. The EVR is actually a controlled vacuum leak. When the EGR valve is not energized, vacuum destined for it is diverted to the atmosphere. When the ECA determines that conditions are right for the EGR valve to open, a variable duty cycle signal is sent to the EVR and vacuum begins to flow to the EGR valve. As the duty cycle to the EGR valve increases, the amount of vacuum sent to the EGR valve increases and the EGR valve opens.

A filter in the EVR is prone to becoming plugged. When the filter plugs, the EGR will open and the engine will begin to idle roughly or die.

EGR Control and EGR Vent

The combination of the EGR control (EGRC) and the EGR vent (EGRV) substitutes for the EVP sensor on many applications. Both are vacuum control solenoids. The ECA controls the EGRC to regulate whether or not vacuum can flow to the EGR valve. When the ECA is not grounding the EGRC, vacuum cannot go to the EGR valve. When the ECA grounds the EGRC, vacuum can flow to the EGR valve. The ground for the EGRV is controlled by a variable duty cycle signal through the ECA. As the duty cycle increases, the amount of vacuum reaching the EGR valve increases and the amount that the EGR valve opens increases.

This is the mounting position for the BYP valve on an early 5.0-liter Mustang. Note the mounting location immediately behind the throttle bore.

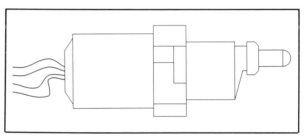

The ISC motor mounts on the side of the throttle assembly of many CFI systems. Four wires are on the ISC motor. Two control the energizing and direction of the motor. The other two are for the ITS, which informs the ECA when the throttle has come to rest on the plunger.

The amount of vacuum to the EGR valve, and therefore the position of the EGR valve, is controlled by the EVR. The EVR is a computer-controlled vacuum leak for the vacuum destined for the EGR valve. The ECA sends a variable duty cycle signal to the EVR. As the duty cycle varies, the amount of vacuum to the EGR varies. As the amount of vacuum to the EGR valve changes, the position of the EGR valve changes.

Inside of the cap on the EVR is a filter. If this filter becomes restricted, the EGR valve will be held open. With an EGR valve that does not close completely, the engine can idle roughly or stall at idle.

Thermactor Air Divert and Thermactor Air Bypass Solenoids

The thermactor air divert (TAD) and thermactor air bypass (TAB) solenoids are used to control the emission control air pump system. When the engine is warming up, the TAD solenoid directs the air from the air pump into the exhaust system ahead of the EGO sensor. This increases the temperature of the exhaust system, which assists the warm-up of the EGO sensor and the catalytic converter. When the engine approaches operating temperature, the TAD solenoid is controlled by the ECA to pump the air into the center of the catalytic converter. This improves the efficiency of the oxidizing section of the catalytic converter.

At certain times, air should not be pumped into the exhaust system at all. During deceleration, pumping air into the exhaust allows for an increased possibility of a backfire. During the enrichment that occurs on heavy acceleration, exhaust temperatures can rise to extremely high levels. During these times, the ECA controls the TAB solenoid to bypass the air to the atmosphere.

Different applications will control the TAB and TAD solenoids in a variety of ways, all of which are some variation of this theme.

Inferred Mileage Sensor

The inferred mileage sensor (IMS), as the name implies, is not an actuator but a sensor. It is discussed here because its use is closely tied to the operation of the TAB and TAD solenoids. As the engine is run, the IMS records time. The ECA sees this time as an estimated mileage. At around 30,000 miles, the IMS signals the ECA to alter the TAB and TAD control program. In addition, the EGR control system may also be affected.

Canister Purge Solenoid

The CANP solenoid is also controlled by the ECA. When the vehicle reaches cruise speed, the ECA energizes the CANP solenoid. This allows the evaporative canister to purge itself. The evaporative canister is a metal or plastic can filled with activated charcoal. The fuel tank vapors vent into the evaporative canister, where they are stored until the engine can burn them with little or no effect on emissions or engine performance. In most cases, the CANP solenoid is energized at cruise speeds.

Wide-Open-Throttle Air Conditioner Cutout Relay

The wide-open-throttle air conditioner cutout relay controls current flow to the air conditioner compressor clutch (ACC). When the ECA senses that the engine is coming under a load, it releases the ground for the wide-open-throttle air conditioner cutout relay. When the ground is released, the relay switch that controls the path to ground for the ACC and the air conditioner compressor shuts off. Shut-ting off the air conditioner compressor when the engine is under a load delivers more power to acceleration. The compressor clutch is also shut off when the engine is overheating and when the ECA detects a prescribed set of sensor failures.

Turbo Boost Control Solenoid

The ECA uses the turbo boost control solenoid to limit the amount of boost the turbocharger can produce. It uses inputs from the BP sensor and KS to determine when safe boost levels have been reached. The boost control solenoid limits the amount of boost by receiving a variable duty cycle signal from the ECA. The waste gate is then controlled by the boost solenoid. Needless to say, only the turbo-charged applications are equipped with a boost control solenoid.

Converter Clutch Override Solenoid

The converter clutch override (CCO) solenoid switches off oil flow to the torque converter clutch in an automatic transmission. Torque converter clutches were introduced in the late 1970s to increase fuel economy. When the engine speed and load conditions indicate cruise, the converter clutch locks up. This connects the transmission input to the output of the crankshaft at a 1:1 ratio. This is a rare condition for a nonlockup automatic transmission. At certain times during the normal operation of the vehicle, this 1:1 ratio is not desirable—for example, in a panic stop, at very low engine speeds, at very low vehicle speeds, and when the engine is cold or

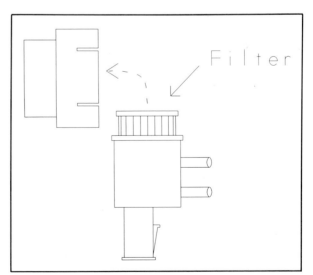

The EGRV is also similar to the EVR. Along with the EGRC, the EGRV controls the EGR on older applications. After the EGRC allows vacuum to go to the EGR valve, the EGRV allows the vacuum to bleed to the atmosphere. When the ECA wants the EGR valve to open, a variable duty cycle signal is sent to the EGRV. The bleeding of the vacuum is reduced and the EGR valve is opened. Like the EVR, the EGRV has a serviceable filter.

overheating. At these times, the ECA disengages the CCO solenoid, which unlocks the converter clutch.

Locking Upshift Solenoid

The locking upshift solenoid (LUS) works in with the CCO solenoid to control the operation of the torque converter clutch. When the ECA senses that the engine is near operating temperature, is not under a load, is at part throttle, and is within a certain rpm band, then it will energize the LUS, which will lock up the torque converter clutch.

Fuel Pump Relay

The fuel pump relay is controlled by the ECA. For most EEC IV–equipped vehicles, the PIP signal is the primary input for the control of the fuel pump relay. When the engine is being cranked, the crank position of the ignition switch energizes the fuel pump relay and the fuel pump runs. When the key is released, the fuel pump relay will shut off the fuel pump unless PIP signals are being received by the ECA. This ensures that the fuel pump is shut off when the engine is not running.

In the event of an accident, a ruptured fuel line could be a severe fire hazard. If a fuel line ruptures, the resulting loss of fuel pressure would cause the engine to die. When the engine dies, the loss of a PIP signal will cause the ECA to shut off the fuel pump by way of the fuel pump relay.

This theory is good unless the fuel line that ruptures is the return line. If the return line ruptures, the engine may continue to run, and therefore the fuel pump would continue to run. The fuel pump would not shut off until the fuel tank was pumped dry. To prevent this, an inertia switch is placed in the fuel pump electrical circuit. When an impact occurs, the inertia switch shuts off the fuel pump. (See the discussion on the inertia switch in the "Electrical Components" section later in this chapter for more detail.)

Integrated Control Module

The integrated control module (ICM) is a metal box, usually located on the radiator firewall, that contains relays to control five functions. Applications such as Thunderbird and Taurus use the ICM in place of the following relays:
EEC power relay
Fuel pump relay
Electro-drive cooling fan (EDF)
High-speed electro-drive cooling fan (HEDF)
Air conditioner relay

Air Conditioner and Cooling Fan Controller Module

The air conditioner and cooling fan controller module is controlled by the ECA on most applications as a way of activating the ACC and the radiator cooling fan. If the vehicle is equipped with an ICM, no air conditioner and cooling fan controller module is used.

Fuel Delivery Components

Fuel Tank

The EEC IV fuel injection fuel tank is in no way unusual when compared with those in carbureted cars.

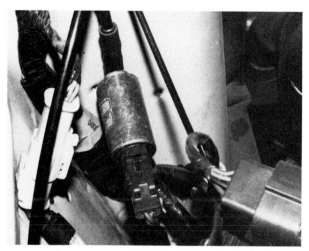

The canister purge solenoid (CANP) is used on many applications to control the purging of the evaporative canister. The evaporative canister is a large can resembling a black tomato juice can. The can is filled with activated charcoal. When fuel vapors are given off by the fuel tank, they are trapped in the canister until the ECA energizes the CANP solenoid to purge the canister.

The fuel pump relay, to the right of the MAP sensor here, controls the fuel pump. When the ignition switch is turned to the on position, the fuel pump will run for about 2 seconds, then shut off. When the engine is cranking or running, the ECA energizes the fuel pump relay. The fuel pump runs continuously while the engine is running.

Fuel Pump

Two types of fuel pumps are used on fuel-injected Ford products: low-pressure and high-pressure.

Low-Pressure Pump

The low-pressure pump is located in the tank and is a vane pump driven by a high-speed electric motor. This pump is used on the low-pressure CFI (Centralized Fuel Injection) cars. It has a deadhead pressure of around 60psi. During operation, it must supply fuel to the injector at a steady pressure of 14.5psi. Therefore, the system pressure should never approach the pump's deadhead pressure.

The low-pressure in-tank pump is also used on high-pressure throttle body and multipoint applications as a lift pump or prepump for a high-pressure chassis-mounted pump. The job of a prepump is to move fuel from the tank to the high-pressure pump.

High-Pressure Pump

The high-pressure pump is a roller vane pump capable of producing a deadhead pressure of nearly 125psi. During operation, this chassis-mounted pump must supply fuel to the injector at a steady pressure of 35psi to 55psi. Therefore, the system pressure should never approach the pump's deadhead pressure.

Most late-model, high-pressure applications have eliminated the need for an in-tank prepump by placing the high-pressure pump in the tank. At first thought, having an electric fuel pump with fuel passing through it in the tank seems to be inviting fire. This practice goes well back into the 1970s with no problems, however.

Filters

Three types of filters are used by Ford: in-tank, main system, and reservoir. A dirty fuel filter—any of the three—can cause a loss of power, stalling, and hesitation.

In-tank Filter

Located on the end of the prepump, fuel pump, or fuel pickup is an in-tank screen or sock. Although this is not the primary filter of the system, it is critical to protecting the pump or pumps from large particles and sediment in the tank. This filter is seldom thought about and almost never replaced. Replacement is never part of a commercial tune-up. To replace this filter, for most applications, it is necessary to remove the fuel tank from the vehicle and then remove the fuel pickup–gas gauge sending unit assembly from the tank. The filter is located on the end of the sending unit or fuel pump.

When this filter becomes restricted, the driver will notice a loss of power under acceleration and eventually at cruise.

Main System Filter

In the fuel line between the pump and the engine is the main system fuel filter. This filter is designed to remove from the fuel passing through it particles that are as small as 10 microns.

This fuel pump is typical of those used on the low-pressure CFI systems. Located in the fuel tank, they supply a much larger volume of fuel than the engine could possibly consume. The excess fuel returns to the tank through the system return line.

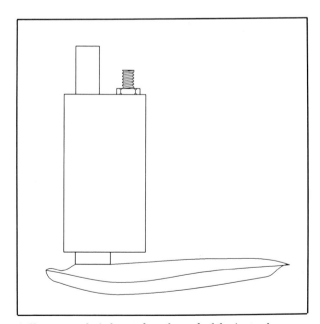

A filter, or sock, is located on the end of the in-tank pump. This is the fuel pump's only defense against damage from hard-particle contamination from the tank. This filter is almost never serviced yet can cause extreme drivability problems.

The service interval described in the owners manual for the fuel filter may be far longer than your driving conditions may warrant. Poor-quality fuel, blowing dust, and other environmental considerations mean that the fuel filter should be changed at least as often as the spark plugs. A group of mechanics working for the city of Los Angeles said that if they do not replace the fuel filters in their police cars at least every 10,000 miles, they begin to have problems.

The filter itself is a paper mesh device in a metal can normally located in the engine compartment.

Reservoir Filter

Some truck applications have an additional filter located on the frame approximately below the driver's feet. It is a plastic container about 5in in diameter and 4in tall. Getting one of these filters from a dealer can be a frustrating experience. The Ford

A fuel injection pump is an electric motor driving a small vane pump or roller vane pump. The motor spins at about 3500rpm. Severe damage can result from cavitating this pump.

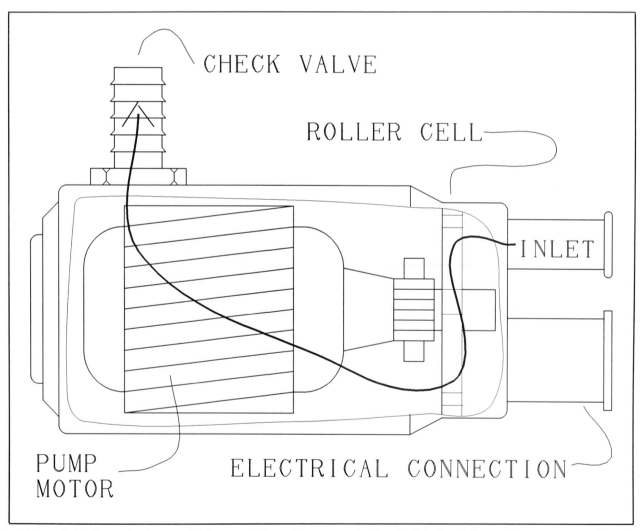

Fuel is pulled in through the pump inlet, pumped through the electric motor, and pumped out through a check valve. As the fuel passes through the electric motor, it acts as a coolant and a lubricant. Severe damage can result to the electric motor when the pump cavitates.

parts manuals do not call it a filter, and many dealership parts people and mechanics do not know that it is a filter. The drivability book identifies it as the "single function reservoir anti-siphon valve" on trucks with only one fuel tank and the "mechanical selector valve reservoir anti-siphon valve" on dual-tank applications. Some dual-tank applications use a single-function reservoir with a separate selector valve.

Pressure Test Point

All the high-pressure applications, both multipoint and CFI, have a test point for checking the fuel pressure. This test point is located on the CFI assembly or on the fuel rail. The low-pressure CFI system does not have such a test point; all pressure testing must be done by teeing the fuel pressure gauge into the throttle body supply hose.

Injectors

Injectors were covered earlier in the "Actuators" section of this chapter. These injectors spray the fuel

on top of the throttle plates or into the intake manifold directly on top of the intake valves.

Fuel Pressure Regulator

MPI Systems

The fuel pressure regulator is mounted on the fuel rail of the multipoint systems. The regulator is a spring-loaded diaphragm in a metal can. The diaphragm controls the opening and closing of a valve. When the fuel pressure exceeds the prescribed level, the diaphragm deflects, opening the valve, and fuel is bled back through the return line to the tank to control the fuel pressure.

Since the injectors of the multipoint systems feed fuel immediately above the intake valve, the pressure into which they are injecting is constantly changing. To compensate for these changes, a vacuum hose connects the intake manifold to the dry side of the fuel pressure regulator diaphragm. When the engine is idling, the pressure in the intake manifold is low and the fuel pressure will be con-

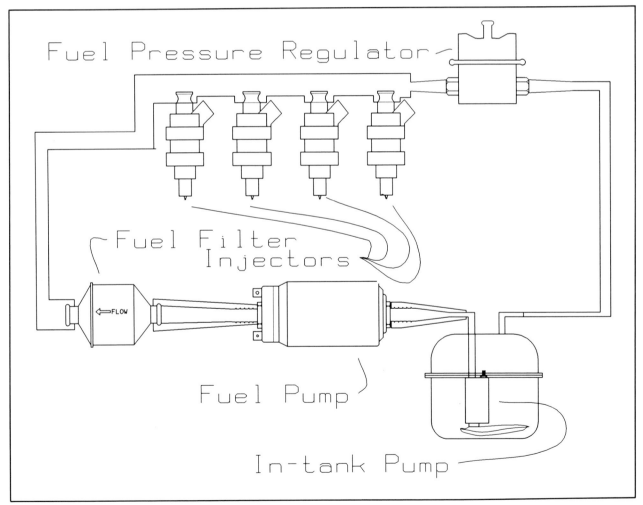

The components through which the fuel passes make up the fuel circuit. These include the fuel tank, the fuel pump or pumps, the fuel filter, the fuel rail, the fuel pressure regulator, the injectors, and the return line to the tank.

trolled at a typical pressure of 30psi to 45psi—45psi to 60psi for the 4.9-liter trucks. When the throttle is opened to accelerate, the intake manifold pressure will increase. The vacuum line carries this increasing pressure to the fuel pressure regulator, increasing the diaphragm spring tension. The result is that the fuel pressure will rise 5psi to 10psi above the idle pressure during acceleration. The rise in fuel pressure overcomes the increasing intake manifold pressure, and a constant flow of fuel to the cylinders results. This feature of the multipoint fuel pressure regulator is similar to the accelerator pump function of a carburetor.

CFI Systems

The fuel pressure regulator used on both the high-pressure and low-pressure CFI systems operates just like that of the multipoint applications except that it has no vacuum port to increase pressure on acceleration.

The fuel pressure on the high-pressure CFI systems is controlled at about 30psi to 40psi. The fuel pressure on the low-pressure CFI systems is controlled at between 13psi and 17psi.

Fuel Lines

Two fuel lines are part of the pressurized fuel supply system: the supply line and the return line.

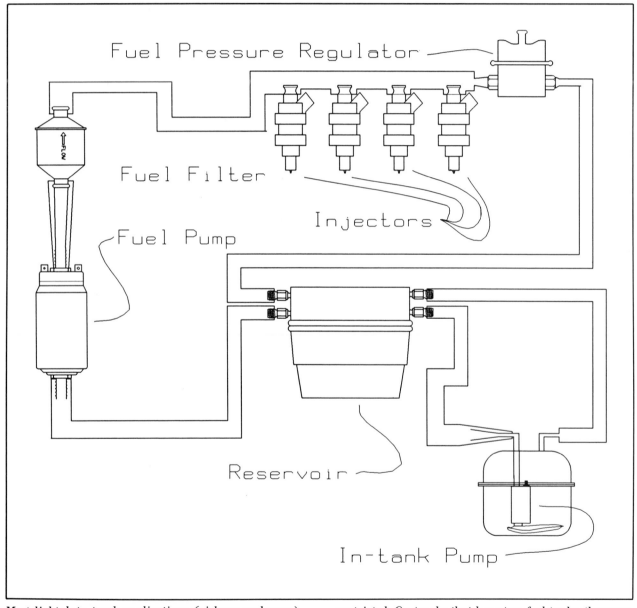

Most light-duty truck applications (pickups and vans) have a reservoir located between the fuel tank and the fuel rail. This reservoir contains a filter, which can become restricted. On trucks that have two fuel tanks, the reservoir contains a switching mechanism to change tanks.

Each is made up of sections that run from one component to another. The supply line carries fuel from the tank to the fuel pressure regulator, whereas the return line carries fuel from the fuel pressure regulator back to the tank. The pressure in the supply line will be relatively low before the pump and at system pressure after the pump. The pressure in the return line should be negligible. A restricted supply line will cause low fuel volume and pressure. A restricted return line will result in high fuel pressure.

Electrical Components

EEC Power Relay

The EEC power relay controls power to the EEC computer. When the ignition switch is turned on, the EEC power relay is energized, closing the switch contacts to the EEC computer. When the engine is shut off, the EEC power relay remains powered up for 2 to 3 seconds. This allows the EEC computer to reset some of the components for the next restart.

Inertia Switch

The inertia switch is a safety device located between the fuel pump power source and the fuel pump. In the event of an impact, such as would occur during an accident, the inertia switch trips. When the inertia switch trips, the fuel pump shuts off. This prevents the fuel pump from continuing to run if a fuel line ruptures during an accident.

The problem with inertia switches is that they have all degrees of sensitivity, ranging from tripping when the vehicle hits a brick wall to tripping when the vehicle receives a relatively light slap from the side of the fist. A reset button is located on the top of the switch. Should the inertia switch accidentally trip, it can be reset by pressing this button.

The inertia switch is located in the trunk of sedans and in the right wheelwell portion of the cargo area of station wagons. The location on the 1984–88 pickups is just to the right of the transmission tunnel, with the reset button just visible above the edge of the carpet. Later-model pickups carry the inertia

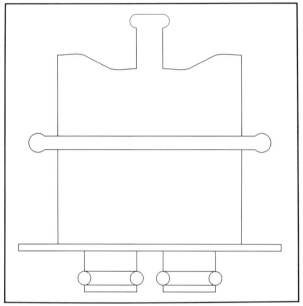

In the fuel pressure regulator fuel enters through one port, and when the pressure rises above a specified point, the excess fuel returns to the tank. The smaller port on the top of this illustration is where the vacuum hose connects. When the pressure in the manifold rises during acceleration, the vacuum at this port drops. As the vacuum drops, the fuel pressure increases. CFI-equipped vehicles do not change fuel pressure during acceleration; therefore, they do not have this vacuum port.

The fuel pressure regulator mounts on the fuel rail. Notice the Schraeder valve for testing fuel pressure.

The plastic hose attached to the top of the pressure regulator increases the fuel pressure as the engine is accelerated. Because of this hose, the fuel pressure will be 5psi to 10psi higher when the engine is not running than when the engine is running.

switch on the firewall, just to the left of the steering column next to the fuse panel. Most vans have it in the passenger's kick panel.

Air Induction Components

Air Cleaner

The air cleaner contains the air filter. All the air that enters the engine and is to be used in combustion passes through the air cleaner. Its job is to filter the air on its way to the intake. On many applications, it also provides a clean air source for the crankcase vents.

Throttle Assembly

The throttle assembly contains a primary throttle bore and the throttle valves. The positions of the throttle valves are controlled by the driver through the accelerator pedal, just as on a carburetor. The BYP valve mounts on the throttle assembly to control the airflow through the idle air bypass. The idle air bypass is an air channel that runs parallel to the primary throttle bore. The BYP valve controls the air through this passage to control the idle speed. CFI systems do not have an idle air bypass; instead, they control the idle speed by means of an ISC motor. The ISC motor is a DC motor that runs a plunger back and forth to control the idle speed and therefore control the engine idle speed.

Intake Manifold

As with any internal-combustion gasoline engine, the Ford fuel-injected engines use a manifold for gathering the air to be used for combustion.

EEC IV System Function

To understand the operation of the EEC IV system, think of a square with a set of events occurring at each corner. At the first corner of the square are the input sensors. These include the MAP, ECT, TP, PIP, and ACT sensors. At the second corner of the square is the ECA, also known as the processor or computer. The ECA gathers information from the sensors, interprets the information to determine the need for fuel and spark advance, and then sends signals to the actuators. At the third corner of the square are the actuators. Although many actuators are used, and although many of these actuators affect the drivability of the vehicle, we will concentrate on only two: the injectors and the ignition module. At the fourth corner of the square are the feedback sensors. The two feedback sensors that apply to our example are the EGO sensor and the KS.

The First Corner

As the journey around the square begins, the

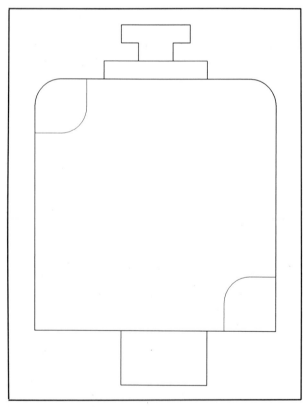

All Ford fuel injection systems use an inertia switch to shut off the fuel pump in the event of an impact. If the vehicle is involved in an accident (impact), a fuel line might rupture. A ruptured fuel line is an extreme fire hazard at an accident scene. With the inertia switch, the fuel pump is shut down as the impact occurs. These switches are sometimes tripped by something as simple as driving too fast over a speed bump. They are reset by pressing the button on top.

The inertia switch location is shown in the owners manual. Even after you consult the manual, it may still be difficult to locate. Normally it will be hiding behind a carpet panel in the trunk on sedans or in the inner fenderwell on station wagons.

basic engine sensors tell the ECA what the operating conditions of the engine are. The MAP sensor sends a frequency that is directly proportional to the pressure in the manifold. The higher the frequency, the greater the pressure; the greater the pressure, the greater the load on the engine. A high-load condition on the engine means a greater demand for fuel but a lesser demand for timing advance. When the MAP sensor indicates a load, the ECA enriches the mixture and retards the timing to prevent detonation (pinging). When load conditions decrease, the ECA permits the timing to advance and allows the mixture to lean out to the ideal 14.7:1 air-fuel ratio.

The second sensor at the input corner is the ECT sensor. A cold engine requires a rich mixture to run properly; this is why carburetors had a choke. When the ECT signal voltage is high, indicating a cold engine, the ECA allows a rich mixture to satisfy the needs of the cold engine. In addition, since the cold air-fuel charge will require additional time to complete its burn, and since a cold engine is not likely to detonate, the ECA allows additional timing advance on a cold engine. As the engine warms up, the air-fuel mixture is leaned out and the ECA allows less advance on the timing control signal to the ignition module.

The TP sensor could be equated to the accelerator pump of a carburetor. When the driver first moves the throttle, the ECA detects an increasing voltage from the TP sensor. The ECA responds by enriching the mixture for acceleration. In addition, if the TP sensor voltage is low, as it will be with a closed throttle, and the MAP frequency is low, as it will be during deceleration, the ECA will shut the injectors off completely. This provides for a little extra fuel economy and cleaner emissions during deceleration.

The PIP signal is an rpm signal originating with the PIP sensor in the distributor, or in the case of the distributorless applications, on the crankshaft. As rpm increase, the need for enrichment also increases. Most engines lose their ability to move fuel through the intake system efficiently at high rpm; therefore, it is necessary to inject extra fuel to be sure enough fuel makes it to the combustion chamber. As important as air-fuel mixture is, perhaps more important is the effect of rpm on timing control. In a standard point-condenser or electronic ignition distributor of the 1970s, a set of spring-loaded weights would swing out as the rotational speed of the distributor increased. As the weights swung out, they would change the position of the point cam or reluctor relative to that of the distributor shaft, and the timing would advance. An increasing PIP frequency (speed) will cause the ECA to advance the timing in a similar manner.

Many EEC IV applications also have an ACT sensor. Although the effects of the ACT sensor are not as readily seen as those of other sensors, the ACT sensor is nonetheless important. The ACT sensor responds to the temperature of the air in the intake manifold. Colder air is denser air; therefore, for every cubic foot of air drawn into the combustion chambers, more fuel is required when the air is cold than when it is hot.

Other input devices include, but on a given application may not be limited to, the EGO sensor, PSPS, BOO switch, EVP sensor, and VSS.

The Second Corner

The information from the input sensors is gathered and processed at the second corner of the square, by the ECA. The ECA uses the information from the sensors to analyze the needs of the vehicle, engine, and operator during the operation of the vehicle.

The throttle assembly of the fuel-injected engine is like that of the carburetor. A throttle cable connects the throttle plate to the accelerator pedal. Note the TP sensor on the left side of the throttle assembly.

The intake manifold is a set of cast-aluminum tubes that connect the throttle assembly to the intake ports of the cylinder head or heads. This is the intake manifold on the 3.8-liter police application Taurus.

The Third Corner

At the third corner of the square, the ECA controls its actuators, or output devices, in an attempt to meet the requirements it has identified. Among these output devices are the following:

ECA Function	Actuator	Sensors
Air-fuel ratio	Injectors	MAP sensor
		ECT sensor
		PIP sensor
		EGO sensor
		TP sensor
Idle speed	Bypass air control	PIP sensor
		BOO switch
		PSPS
Ignition timing	TFI ignition	MAP sensor
		PIP sensor
		ECT sensor
Emissions	EVR (or EGRV and EGRC)	MAP sensor
		BOO switch
	TAB solenoid	ECT sensor
	TAD solenoid	TP sensor
		PIP sensor

The Fourth Corner

The fourth corner of the square contains the feedback sensors. You have probably worked with people who operate like these sensors. They are not there for the decision-making process—how much fuel, how much air—but they are certainly there to tell you about the mistakes. In the case of fuel and timing control, the feedback sensors are the EGO sensor for fuel and the KS for timing. Let's look at how these sensors work.

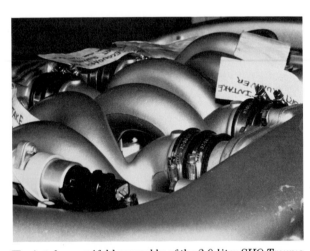

The intake manifold assembly of the 3.0-liter SHO Taurus engine has two runners for each cylinder. A long set of runners provides good torque for acceleration off the line. At about 2200rpm, the ECA switches the manifold from the long runners to a short set of runners. The short set of runners provides high-end horsepower. The use of this type of intake manifold configuration eliminates the compromise between torque and horsepower found in most engines.

After the MAP, ECT, TP, PIP, and ACT sensor inputs are analyzed, the ECA opens the injectors for a length of time it feels is appropriate to inject the proper amount of fuel. The EGO sensor then analyzes the exhaust gases resulting from that combustion. If these exhaust gases have a high oxygen content, the EGO sensor will signal the ECA to enrich the mixture. If the oxygen content of the exhaust is extremely low, the EGO sensor will signal the ECA to lean out the mixture.

After the MAP, ECT, and PIP sensor inputs are analyzed, the ECA advances the timing to a point it feels is appropriate for the temperature, load, and speed of the engine. If the decision of the ECA is correct, maximum advance without detonation will occur. For popular engines such as the 2.3-liter overhead cam (ohc), 2.3-liter Turbo, 3.0-liter EFI and super-high-output (SHO), and 3.8-liter supercharged (SC) engines—as well as the 2.9-, 4.9-, and 5.0-liter light truck engines—a knock sensor signals the ECA when it has overadvanced the timing, resulting in detonation (pinging).

Closed-Loop Systems

Systems that incorporate feedback sensors are referred to as closed-loop systems. Although the two

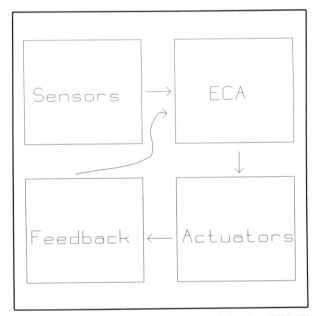

Four groups of components are found in the EEC IV system. The sensors gather information about the operating conditions of the engine. This information is sent to the ECA. The ECA processes the information, makes decisions about injector on-time and ignition timing, and then sends these decisions to the actuators. The actuators are devices such as the injectors and ignition module. The results of the actions of the actuators are monitored by the feedback sensors. The feedback sensors send their information to the ECA so that the ECA can correct the signals it is sending to the actuators.

closed-loop systems discussed in the preceding example—fuel control and timing control—are critical to engine operation, they are by no means the only ones in the EEC IV system. Let's look at a few others in a little more detail.

EGR Control

Primary Input Sensors

MAP The EGR valve will open an amount proportional to engine load.

ECT The EGR valve will only open when the engine is near, at, or above operating temperature.

PIP The EGR valve will not open when the engine is at or near idle speed.

Feedback Sensors

EVP

Pressure feedback EGR (PFE)

The ECA analyzes the data from the MAP, ECT, and PIP input sensors and decides if the EGR valve should be opened. The ECA then signals the EVR solenoid to open the EGR valve. By altering the duty cycle of the signal to the EVR, the ECA is able to control the amount that the EGR valve is opened. Altering the duty cycle alters the amount of vacuum, and changing the amount of vacuum changes the amount that the EGR valve is opened.

Two feedback sensors might be used to monitor the ECA's control of the EGR: the EVP sensor and the PFE sensor. The ECA determines how much the EGR should open based on rpm and the input signal from the MAP and ECT sensors. It then estimates how much vacuum will be needed to open the EGR valve that amount, and the signal to the EVR is adjusted accordingly. As the EGR valve opens, the EVP potentiometer reports the EGR diaphragm position back to the ECA. If the reported position is not what the ECA expected, then the ECA can modify the signal to the EVR.

The job of the PFE sensor is the same as that of the EVP sensor. Instead of using a potentiometer to monitor the position of the EGR diaphragm, however, the PFE sensor measures exhaust back pressure to reinforce the accuracy of the ECA's decisions.

Some applications use a pair of solenoids to control the opening and positioning of the EGR valve. These solenoids are known as the EGRC and EGRV. The EGRC is a normally closed solenoid-operated valve controlled by the ECA, primarily in response to the ECT sensor. When the engine approaches operating temperature, the ECA opens the EGRC, permitting vacuum to flow from the intake manifold toward the EGR and the EGRV. The normal state for the EGRV valve is open. When the EGRC opens, the

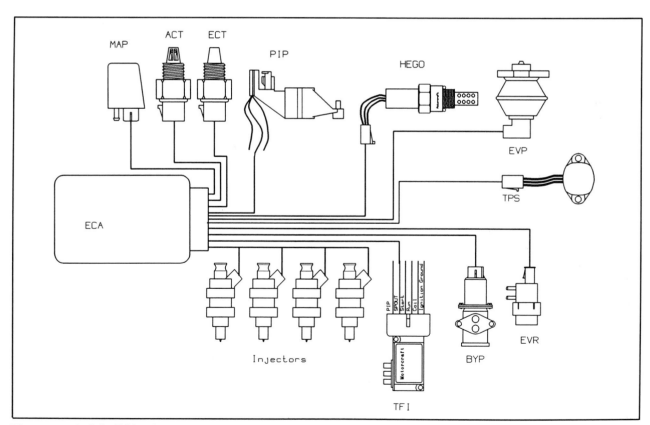

The sensors feed the ECA information about the operating conditions of the engine. The actuators are controlled by the ECA to regulate the operation of emission, fuel injection, and timing control systems.

EGRV bleeds the vacuum headed to the EGR valve off to the atmosphere. The result is that the EGR valve does not open. When the load conditions and speed of the engine indicate that the EGR valve should be opened, then the ECA begins to send a variable duty cycle pulse to the EGRV. As the duty cycle of this pulse increases, the amount of vacuum bled to the atmosphere begins to decrease and more is held back to open the EGR valve. The EVP sensor then reports the EGR position back to the ECA. If the EGR is in the proper position for current engine operating conditions, then the ECA will not modify the position; if it is not, then the ECA will modify the duty cycle of the EGRV pulse until the correct position is attained.

Idle Speed Control

Primary Input Sensors
PIP   The ECA monitors engine rpm and controls either a BYP air control valve or an ISC motor.

ECT   A cold engine requires a high idle speed to overcome the extra rotational resistance of thick oil and the poor atomization qualities of the cold air-fuel charge.

Feedback Sensor
PIP   The same sensor that provides a primary input for the control of EGR is the feedback sensor.

Two types of automatic ISC devices are used by Ford: the idle speed control and idle tracking switch (ISC/ITS) and the BYP air control valve. The ISC/ITS is a DC motor used to open and close the throttle plates when the engine is at idle. It is limited to use on the CFI, or throttle body, applications. The ECA controls current through the ISC motor. When the ECA is not applying current, the ISC motor remains stationary. When a change in idle speed is required, the ECA will select the direction that the motor needs to turn and deliver current to it in the appropriate direction. When the correct idle speed is reached, the ECA will cut off the current.

The ISC system detects that the throttle is closed and that the ECA should control the speed of the engine by means of the ITS. Inside of the ISC motor, on the internal end of the plunger that opens and closes the throttle, is a small switch. When the throttle comes to rest on the end of the plunger, the switch is closed. The closed switch signals the ECA that it should open and close the throttle to control the speed of the engine.

The multipoint applications—those with one injector for each cylinder—use a BYP air control valve to control the idle speed of the engine. This device might best be described as an opened valve. It is a spring-loaded, normally closed, solenoid-operated valve. The ECA sends a pulse at about 60 hertz to the solenoid to control the amount of opening and thereby the idle speed. When the ECA energizes the BYP valve, the valve begins to open. Before it can open completely, the ECA deenergizes the BYP valve and the valve begins to close. Before the valve has a chance to close fully, the ECA reenergizes the BYP valve. The result is that the valve dithers rather than opening and closing completely. As the ECA alters the duty cycle on the pulse, the opened position changes. As the opened position changes, it alters the amount of air allowed through the valve.

The idle speed changes the amount of air going through the BYP valve. The BYP valve mounts on the

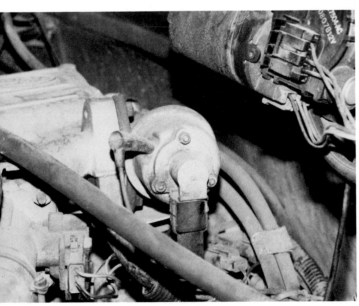

This view of the 4.9-liter shows the locations of the EVP (EGR Valve Position sensor) and the TP sensor.

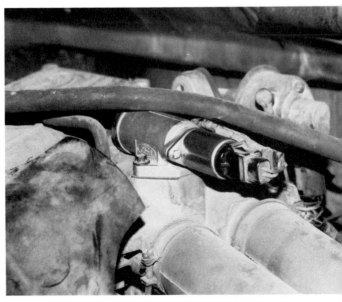

The BYP air control valve is used to control idle speed on the MPI engines. This is the location of the BYP valve on the 4.9-liter truck engine.

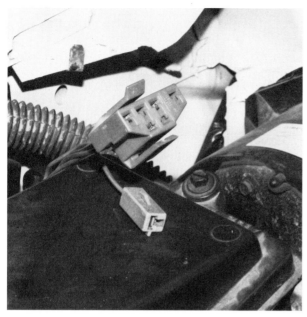

The bulk of the testing required on the EEC IV fuel injection system is done at the STAR test connector. This connector is located under the hood, usually on the right or left fenderwell. The test connector might be red, black, or gray.

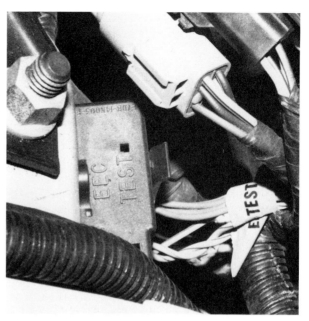

On most newer applications, the STAR connector is located in a plastic protective cover, which is clearly marked.

throttle assembly to control the amount of air allowed around the throttle plates and thus regulate idle speed.

Air Conditioner and Radiator Fan Control

Input Sensors

ECT   Although the ECT input is primarily for radiator fan control, the ECT sensor is also used to inform the ECA when the engine is overheating. When the engine overheats, the ECA will turn off the ACC.

MAP   When the manifold pressure indicates a high load or demand on the engine, the ECA will turn off the compressor clutch to allow more power from the engine to be used to handle that load.

TP   When the TP sensor indicates a wide-open-throttle condition, it assumes this is a signal from the driver that acceleration is desired. The ACC will be shut off to meet this desire.

The air conditioner compressor clutch and the radiator cooling fan are both controlled by the ECA on most applications. The ECA control relays are located in one of two control units to apply these devices.

The first of these units is called the air conditioner and fan controller module. This unit contains two relays: the fan relay and the ACC relay. Acting as an interface, this module is controlled by the ECA to control the ACC and the radiator cooling fan.

The second unit is known as the ICM. This unit is used in place of the air conditioner and fan controller module on applications such as the Sable, Taurus, and SC Coupe. In addition to being used by the ECA to control the ACC and the radiator fan, the ICM is also an interface for control of the fuel pump, power to the ECA, power to the fuel pump, and a second speed on the radiator cooling fan.

Canister Purge

The ECA also controls the purging of the fuel evaporation emission control system. When the ECA detects—through the monitoring of the PIP, TP, ECT, and MAP sensors—that engine conditions are such that the evaporative canister can be purged, the ECA grounds the CANP (Canister Purge solenoid). When the CANP solenoid is grounded, vacuum goes to the CANP valve and the contents of the activated charcoal evaporative control canister are emptied into the intake system.

ECA Modes of Operation

The ECA has seven modes of operation. Although the technician, least of all the amateur enthusiast, does not need to be continuously aware of these modes, an understanding of them helps to better comprehend the thinking processes of the ECA. These modes of operation are as follows:

Crank mode
Underspeed mode
Closed-throttle mode (idle or deceleration)
Part-throttle mode
Wide-open-throttle mode
Cold or hot engine operation mode
Limited operation strategy (LOS) or failure mode effects management (FMEM) mode
Note: LOS and FMEM are limp-in modes; a given

application will have one or the other. The result of either is improved drivability in the event of a circuit or system failure, but the FMEM is far more sophisticated than the LOS mode.

Example: A lead technician at a dealership outside Vancouver, British Columbia, Canada, and I decided to test the abilities of FMEM on a new 1989 Taurus. We disconnected the MAP, TP, ECT, ACT, and EGO sensors. This left only the PIP of the basic engine sensors to send information to the ECA. Although the car did not run perfectly, it drove as though it only needed a tune-up.

Crank Mode

When the ignition switch is in the crank position, the ECA uses only the ECT sensor to determine what the injector pulse width should be. In addition, the ignition timing becomes fixed. The TFI module receives cranking voltage at the third wire from the top, which causes the module to ignore the SPOUT timing control signal and operate exclusively from the PIP signal. As a result, the timing becomes fixed at base timing.

Underspeed Mode

The underspeed mode is peculiar to applications that use a VAF meter. These applications include the 2.3-liter Thunderbirds and the 1.9-liter engines. Since the VAF sensor relies on steady airflow to prevent high-frequency fluctuations of the sensor vane and since these fluctuations increase dramatically when the engine rpm drop below 500, at speeds below 500rpm, the VAF signal is ignored.

Closed-Throttle Mode

When the throttle is closed, one of two things is indicated: either the engine is decelerating or the engine is idling. If the rpm are low, the ECA assumes that the engine is idling. The ECA will control the engine speed through the ISC motor or the BYP valve. On some engines, the air-fuel ratio will be leaned out slightly to increase fuel economy and decrease emissions.

If the rpm are high, the ECA will assume the engine is decelerating. The EGR will immediately close, and the injectors will be shut off. The injectors will remain shut off until the PIP sensor indicates engine rpm below about 1500.

Part-Throttle Mode

Partial throttle is interpreted by the ECA as a cruise condition. During part-throttle operation, the ECA will use information from the ECT, MAP, TP, and PIP sensors to decide on an injector on-time. The EGO sensor then provides feedback for the accuracy of that decision.

Wide-Open-Throttle Mode

When the TP sensor indicates a wide-open condition, the ECA increases the injector pulse width, closes the EGR valve, advances the timing, and ignores the EGO sensor. In the case of the dual-injector CFI systems, the injectors, which normally alternate opening, will begin to pulse together.

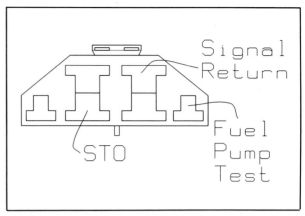

Three of the terminals of the STAR connector are important. The lower left of the center four is the STO, and the upper right of the center four is a ground called signal return. These two terminals are used to retrieve the trouble codes. The third important terminal is the fuel pump test connector. Grounding the fuel pump test will activate the fuel pump to test the fuel pressure without starting the engine.

Cold or Hot Engine Operation Mode

During a cold or hot mode of engine operation, the ECA enriches the mixture. This should help cool the engine if it is running hot. If the engine is running cold, then the extra fuel is needed to keep it running properly. If the hot or cold signal is erroneous—as it often is—the extra enrichment will not significantly affect the drivability of the car. If the signal is erroneous, performing the self-test automatic readout (STAR) test will point this out.

Limited Operation Strategy or Failure Mode Effects Management Mode

LOS is a limp-in mode. When the ECA detects a defect in the EEC IV system, it enters the LOS mode and the EGR valve is shut off. The BYP valve goes to a fixed position (usually a relatively high idle speed), timing becomes fixed at a calibrated amount of advance, and the injector pulse width becomes fixed. When the vehicle is in the LOS mode, the quality of drivability will be greatly reduced; however, the driver will be able to get the car home.

Later applications have forfeited the LOS mode in favor of the FMEM mode. This is a sophisticated limp-in mode that maintains relatively good drivability even when the system has suffered a major failure. The ECA uses values stored within its memory to substitute for missing values from failed sensors.

The FMEM mode is so effective that on several occasions, while teaching Ford fuel injection systems to technicians, I have disconnected several sensors simultaneously. Although a noticeable change occurred in the way the engine ran, these cars equipped with FMEM remained drivable. In fact, they ran as if they needed a tune-up, nothing more.

8

EEC IV Onboard Diagnostics

EEC IV STAR Test

Ford's EEC IV onboard diagnostic system is a marvel of computer technology and programming. Most of the other automobile manufacturers have chosen simply to report defective circuits to the technician. When the EEC IV STAR test, or quick test, is initiated by the technician, the ECA begins a real-time cause and effect test procedure. This test procedure determines not only if the system has any open circuits but also if the devices are actually working. For example, at one point during the engine-running test, the ECA switches air from the air pump to the exhaust system upstream of the EGO sensor. At this point, the ECA expects to see the voltage from the EGO sensor drop. If the EGO voltage drops, then the ECA will know that the air pump upstream-downstream control valve—known as the TAD valve—is working and that the EGO sensor is working.

The EEC IV STAR test can be divided into two categories: the KOEO test and the KOER test. To get a complete and accurate picture of the operating condition of the EEC system, it is advisable to run both sections of the test.

Philosophy of the Results

Before actually examining the test procedure, let's look at the philosophy of its results, which will be in the form of two-digit—or, beginning with the 1991 model year on some applications, three-digit—service codes. These codes indicate systems or circuits where the ECA has detected the need for service, repair, or correction. Often, many codes will be delivered by the ECA, and all may be the result of a single problem or each may be the result of a separate problem. Before jumping into locating the source of one code, look at it in the light of the other codes.

As was mentioned earlier, during one portion of the engine-running test, the ECA pumps air across the EGO sensor. If the TAD valve fails to redirect the air from the air pump across the EGO sensor, the ECA might generate codes relating to TAD function, EGO function, or both. If both codes are received, the wise technician would look at them to determine which of the components relating to them could be responsible for both codes. It is not likely that the EGO sensor would affect the operation of the TAD valve, but it is likely that the TAD valve could affect the operation of the EGO sensor. The wise technician would address the code related to the TAD valve first.

Test Procedure

To begin the EEC IV STAR test, locate the test terminal, which will be in the engine compartment, under the hood. It is a six-terminal connector usually found on one of the inner fenderwells. Although this connector has pockets for six wires, normally only three or four of these wires are in the connector. Located near the connector is a single pigtail connector. This is an essential part of the diagnostic hookup.

Once the test connectors are located, you have a choice of several tools to connect to acquire the self-diagnostic information. Ford Motor Company provides its dealer service facilities with a dedicated tester known as the STAR tester. Several manufacturers of automotive tools and test equipment market testers to access the service codes. All the specialized testers make the job of extracting the service codes easier and usually faster. These testers do not do anything that cannot be done with much simpler tools, however. I prefer to use an analog voltmeter to extract the codes. In the following description of the use of the analog voltmeter, you could substitute the use of a test light or even a buzzer.

KOEO Test

Ensure that the temperature of the engine is between 50 and 250 degrees Fahrenheit. If the temperature of the engine is outside this parameter, false codes related to engine temperature will be generated. Locate the test connector, and connect the red lead of an analog voltmeter to the positive terminal of the battery. Connect the black lead of the voltmeter to the lower left terminal of the center four terminals of the six-pocket test connector. This terminal is known as the self-test output (STO). At this point, the voltmeter should read 12 volts. Now connect a jumper

As an alternative to being displayed by the analog voltmeter, the trouble codes, which are also called service codes, can be read as a flashing light on the instrument panel. The auto repair industry calls this a "Check Engine" light. When using the check engine light, a code 12 would appear as a blink, a pause, then two blinks, as shown here.

During the KOEO test, the fast codes confirm that the test procedure has been entered. The on-demand, or hard, codes relate to problems that still exist. The memory codes relate to problems that existed the last time the engine ran or earlier.

wire between the upper right terminal of the center four terminals and the single pigtail wire. This single pigtail is known as the self-test input (STI). The setup is now complete for the engine-off test. Turn the ignition switch on and count the needle sweeps. During the engine-off self-test, five events will occur:
1. The first event is a series of clicks heard in the engine compartment. During this series of clicks, the ECA is taking readings from all the sensors that are operating with the engine off. It is also switching actuators on and off to test their operation.
2. The second event is the fast codes. These will be seen on the voltmeter as a series of short, fast pulses of from 0 to 1 or 2 volts. The fast codes contain all the codes that will be seen later. They are read by the STAR tester and other diagnostic tools. As far as the use of the analog voltmeter is concerned, these pulses have no purpose other than to verify that the KOEO test has been successfully entered.
3. The third event is the KOEO on-demand codes, which are hard codes. These will be a series of needle sweeps of from 0 to a full 12 volts. They are two-digit codes that are read in the needle sweeps. For example, the code 21 would be seen as follows:
pulse–pulse
pause
pulse

A code 24 would be seen as:
pulse–pulse
pause
pulse–pulse–pulse–pulse.

Each on-demand code will be repeated twice. If several codes are reported, they will be repeated twice in sequence, as follows:
21–24–21–24.

The KOEO on-demand codes represent problems that were detected during the clicking that occurred at the beginning of the test. These are problems that exist now, as the test is being performed.
4. The fourth event is the separator code. After the last on-demand code comes a 5- to 6-second pause followed by a single needle sweep. This single needle sweep is called the separator code. It marks the end of the on-demand codes and indicates that the next set of codes will be the memory codes. The Ford service manuals refer to it as the code 10, which stands for one needle sweep followed by zero needle sweeps.
5. The fifth event is the memory codes. About 5 or 6 seconds after the separator code, the memory codes—also known as continuous codes—will be pulsed. These will be needle sweeps exactly like those of the KOEO on-demand codes. A code will be set into memory when a major engine sensor circuit is detected to have an open, short, or ground. On late-model EEC IV systems, when the memory code sets, the malfunction indicator light (MIL) will turn on.

Memory codes represent problems that were detected the last time the engine ran or earlier. These are problems that the ECA detected in sensor or actuator circuits and that can have a major effect on the operation of the engine. These problems existed in the past and, for the purpose of interpretation, no longer exist. They can be contrasted with the on-demand codes, which represent problems that exist now, not in the past.

If a serious problem existed in the past, a code would be stored in memory. If the problem existed in the past and still exists, both an on-demand code and a memory code will appear.

KOER Test

The KOER self-test is a little more complicated to perform than the KOEO test. As in the KOEO test, engine temperature is critical. The engine temperature for this test must be between 180 and 250 degrees Fahrenheit. To ensure that the test and the results of the test are accurate, follow this procedure:

1. Disconnect the jumper between the upper right terminal of the center four terminals of the six-pocket test connector and the STI pigtail. Start the engine and allow it to run at 2000rpm for 2 minutes. This is to ensure that the ECT and EGO sensors are heated to their normal operating levels.

2. Shut the engine off, reconnect the jumper, and start the engine. Almost immediately after starting the engine, the engine identification (ID) codes will be pulsed. These will be two, three, or four pulses of the voltmeter. Two pulses means that the ECA believes it is connected to a four-cylinder engine, three means a six-cylinder engine, and four means an eight-cylinder engine. If the number of pulses does not match the number of cylinders, the wrong ECA has been installed in the vehicle.

Note: Some scanners and engine analyzers may miss the first engine ID pulse. This gives an indication of two fewer cylinders than the engine really has. If you are using a scanner and get an indication of fewer cylinders than the engine actually has, connect a voltmeter and repeat the test. It is possible that the scanner missed the first pulse.

3. Following the engine ID codes, the ECA will begin to switch actuators on and off and modify the idle speed. As the ECA does this, it is looking for a response from its sensors. An example of this is when the TAD valve pumps air across the EGO sensor. The ECA expects to see the EGO sensor voltage drop low. If it does not, it will generate codes. During this time, the engine rpm will go up and down, the engine will misfire, and the catalytic converter will stink.

4. During the odd events that occur in step 3, you need to perform the brake on-off, power steering (BOOPS) procedure. You must turn the steering wheel one-half turn and touch the brake pedal. If the vehicle has a standard, or manual, transmission, depress the brake pedal only. As you do these things, the ECA takes the opportunity to confirm their operation. Although it is not necessary to perform the BOOPS procedure on many applications, if it is not done on a vehicle that requires it, false codes will be generated. If the BOOPS procedure is done on a vehicle that did not require it, no false codes will be generated.

5. After several seconds, the engine will smooth out. At this point, the ECA has advanced the timing to approximately 20 degrees before initial timing. A pause lasting several seconds will occur. This will be followed by a single needle sweep called the dynamic

```
EEC IV KOER

Disconnect jumper
Start & warm Engine
Shut engine off
Reconnect jumper
Restart engine
Engine I.D. codes
BOO/PS
Dynamic response
Fast
On-demand
```

Here is a summary of the procedure for retrieving the KOER codes. The only codes retrieved during this test are on-demand codes.

response code, or code 10. Following the single needle sweep, you have 10 seconds to snap the throttle to the wide-open position. The engine speed must exceed 2000rpm. As soon as the target rpm is exceeded, the throttle should be closed.

This is called the goose test. The purpose of this test is to allow the ECA to see changes in the signals from the MAP sensor and the TP sensor. In addition to the sensor changes, the ECA wants to see that the speed of the engine returns to the proper idle speed following the snap.

6. The goose test is followed almost immediately by fast codes. Like the KOEO fast codes, the KOER fast codes have all the information about what was discovered during the KOER test. The fast codes require a scanner or a STAR tester to read.

7. The KOER on-demand codes represent problems that were found as the ECA went through the KOER test. These, like the KOEO on-demand codes, are two-digit codes read in needle sweeps.

Supplemental Tests

It could be said that the procedure ends here, and the acquisition of the codes does end here. You must be familiar with several additional procedures, however, to effectively work through the trouble code procedures. These procedures are listed below and are discussed in the "Supplemental EEC IV Tests" section at the end of this chapter.

Supplemental KOEO Tests
Continuous monitor test, also known as the wiggle test
Output state test

Supplemental KOER Tests
Continuous monitor test
Computed timing test
SEFI test (available only on sequentially injected engines)

EEC IV Two-Digit Test Codes

Code 11

The Code 11 means that the ECA has detected no problems during the section of the test where the code was delivered. This does not mean that the codes found in the other sections of the test are invalid; each section of codes should be thought of separately.

Code 12

MPI Applications

The code 12 comes up only during the engine-running test and means that the engine idle speed was unable to reach the upper test limit. This code, when pulsed out by an MPI system, is often the result of throttle body coking. Coking restricts the flow of air across the throttle plates when the throttle is closed. Remove the rubber or plastic tube that connects the air cleaner to the throttle plates, open the throttle plates, and inspect the area behind them. If you find evidence of a carbon build-up, spray carburetor cleaner on a shop towel and wipe the carbon out from behind the throttle. If the code 12 persists after the cleaning of the throttle bore, adjust the minimum air.

To adjust the minimum air for MPI systems, start the engine and allow it to warm up thoroughly. Allow the engine idle to stabilize. Disconnect the BYP valve. The engine speed should slowly decrease until it dies.

To check the minimum air adjustment on the MPI engine, disconnect the electrical connector on the BYP valve. The engine rpm should drop immediately. After struggling for a few seconds, the engine should die.

If the engine dies abruptly, adjust the throttle stop screw until it dies slowly.

Code 12 - Central Fuel Injection

The code 12 on CFI, or throttle body injection, systems means that during the engine-running portion of the test procedure, the ISC motor was not able to raise the idle speed of the engine to the proper high idle speed.

Disconnect the electrical connector to the ISC motor located on the side of the throttle body assembly. This connector has four wires. Two of the wires are for the ITS and two are for the electric motor. The two wires for the ITS should have infinite resistance between them when no pressure is applied to the end of the plunger. The resistance should drop almost to 0 when the end of the plunger is depressed. The two wires dedicated to the electric motor should have a few dozen ohms of resistance. This resistance should not change when the plunger is depressed.

Connect a jumper wire to the positive terminal of the battery. Connect another jumper wire to the negative terminal of the battery. Apply current to the electric motor. The plunger should extend or retract. If it does not move, reverse the jumper wires. If it still does not move, replace the ISC motor. If the plunger does move, allow it to travel to the fully extended or retracted position. Measure the distance from the tip of the ISC motor to the flat of the ISC mounting bracket. In the fully extended position, this distance should be greater than 2in; in the fully retracted position, it should be less than 1¾in. If the plunger moves according to these parameters, inspect the wiring to the ECA. If the wiring is in good condition, replace the ECA.

Code 13

When the ECA was performing the engine-running test, it attempted to lower the idle speed to less than curb idle. The code 13 indicates that it was unable to do so. As with the code 12, the procedure for correcting the code 13 will differ depending on whether the vehicle is equipped with MPI (EFI) or CFI (throttle body injection).

MPI Applications

If the vehicle is equipped with an MPI system, the BYP air control valve was unable to lower the engine idle speed. When the electrical connector of this unit is disconnected, the engine should die; therefore, the BYP valve should easily be able to lower the engine rpm to the lower test parameter. This problem has two likely causes. The first, and most likely, is improperly adjusted minimum air.

To adjust the minimum air, first ensure that the throttle linkage and cables are not binding to hold the throttle open. Once this is confirmed, start the engine and allow it to warm up thoroughly. Allow the engine idle to stabilize. Disconnect the BYP valve. The engine speed should slowly decrease until it dies. If the engine dies abruptly, adjust the throttle stop screw until it dies slowly.

If the minimum air adjustment is correct or if adjustment does not correct the code, check for vacuum leaks or other sources of air entering the engine.

CFI Applications

If the car is CFI equipped, disconnect the electrical connector to the ISC motor located on the side of the throttle body assembly. This connector has four wires. Two of the wires are for the ITS and two are for the electric motor. The two wires for the ITS should have infinite resistance between them when no pressure is applied to the end of the plunger. The resistance should drop to almost 0 when the end of the plunger is depressed. The two wires dedicated to the electric motor should have a few dozen ohms of resistance. This resistance should not change when the plunger is depressed.

With a pair of jumper wires—one connected to the positive terminal of the battery, the other to the negative terminal of the battery—apply current to the electric motor. The plunger should extend or retract. If it does not move, reverse the jumper wires. If it still does not move, replace the ISC motor. If the plunger does move, allow it to travel to the fully extended or retracted position. Measure the distance from the tip of the ISC motor to the flat of the ISC mounting bracket. In the fully extended position, this distance should be greater than 2in; in the fully retracted position, it should be less than $1\frac{3}{4}$in. If the plunger moves according to these parameters, inspect the wiring to the ECA. If the wiring is good, replace the ECA.

Code 14

The code 14 indicates a failure in the PIP circuit. This code will never be found in either the KOER or KOEO on-demand codes; it will only be pulsed out as a memory code. If this memory code is present, it is a result of erratic pulses from the PIP sensor. This condition could be caused by magnetic or radio interference. Be sure that the antenna coax for two-way radios is not routed near the EEC IV wiring harness.

If radio or induction sources are not indicated, locate the ignition diagnostic monitor (IDM) wire.

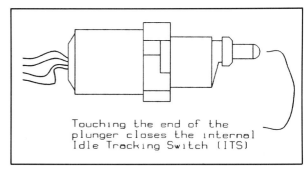

When the code 13 is received on a CFI application, check the condition of the ITS, which is located inside the ISC motor. Two of the four wires to the ISC motor are for the ITS. With the key on but the engine off, the voltage on one of these wires should go high and low. Connect a test light to the wires one at a time. Open and close the throttle. One of these wires should turn the light on and off as the throttle is opened and closed.

Sometimes the BYP valve can become plugged with carbon and soot. When the code 12 or 13 is received on an MPI car, check for soot in the BYP valve before adjusting minimum air or replacing parts.

The code 14 indicates a problem in the PIP circuit. An early version of this sensor had a fairly high failure rate. This is an early PIP sensor.

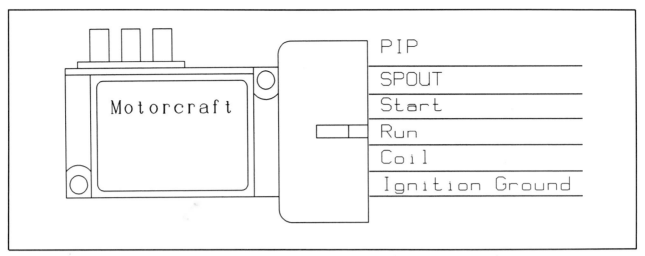

| PIP |
| SPOUT |
| Start |
| Run |
| Coil |
| Ignition Ground |

Motorcraft

The PIP signal goes into the top terminals of the TFI module and splits inside the TFI module. This signal is used in place of the SPOUT signal to turn the ignition coil *on and off if the SPOUT signal should be missing for any reason.*

To replace the PIP sensor, it is necessary to remove the distributor shaft from the distributor. A roll pin holds the gear on the bottom of the distributor. Once the roll pin and the gear are removed, the replacement of the PIP sensor is simple.

The IDM wire on the TFI (distributor-type) ignition system is the second wire from the bottom on the six-wire connector to the ignition module. For applications equipped with the DIS, this is pin 12. Disconnect the TFI or DIS module. Disconnect the coil or coil pack. Disconnect the sixty-pin connector from the ECA. This isolates the IDM wire from the electronic components. Connect an ohmmeter between the IDM wire and ground. The ohmmeter should read infinity. If the ohmmeter reads less than infinity, repair the short to ground in the IDM wire. If the circuit does read infinity, with the ohmmeter still connected, wiggle the IDM wire. This will check for an intermittent short to ground.

If the IDM wire is not shorted-to-ground, connect the black lead of the ohmmeter to ground. Connect the red lead of the ohmmeter to pins 4, 40, 46, and 60, in turn. For each of these pins, the resistance to ground should be infinity. If any show a resistance of less than 10,000 ohms, replace the ECA.

If the resistance to ground for the ECA checks out good, reconnect the coils, the ignition module, and the ECA. Perform the continuous monitor test on the ignition module wiring harness and the ECA harness. As part of this test, lightly tap on the TFI or DIS module and on the ECA, simulating road shock. (For information about performing the continuous monitor test, refer to the "Supplemental EEC IV Tests" section at the end of this chapter.)

If the system passes the continuous monitor test, you have reached an impasse: the problem that generated the code 14 is intermittent and is not currently presenting itself. Put everything back together and erase the code. Assume that the code was set by a passing radio signal. If it returns, repeat the above procedure. Remember that when a memory code is set, the MIL will illuminate.

Code 15

The code 15 indicates an ROM test failure. It can be generated as either a KOEO on-demand code or a memory code.

If the code 15 is obtained during the KOEO test, check the power to pin 1 of the ECA. With the key on or off, 12 volts should be at ECA pin 1. If 12 volts is not at terminal 1, repair the wire. If 12 volts is at terminal 1, check the grounds at pins 40 and 60.

The code 15 is obtained as a continuous code the first time the KOEO test is performed following an interruption of power to ECA pin 1. If this code is generated during the KOEO memory codes, clear the codes (the procedure for this is described under the

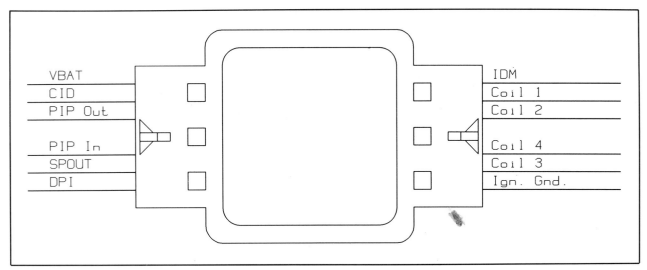

On DIS applications, the code 14 means the computer has detected a problem in either the PIP wires or the IDM wire. The PIP wires are the third (PIP out) and fourth (PIP in) *from the top on the left. The IDM wire is the top wire on the right.*

"Continuous Monitor Test" discussion in the "Supplemental EEC IV Tests" section at the end of this chapter). Rerun the KOER test. If the code does not return, service any other codes that are generated. If the code 15 returns, check the power to pin 1 of the ECA. With the key on or off, 12 volts should be at ECA pin 1. If 12 volts is not at terminal 1, repair the wire. If 12 volts is at terminal 1, check the grounds at pins 40 and 60.

Code 16

The code 16 during the engine-running test indicates that the idle speed of the engine is beyond the self-test limit as the ECA begins the idle control tests. In summary, this is an indication of excessive air entering the engine. Some sources of this extra air include a vacuum leak, improperly adjusted minimum air, and binding or improperly adjusted throttle linkage.

If the code 16 is received on the 2.3- and 5.0-liter applications, it is an indication that the rpm during the test are not high enough to perform the test properly. The possible causes of this code are an open or shorted wiring harness to the BYP air control valve, incorrect throttle linkage adjustment, a faulty BYP air control valve, and contamination in the throttle bore or BYP air control valve.

To begin the code 16 testing, note if codes 31, 32, 33, and 34 are present. These codes are related to the EGR valve and its control system. A faulty EGR system can affect the idling of the engine. If these codes are not present, test the resistance of the BYP air control valve. This valve contains a diode; for this reason, the ohmmeter will show extremely high resistance—or an open circuit—with the leads connected in one direction and about 7 to 13 ohms with the leads reversed.

The six-cylinder DIS coil pack has three wires connected between the module and the coil pack. These wires control the firing of the coils by making and breaking ground. A fourth wire carries power to the coils.

The code 15 means the ROM chip in the computer has apparently failed.

The code 16 means the computer was unable to raise the rpm of the engine to the expected level during the KOER test. Reasons could include a defective BYP valve or an open or short in the wiring harness.

If these specs are met, check the resistance of each BYP terminal to the case of the BYP valve. This test should show an open circuit between each terminal and the case. If you find less-than-infinite resistance, replace the BYP valve.

If you find infinite resistance between the BYP case and the BYP terminals, check the voltage at the BYP harness terminals. Turn the ignition switch to the run position. One of the two wires should carry VBAT. If neither of the wires has 12 volts, repair the open circuit between the BYP valve and the ECA. If both of the wires have 12 volts, this means that the BYP control wire is shorted-to-voltage. Trace the short and repair if necessary. If one of the wires has 12 volts, check for continuity between the BYP harness and pin 21 of the ECA. The resistance should be less than 5 ohms. If the resistance is less than 5 ohms, check for a short in the ECA wiring harness between the BYP harness wire that did not have 12 volts and ECA pins 40, 46, and 60.

If the source of the code 16 is still not found, reconnect the BYP valve and start the engine. Allow the engine to idle. Set a dwell meter on the four-cylinder scale and connect it to the BYP control wire (this is the previously mentioned wire that runs from the BYP valve to pin 21 of the ECA). With the engine idling, the dwell meter should read something other than 0 or 90. If it reads 0 or 90, replace the ECA.

If all the above check out good, look again at the engine basics that can cause idling problems:
Is the throttle bore sooted up?
Are the tune-up components in poor condition?
Are defective or disconnected hoses causing
    vacuum leaks?
Are vacuum leaks occurring around the intake
    manifold?
If no source for the problem is found, repeat the self-test procedure.

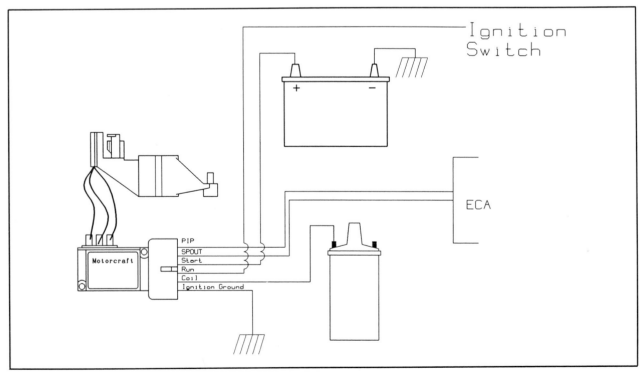

A perceived problem in the SPOUT circuit will cause the code 18 to be generated. This problem could be in the SPOUT or PIP wiring. It could also be an intermittent open in the PIP circuit or the TFI module.

Code 17

The code 17 indicates that the rpm are below the self-test limit. This code is the opposite of the code 16. (Note that no code 17 exists for the 2.3- and 5.0-liter applications.) The possible causes of the code 17 can be determined by asking the following questions:

Were all the engine accessories off?
Was the engine at normal operating temperature?
Is soot built up in the throttle bore or BYP valve?
Is the minimum air set correctly?
Are the throttle plates sticking or binding?

Code 18

The code 18 relates to the loss of the tach signal to the ECA. If this code comes up during the engine-running test, it means that the ECA has detected an open in the SPOUT circuit during the on-demand codes. Because the code came up during the on-demand codes, the problem causing it is a hard fault—an existing problem—and therefore should be easy to trace.

If the code 18 is in the memory codes; it will be a little more difficult to trace. A memory code 18 indicates that the IDM signal between the TFI module and the ECA has been lost sometime in the past. Because the code 18 did not come up in the on-demand codes, the problem is intermittent—no longer exists—and may be difficult to locate.

KOER On-Demand Code

Troubleshooting the KOER on-demand code is fairly simple. Begin by locating the SPOUT connector. This is the connector in the yellow and green wire that runs from terminal 2 of the TFI module to terminal 36 of the ECA. It is disconnected to check or set the initial timing. The code 18 could result if the connector was left out or disconnected during the last tune-up.

If the connector is in place, perform the computed timing test (see the "Supplemental EEC IV Tests" section at the end of this chapter). Connect a timing light. Run the KOER self-test. After the last on-

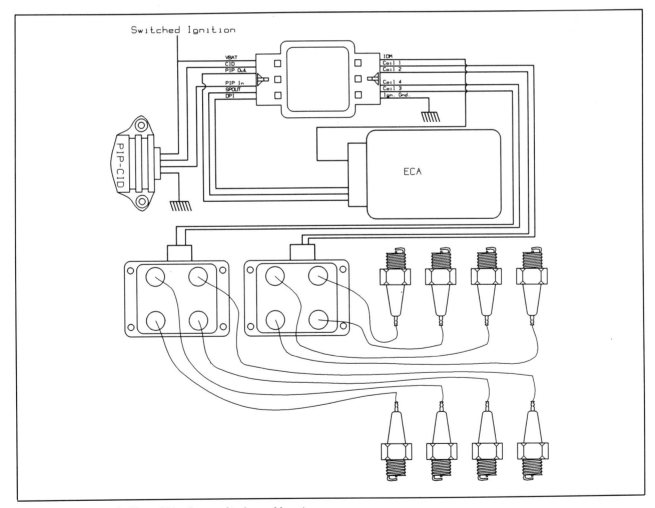

With the DIS, the code 18 could be the result of a problem in the DIS module, the PIP sensor, or the PIP or SPOUT wiring. This diagram is for the 2.3-liter dual-plug engine.

demand code is received, check the timing. It should be initial timing—usually 10 degrees before top dead center on EEC IV engines—plus 20 degrees, plus or minus 3 degrees. If the computed timing test meets this spec and the code 18 was again received as you prepared for computed timing, you have a puzzle. Logically, these results are mutually exclusive. Repeat the computed timing test and again watch for the code 18. If the code 18 repeats and the computed timing is within spec, the ECA is making erroneous decisions and should be replaced.

If the computed timing is not correct, shut the engine off, disconnect the self-test hookup, disconnect the SPOUT wire, and check the initial timing. The initial timing is 10 to 12 degrees on most EEC IV applications, but it would be wise to check this against the EPA decal located under the hood of the vehicle. If the initial timing is okay but the computed timing was incorrect, check the power supply voltage to the ECA. With the ECA harness connector connected and the key on but the engine off, measure the voltage between ECA terminal pin 37 and pins 57 and 60. It should be battery voltage. If these voltages are okay, check the voltages between pins 40 and 57 as well as pins 40 and 60; the voltage should be battery voltage.

If all these voltages are okay, connect a digital tachometer to the yellow and green wire that runs from ECA pin 36 and terminal 2 of the TFI module (this is the SPOUT wire). Start the engine. The tachometer should read an rpm greater than 0. If the tach reads 0, inspect the SPOUT wire for opens or shorts to either ground or voltage. If the wire is okay,

replace the ECA. A reading greater than 0 on the tach means that the ECA is producing the SPOUT (timing control) signal and the TFI module must be impeding the timing control ability of the system.

If the initial timing is incorrect, adjust as necessary and repeat the self-test. If the computed timing is still incorrect, replace the ECA.
Note: If the vehicle being diagnosed is equipped with a distributorless ignition, the SPOUT wire is connected to pin 5 of the DIS module.

Memory Code

The memory code 18 means that during an earlier operation of the engine, the ECA detected a loss of the IDM signal to the ECA. This condition could be caused by a shorted or open harness between the ignition module and the ECA, a defective ignition module, or a defective ECA. If the vehicle is equipped with the TFI (distributor-type) ignition system, disconnect the E-core coil and the sixty-pin connector from the ECA. With an ohmmeter set on the 20,000-ohm scale (or the equivalent), check the resistance between pin 4 of the ECA harness and the negative terminal of the E-core coil primary. The resistance should be between 20,000 and 24,000 ohms. If the resistance is greater than 24,000 ohms, repair the open circuit in the wire. If it is less than 20,000 ohms, check the resistances between pin 4 and pins 40, 46, and 60 of the ECA harness. If any of the resistances is less than 10,000 ohms, repair the short between the affected wires.

If all the resistances check out okay, reconnect the sixty-pin connector to the ECA. Leave the E-core coil disconnected. Again check the resistances between terminals 4 and 40, 4 and 46, and 4 and 60. The resistance for each test should be greater than 10,000

If the PIP sensor indicates an inappropriate number of cylinders during two consecutive camshaft rotations, the code 18 will set. The armature should determine the number of pulses created by the PIP sensor. This armature is from a six-cylinder engine. The narrow blade identifies it as being from a sequential engine.

On many applications, the code 18 can result from accidentally forgetting to reinstall the SPOUT connector after checking or setting the initial timing.

ohms. If it is not, replace the ECA. If the resistance is greater than 10,000 ohms, reconnect the E-core coil and perform the continuous monitor test.

Enter the continuous monitor test as described in the "Supplemental EEC IV Tests" section at the end of this chapter. Wiggle the TFI module harness and connector. Pay particular attention to the six wires at the TFI module. Tap on the TFI module. If a fault is indicated, make the appropriate repair. If no fault is indicated, replace the ECA.

If the vehicle you are working on is equipped with the DIS, the test procedure is the same except that where the instructions say to connect or disconnect the E-core coil, you should connect the pin 7-to-pin-12 connector of the DIS module.

Code 19

If the code 19 is received during the KOEO portion of the test, it indicates a loss of power to the ECA. If the car is equipped with DIS and the code is obtained during the memory codes, a failure of the cylinder identification (CID), or camshaft input, signal has been detected.

For all vehicles, when the code 19 is received during the KOEO portion of the test, replace the ECA.

If the code is a memory code, which is only possible on DIS-equipped engines, it indicates a problem with the cam sensor. To begin troubleshooting the memory code 19, connect a digital tachometer to pin 24 of the ECA harness. Crank the engine. Does the tachometer indicate anything other than 0? If it does, replace the ECA. If it does not, disconnect the harness from the ECA and the left connector (looking at the module upright) from the DIS module. Check

the resistance of the wire that runs between the second wire from the top of the DIS connector to pin 24 of the ECA harness. If the resistance is greater than 5 ohms, repair the defective wire. If the resistance is less than 5 ohms, ensure that the wire connected to ECA pin 24 is not shorted to the wires connected to pins 16, 37, and 40. If you find no short

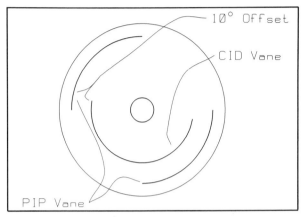

The CID sensor is found behind the harmonic balancer on the 2.3-liter dual-plug engine. The CID sensor on most other engines is located in the hole where the distributor used to be mounted.

The ECT sensor is a negative temperature coefficient thermistor. As this sensor heats up, its resistance drops. To locate the ECT sensor, begin looking near the thermostat housing. On this engine, it is located between the upper radiator hose and a heater hose. A problem with the ECT sensor, even something as simple as not having the engine warmed up for the test, can cause the code 21 to be generated. This code is common when the engine is not properly warmed before the KOER test.

On the 3.0-liter SHO engine, the CID sensor is located on the right inner camshaft. The pulse from this sensor tells the DIS module which coil to fire next.

between these wires, replace the DIS module. If the wires are shorted, repair the short.

Code 21

The code 21 relates to the ECT (Engine Coolant Temperature sensor). If the temperature of the engine during the KOEO test is less than 50 degrees Fahrenheit or greater than 250 degrees Fahrenheit, the code 21 will be received. This code will be received during the KOER test if the temperature of the engine is less than 180 degrees Fahrenheit or greater than 250 degrees Fahrenheit. When performing the quick test to extract the trouble codes, be sure that the engine temperature is within these guidelines.

If the code 21 is received during either the KOEO test or the KOER test, ensure that the temperature of the engine is within the specs. If necessary, disconnect the jumper from the test connector and run the engine until the operating temperature is reached. Repeat the test. If the code 21 is still received, verify that the 5-volt VREF regulator of the ECA is working. To preclude the possibility of a bad ECT wire causing a deceptive reading, check the VREF at the TP sensor. If 5 volts is present at the TP connector, check the resistance of the ECT sensor. The resistance of the sensor should be as shown in the following chart:

ECT Temperature vs. Resistance

Temperature of the Engine (Degrees Fahrenheit)	Resistance (Ohms)
50	58,750
68	37,300
86	24,270
104	16,150
122	10,970
140	7,700
158	5,370
176	3,840
194	2,800
212	2,070
230	1,550
248	1,180

The exact temperature of the engine coolant at the point where the ECT sensor is located is impossible to determine accurately, and the sensors may vary slightly. Therefore, do not expect the resistance reading to be exactly as indicated in the above chart. *Note:* A rule of thumb is that the ECT sensors seldom become slightly defective. As a result, if the sensor reading falls anywhere on or near the chart, the sensor is probably good. It is usually sufficient to estimate the temperature of the engine as simply cold, warm, or hot.

If the resistance is good, leave the ECT sensor disconnected. Connect a digital voltmeter to the ECT signal wire. It should read 5 volts. If it does not, repair the defective wire or connection at the ECA. If the wire is not damaged, replace the ECA.

If the voltmeter does read 5 volts, leave it connected and connect a jumper wire between the

ECT signal wire and the signal return wire at the ECT connector. The voltage displayed on the meter should drop to 0. If it does not, repair the signal return wire. If it does, replace the ECA.

Code 22

The code 22 means the ECA does not see a signal from the MAP sensor or BP sensor, depending on the application. This code can be received as a KOEO code, a KOER code, or a memory code.

KOEO or KOER Code

If the code 22 is received during the KOEO or KOER test, it means that the pulse from the MAP sensor is either missing or out of the expected frequency range. Connect a high-impedance voltmeter to the middle wire of the MAP sensor connector. Turn the ignition switch on, and the voltmeter should read 2.5 volts. If it does not, check the other two wires. One wire (usually orange) should have 5 volts. If it does not, repair as necessary. The other wire should be a ground. Repair as necessary.

Note: If the code 22 is received during the engine-running test, make sure the EGR valve is closing and seating properly. If the EGR valve is not seating properly, this can cause erratic manifold pressures, which can result in erratic readings from the MAP sensor. Erratic readings from the MAP sensor can set the code 22.

Memory Code

If the code 22 is received during the memory codes, it means that the problem occurred in the past

The code 22 relates to the MAP sensor. Code 22 problems almost always end up being connections or wires. On some models, the MAP sensor may be difficult to locate. With the MAP sensor on a 1991 Taurus, for example, only the vacuum and electrical connectors can be seen through the firewall.

and no longer exists. Enter the continuous monitor test mode (as described in the "Supplemental EEC IV Tests" section at the end of this chapter) and test for intermittent opens, shorts, or grounds in the MAP sensor circuit.

Code 23

The code 23 indicates a problem with the TP sensor. This code can be generated during the KOEO or KOER test. It will be received when the ECA sees a voltage from the TP sensor that is outside the expected parameters during the test. The low-end spec for this voltage is between 0.2 and 0.39 volt, depending on the application. The high-end spec is 4.84 volts for all applications except the 3.0-liter SHO engine, for which it is 4.89 volts.

Begin troubleshooting the code 23 by checking the voltage on the TP signal wire (ECA pin 47, usually a green wire) with the throttle closed. It should be within the specs listed above. If the voltage is lower than the specified minimum voltage, disconnect the harness from the TP sensor. The voltage on the orange wire should be approximately 5 volts (VREF). If it is not, disconnect the sixty-pin connector from the ECA. Inspect the connection of pin 47 to the ECA. If this connection is good, check the resistance between the orange VREF wire and the signal return (TP ground) wire, which is usually black. The resistance should be infinity. If the resistance is less than infinity, repair the short between the VREF wire and the signal return wire.

If the resistance between the VREF and signal return wires is okay, connect an ohmmeter between the VREF and signal return terminals of the TP sensor. Move the throttle back and forth. If the resistance changes, replace the ECA. If the resistance does not change, replace the TP sensor.

If when the TP signal voltage was checked, it was more than 4.84 volts (4.89 for the SHO engine), check for a short between the VREF wire and the TP signal wire. Also check for a short between the TP signal wire and any other voltage source. If all of this checks out okay, replace the TP sensor.

Code 24

If the code 24 is received during the KOEO or KOER test, it is an indication that the air temperature sensor is transmitting outside the expected range.

If the temperature of the air in the intake manifold is less than 50 degrees Fahrenheit or greater than 250 degrees Fahrenheit, this code will be received. When performing the quick test to extract the trouble codes, be sure that the engine temperature is within these guidelines.

If the code 24 is received during either the KOEO test or the KOER test, be sure that the temperature of the engine is within these specs. If necessary, disconnect the jumper from the test connector and run the engine until the operating temperature is reached. Repeat the test. If the code 24 is still received, verify that the 5-volt reference voltage regulator of the ECA is working. To preclude the possibility of a bad ACT wire causing a deceptive reading, check the VREF at the TP sensor. If 5 volts is at the TP connector, check the resistance of the ACT sensor, which should be as shown in the following chart:

In many cases, the TP sensor is difficult to see. Regardless of the application, however, the sensor is always located on the throttle assembly. The code 23 relates to adjustment problems or perceived failure in the TP sensor.

The code 24 relates to the Air Charge Temperature (ACT) sensor. On almost all Ford EFI products, the ACT sensor is located in the intake manifold. The code 24 means the sensor is indicating a temperature that is outside the expected test range. This code is common when the engine is not properly warmed before the KOER test.

ACT Temperature vs. Resistance

Temperature of the Intake Manifold Air (Degrees Fahrenheit)	Resistance (Ohms)
50	58,750
68	37,300
86	24,270
104	16,150
122	10,970
140	7,700
158	5,370
176	3,840
194	2,800
212	2,070
230	1,550
248	1,180

The exact temperature of the air in the intake manifold at the point where the ACT sensor is located is impossible to determine accurately, and the sensors may vary slightly. Therefore, do not expect the resistance reading to be exactly as indicated in the above chart.

Note: A rule of thumb is that ACT sensors seldom become slightly defective. As a result, if the sensor reading falls anywhere on or near the chart, the sensor is probably good. It is usually sufficient to estimate the temperature of the engine as simply cold, warm, or hot.

If the resistance is good, leave the ACT sensor disconnected. Connect a digital voltmeter to the ACT signal wire (pin 25). It should read 5 volts. If it does not, repair the defective wire or connection at the ECA. If the wire is not damaged, replace the ECA.

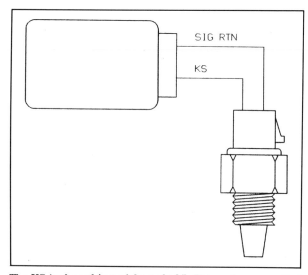

The KS is the subject of the code 25. This code means that during the goose test section of the KOER test, the voltage did not rise on the KS wire. Another way of saying this is that the ECA, through the KS, did not detect a detonation. Causes for this range from problems in the KS circuit to fuel with too high an octane rating.

If the voltmeter does read 5 volts, leave it connected and connect a jumper wire between the ACT signal wire and the signal return wire at the ACT connector. The voltage displayed on the meter should drop to 0. If it does not, repair the signal return wire. If it does, replace the ECA.

Code 25

The code 25 is one of my favorite codes to troubleshoot because it allows me to use one of my favorite diagnostic tools—a hammer.

The code 25 means no detonation was detected by the KS or the ECA when the engine was goosed during the KOER test. Just before the dynamic response code, the ECA advances the timing to 20 degrees before initial timing and locks it. With the timing at 30 degrees before top dead center, the engine should detonate when the throttle is goosed.

Several things can keep the engine from detonating during the goose test, including the following:

Fuel quality: In the world of the 1990s, fuel quality as a cause of the code 25 is highly unlikely. Remember, for the code 25 to be generated, a detonation must not be detected during the goose test. The implication here is that the fuel must be too good—that is, it must have an octane rating that is too high. (Yeah, right.)

Engine problems: If the engine compression is reduced for any reason, it will inhibit the engine's ability to detonate.

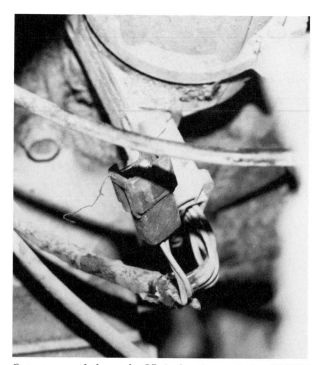

One cause of the code 25 is leaving out the SPOUT connector after checking or setting the initial timing. Check the SPOUT connector early in the troubleshooting of the code 25.

Initial timing: If the initial timing of the engine is retarded, the engine will be less likely to detonate.

If the fuel, engine, and initial timing have been ruled out as possible causes of the code 25, begin the test procedure by repeating the KOER test. This time, when the code 10 dynamic response code is given, do not goose the throttle. Instead, tap smartly on the exhaust manifold immediately above the KS with a 4-ounce hammer. Ignore all the codes except the code 25. If the code 25 does not return, the system is working properly.

If the code 25 does return, check the voltage between pins 23 and 46. This voltage should be between 1 and 4 volts. If it is, replace the KS.

If the voltage is less than 1 volt, check for a short between the KS wire and the KS signal return wire. Check also for a grounded KS wire. If the wires are okay, replace the KS.

If the voltage is greater than 4 volts, check for an open in the KS wire (pin 23 at the ECA) or the KS signal return wire (pin 46). If the KS and signal return wires are not damaged, replace the KS.

Code 26

The code 26 has three possible meanings, depending on the application:

1.9- and 2.3-liter Turbo applications: VAF was out of range

3.0-liter SHO, 3.8-liter SC, and some 5.0-liter applications: MAF was out of range

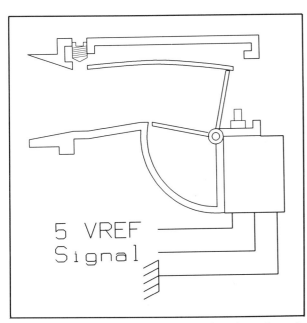

For the 1.9-liter and 2.3-liter Turbo applications, the code 26 relates to a problem in the circuitry of the VAF sensor. The 5-volt reference is sent to the VAF sensor, which is connected to ground. A third wire carries a variable voltage signal from the VAF sensor to the ECA. As the volume of air entering the engine increases, the signal voltage to the ECA increases.

5.8- and 7.4-liter trucks with E4OD transmission: Transmission oil temperature (TOT) was out of range

1.9- and 2.3-Liter Turbo Applications

The code 26 for 1.9- and 2.3-liter Turbo applications obtained during the KOEO or KOER test means that the output voltage of the Vane Air Flow sensor is outside the expected range. During the KOEO test, the ECA expects to see a voltage between 0.17 and 0.5 volt. During the KOER test, the ECA expects to see a reading between 1.1 and 1.7 volts. If the voltage is outside these specs, the code 26 will be generated.

If the code 26 is delivered during the KOEO test, check the voltage at pin 43 of the ECA. This voltage should be between 0.17 and 0.5 volt. If it falls outside of this range, remove the VAF sensor from the car. Inside the VAF sensor is a movable flap. Although the flap should be under spring tension, it should move freely when pushed with a finger or pencil. If the flap does not move freely, replace the VAF sensor.

If the code 26 is received during the KOER test, check the voltage at pin 43 of the ECA while the engine is idling. This voltage should be between 1.1 and 1.7 volts. If it is outside of these specs, check the rubber tube that connects the VAF sensor to the throttle assembly for leaks. If air leaks into the intake system through this tube, this leaking air will not be pushing on the flap. The result is that the flap will not move as far as it should at idle. Therefore, the output voltage will be lower than it should be.

If the throttle-body-to-VAF connector tube has no leaks, check for the free movement of the VAF flap as described previously for the KOEO code 26. A binding or sticking flap warrants the replacement of

The code 26 on vehicles equipped with the MAF sensor means the signal detected by the ECA is outside the expected range. The MAF sensor is located in the air tube that runs between the air cleaner and the throttle assembly.

the VAF sensor. If the flap does not stick or bind, check the engine for proper idle speed.

3.0-Liter SHO, 3.8-Liter SC, and Some 5.0-Liter Applications

If the code 26 is received on an engine equipped with a Mass Air Flow sensor, it means the MAF reading was outside the expected range during the test. During the KOEO test, the voltage output of this sensor should be less than 0.7 volt. During the KOER test, the voltage output should be between 0.2 and 1.5 volts (idle spec). Four wires are connected to the MAF sensor. These wires connect to five terminals on the ECA. Terminal A of the MAF sensor is connected to terminals 37 and 57 of the ECA. This wire carries the vehicle power (VPWR) supply, or switched ignition voltage. Terminal B is connected to pins 40 and 60 of the ECA and supplies ground for the MAF electronics. Terminal C is the signal ground, which is called the signal return by Ford. Terminal D carries the actual information or signal to the ECA; Ford calls this the MAF signal.

During the KOER test, the ECA expects to see about 0.8 volt from the MAF sensor when the engine is idling. If the code 26 is received, check the 12-volt power supply (MAF terminal A) to the MAF sensor. Check the ground for the MAF power supply (MAF terminal B) as well. If these are good, check the signal return wire (MAF terminal C). If this is also good, check the wire that carries the MAF signal to the ECA (MAF terminal D). This wire is connected to pin 50 of the ECA. Using a thin safety pin or an insulation-probing alligator clip, connect a voltmeter to the wire

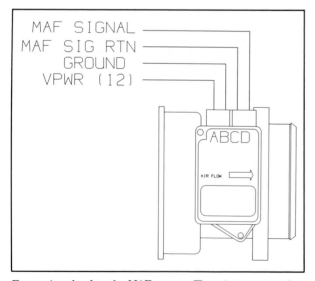

Four wires lead to the MAF sensor. The wire connected to terminal A carries a 12-volt power supply to the sensor. The wire connected to terminal B is a ground for the sensor power supply. Terminal C is the signal return or ground for the MAF signal. The wire connected to terminal D carries the MAF signal to the ECA.

going into pin 50 as close to the sixty-pin ECA connector as possible. Start the engine. The voltage displayed on the meter should be about 0.8 volt. If it is not, check the voltage at terminal D of the MAF sensor. If the voltage there is not approximately 0.8 volt, check the connection at the MAF sensor. If the connection is good, replace the MAF sensor. If the voltage at MAF terminal A is 0.8 volt, repair the wire between pin 50 of the ECA and terminal D of the MAF sensor. If 0.8 volt is at terminal 50, carefully inspect the connection. If you find no defects in the MAF sensor or the wiring harness, replace the ECA.

Code 26

5.8- and 7.4-Liter Trucks with E4OD Transmission

Transmission oil temperature (TOT) sensor: To pass the KOEO or KOER test, the voltage from the TOT sensor must be between 0.21 and 3.5 volts. When the code 26 is received on one of these applications, drive the vehicle in city traffic for 20 to 30 minutes. Repeat the KOEO or KOER test or both. If the code 26 is still received, verify that the 5-volt reference voltage regulator of the ECA is working. To preclude the possibility of a bad TOT wire causing a deceptive reading, check the VREF at the TP sensor. If 5 volts is at the TP connector, check the resistance of the TOT sensor. The resistance of the sensor should be as shown in the following chart:

Temperature of the Transmission (Degrees Fahrenheit)	Resistance (Ohms)
50	58,750
68	37,300
86	24,270
104	16,150
122	10,970
140	7,700
158	5,370
176	3,840
194	2,800
212	2,070
230	1,550
248	1,180

The exact temperature of the transmission fluid at the point where the TOT sensor is located is impossible to determine accurately, and the sensors may vary slightly. Therefore, do not expect the resistance reading to be exactly as indicated in the above chart.

Note: A rule of thumb is that TOT sensors seldom become slightly defective. As a result, if the sensor reading falls anywhere on or near the chart, the sensor is probably good. It is usually sufficient to estimate the temperature of the transmission as simply cold, warm, or hot.

If the resistance is good, leave the TOT sensor disconnected. Connect a digital voltmeter to the TOT signal wire. It should read 5 volts. If it does not, repair the defective wire or connection at the ECA. If the wire is not damaged, replace the ECA.

If the voltmeter does read 5 volts, leave it connected and connect a jumper wire between the TOT signal wire and the signal return wire at the TOT connector. The voltage displayed on the meter should drop to 0. If it does not, repair the signal return wire. If it does, replace the ECA.

Code 28

The code 28 has two different meanings, depending on the car or truck being worked on:

1.9- and 2.3-liter Turbo applications: VAT was out of range

2.3-liter dual-plug engine applications: Primary tach signal was lost, right side

1.9- and 2.3-Liter Turbo Applications

Verify that the 5-volt reference voltage regulator of the ECA is working. To preclude the possibility of a bad ACT wire causing a deceptive reading, check the VREF at the TP sensor. If 5 volts is found at the TP connector, check the resistance of the ACT sensor. The resistance of the sensor should be as shown in the following chart:

VAT Temperature vs. Resistance

Temperature of the Intake Air (Degrees Fahrenheit)	Resistance (Ohms)
50	3,700
240	125

The exact temperature of the air in the intake manifold at the point where the ACT sensor is located is impossible to determine accurately, and the sensors may vary slightly. Therefore, do not expect the resistance reading to be exactly as indicated in the above chart.

Note: A rule of thumb is that ACT sensors seldom become slightly defective. As a result, if the sensor reading falls anywhere on or near the chart, the sensor is probably good. It is usually sufficient to estimate the temperature of the engine as simply cold, warm, or hot.

If the resistance is good, leave the ACT sensor disconnected. Connect a digital voltmeter to the ACT signal wire (pin 25). It should read 5 volts. If it does not, repair the defective wire or connection at the ECA. If the wire is not damaged, replace the ECA.

If the voltmeter does read 5 volts, leave it connected and connect a jumper wire between the ACT signal wire and the signal return wire at the ACT connector. The voltage displayed on the meter should drop to 0. If it does not, repair the signal return wire. If it does, replace the ECA.

2.3-Liter Dual-Plug Engine Applications

Code 28 on these engines means the portion of the ignition module responsible for firing the right bank spark plugs failed to deliver a tach signal to the ECA. Check the resistance of the wire that runs between pin 4 of the ECA and DIS (distributorless ignition system) module pin 11. Inspect these terminals for corrosion and damaged pins. If the wire and

For the 1.9-liter and 2.3-liter Turbo applications, the code 28 relates to a problem in the circuitry of the VAT sensor. The VAT sensor is a standard thermistor circuit. Located in the VAF sensor, it cannot be replaced without replacing the VAF sensor.

This VSS is located in the transmission. It has two wires and produces an AC signal. The internal structure of this sensor is similar to that of the old-style pickup coils used in electronic ignition systems since the early 1970s.

the pins are in good condition, replace the DIS module.

Code 29

When the code 29 is received during the memory codes, it is an indication that the VSS did not deliver a signal to the ECA when other inputs to the ECA indicate that the vehicle is moving.

Begin the test procedure by clearing the memory codes. To clear the memory codes, reenter the KOEO self-test. When the first KOEO code is received, disconnect the STI, which is the jumper wire that was placed between the six-terminal test connector and the single-terminal test connector. As the STI is disconnected, a clicking and whirring sound will be heard. This sound verifies that the memory codes have cleared.

Now testdrive the vehicle. If the car is equipped with an automatic transmission, place the transmission in low and accelerate to 25mph. Allow the vehicle to coast to a stop. If the car is equipped with a manual transmission, place the transmission in first gear. Slowly accelerate, shift to second gear, and accelerate to 40mph. Bring the car to a stop.

Extract the service codes again. If the memory code 29 returns, carefully inspect the VSS wiring harness. Look for frayed wires, damage to the insulation, and loose connections. If the wiring harness looks good, replace the VSS.

Code 31

Most of the 30-series codes relate to the EGR control system. The code 31 can be received during any stage of the self-test. If it is received during the KOEO on-demand section of the test, it indicates that the EGR position-sensing device is transmitting a voltage lower than the ECA expected to see during the test.

The EEC IV system uses two types of EGR positioning sensors. The first type is the EGR Valve Position sensor. This is a potentiometer similar to the TP sensor and is located on top of the EGR. When the EGR valve is closed, the EVP sensor should be sending approximately 0.5 volt to terminal 27 of the ECA. As the EGR valve opens, the voltage rises until it reaches just under 4.8 volts. Through this means, the ECA knows at all times if the EGR control system is responding to the signals it is being sent.

The second EGR monitoring device is the PFE sensor. This device senses the pressure in a tube that runs from the exhaust system to the EGR valve. When the EGR valve is closed, a pressure exists in this tube. As the EGR valve opens, the pressure in the tube drops. As the EGR valve continues to open, the pressure in the tube continues to drop until it becomes a vacuum. While this pressure is dropping, the voltage from the PFE sensor to terminal 27 slowly drops. At idle, the voltage to pin 27 is about 2 volts.

For either sensor, the code 31 is generated when the voltage to pin 27 is less than 0.2 volt during the KOEO self-test. Troubleshoot the code 31 for each type of application as discussed here.

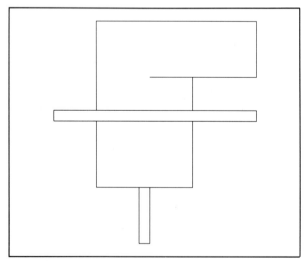

The EVP sensor is a potentiometer. Three wires are attached to it. One wire carries a 5-volt reference to the sensor. The second wire provides a ground. The third wire carries a variable voltage signal to the ECA. When the EGR is closed, the TP sensor is delivering about 0.8 volt to the ECA. As the EGR is opened, the voltage to the ECA slowly rises to over 4 volts. The code 31 means the sensor voltage to the ECA was outside the expected range.

The PFE sensor measures the pressure in the tube that runs from the exhaust system to the EGR valve. When the pressure in this tube is high, it indicates the EGR valve is closed. As the pressure drops, the PFE assumes that it is because the EGR valve is opening. When the EGR valve opens, it exposes the EGR tube to manifold vacuum and the pressure in the tube drops. The code 31 indicates an unexpected voltage when this sensor is used in place of the EVP sensor.

EVP Applications

If the code 31 is received during the KOEO or KOER test, begin by attempting to generate the code 35, which represents a condition that is the opposite of the code 31. Disconnect the connector from the EVP sensor and place a jumper wire between the EVP signal terminal and the VREF terminal. Run the KOEO self-test again. If the code 35 is received during this test, it proves that the wiring, connections, and ECA are in good condition. By the process of elimination, the fault that caused the code 31 is in the ECA.

If the code 31 returns during the second KOEO test, connect a voltmeter between the VREF wire (usually orange) and the signal return wire (usually black). The voltmeter should read between 4 and 6 volts (it really should read 5 volts). If it does not, check the voltage at the VREF wire. If you find 5 volts at the VREF wire, check and repair the signal return wire. If the voltage between the VREF and signal return wires is 5 volts, check the voltage between the VREF wire and the EVP signal wire. Again, the voltage should be between 4 and 6 volts. If it is not, repair the EVP signal wire.

If the wiring for the EVP sensor tests good, disconnect the EEC IV harness from the ECA and the EVP sensor. Check the resistances between ECA pin 27 and pins 40, 46, and 60. The resistance should in each case be greater than 10,000 ohms (actually, it should be infinity ohms). If the resistance is less than 10,000 ohms, repair the short between the affected wires. If the resistances check out good, replace the ECA.

PFE Applications

If the vehicle is equipped with a PFE sensor, the code 31 during the KOEO self-test indicates the voltage at terminal 27 of the ECA was below 0.2 volt. Begin by attempting to generate the code 35, which represents a condition that is the opposite of the code 31. Disconnect the connector from the PFE sensor and place a jumper wire between the PFE signal terminal and the VREF terminal. Run the KOEO self-test again. If the code 35 is received during this test, it proves that the wiring, connections, and ECA are in

This is the PFE sensor used on the 3.0-liter SHO engine.

The EVR (EGR Valve Regulator) controls the operation of the EGR valve. Controlled by a variable duty cycle signal from the ECA, the EVR regulates the amount of vacuum to the EGR valve. Many of the 30-series codes can be the result of problems with the EVR.

Under the EVR cap, which is white in this photo, is a filter. When this filter is plugged, it can affect the operation of the EGR valve. Check this filter early in the troubleshooting of any EGR-related code.

good condition. By the process of elimination, the fault that caused the code 31 is in the ECA.

If the code 31 returns during the second KOEO test, connect a voltmeter between the VREF wire (usually orange and white) and the signal return wire (usually black and white). The voltmeter should read between 4 and 6 volts (it really should read 5 volts). If it does not, check the voltage at the VREF wire. If you find 5 volts at the VREF wire, check and repair the signal return wire. If the voltage between the VREF and signal return wires is 5 volts, check the voltage between the VREF wire and the PFE signal wire. Again, the voltage should be between 4 and 6 volts. If it is not, repair the PFE signal wire.

If the wiring for the PFE tests good, disconnect the EEC IV harness from the ECA and the PFE sensor. Check the resistances between ECA pin 27 and pins 40, 46, and 60. The resistance should in each case be greater than 10,000 ohms (actually, it should be infinity ohms). If the resistance is less than 10,000 ohms, repair the short between the affected wires. If the resistances check out good, replace the ECA.

If the code 31 was received during the KOER test on a PFE sensor–equipped vehicle, begin the best procedure by disconnecting the EGR valve vacuum hose and repeating the KOER self-test. If the code 31 returns or if the code 32 is generated, check the tube from the exhaust tube to the PFE sensor for restrictions. If you find no restrictions, check the EGR valve for proper seating and replace it if necessary.

If the code 31 does not repeat and if the code 32 is not generated, inspect the EVR filter. The EVR controls the amount of vacuum available to the EGR valve by controlling a vacuum leak. A filter over the bleed port prevents dirt from being pulled into the engine through this opening. If the filter becomes restricted, it will cause the EGR valve to hang open when the engine is running. If the EVR filter is okay, replace the EVR solenoid.

If the code 31 was received during the memory codes, it indicates that the code 31 condition existed during the last time that the engine ran. If the code 31 also existed in the KOEO or KOER self-test on-demand codes, make those repairs first. If it did not exist in the on-demand codes, it indicates the problem is intermittent.

To test for an intermittent code 31 on either PFE or EVP applications, enter the continuous monitor mode (see the "Continuous Monitor Test" discussion in the "Supplemental EEC IV Tests" section at the end of this chapter). If the vehicle is equipped with a PFE sensor, connect a hand-held vacuum pump to the PFE pressure port. Apply vacuum while watching the continuous monitor test voltmeter. If the voltmeter goes to 12 volts while you are applying the vacuum, replace the PFE sensor.

If the vehicle is equipped with an EVP sensor, attach the vacuum pump to the EGR valve. Apply vacuum to the valve. If the continuous monitor voltmeter goes to 12 volts while you are applying the vacuum, replace the EVP sensor.

If the application of vacuum does not affect the continuous monitor voltmeter, continue the test by wiggling the sensor wiring harness and tapping lightly on the sensor. This tapping is intended to simulate road shock, not the shock of a 60mph collision; be gentle. If wiggling the wires causes the voltmeter to rise to 12 volts, repair the wire or connection as necessary. If tapping on the sensor causes the voltmeter to rise, replace the sensor. If the voltmeter does not rise to 12 volts during this test, the problem cannot be simulated at this time. Service any other codes that exist and clear the codes.

Code 32

EVP Applications

For EVP applications, if the code 32 is received during the KOEO or KOER test, disconnect the EVP harness connector and inspect for loose or damaged connections. Install a hand-held vacuum pump on the EGR valve. Apply and release the vacuum several times. Reconnect the EGR valve and run the KOER self-test. If the code 32 does not return, the problem was a binding EGR valve. If the code 32 does return, replace the EVP sensor. Repeat the self-test. If the code 32 is still present, replace the EGR valve.

The code 32 during the memory codes means that the EVP signal voltage was below the closed EGR voltage limit of 0.29 volt. Carefully inspect the EVP harness and connectors. Make any repairs that are obviously needed. Attach a hand-held vacuum pump to the EGR valve. Connect a digital voltmeter to pin 27 of the ECA. Slowly apply vacuum to 6in of mercury. Now, slowly bleed the vacuum off. Lightly tap on the EVP sensor. Is the voltage to pin 27 less than 0.29 volt? If it is, replace the EGR valve. If it is

This is the EVR used on the 3.0-liter SHO engine.

not, then the condition that generated the code no longer exists.

PFE Applications

If the code 32 is received during the KOER test, carefully inspect the EVR and the EVR filter. Check the tube that connects the PFE sensor to the EGR port for restrictions and blockages.

If the EVR and the PFE sensor look good, disconnect the vacuum line to the EGR valve and plug the hose. Repeat the KOER test. If the code 31 or the code 32 is generated, verify that the PFE supply tube has no leaks. If neither the code 31 nor the code 32 is generated, verify that the EVR filter is not restricted (dirty) and replace the EVR.

If the code 32 is a memory code, connect a hand-held vacuum pump to the EGR valve. Slowly apply a vacuum to the valve. If the valve opens smoothly, check the EVR filter, the EVR connections, and the pressure supply hose to the PFE sensor. If all of these are good and the code did not show up during the KOEO codes or the KOER codes, the problem no longer exists. No further testing for this problem need be done.

Code 33

When the code 33 is received during the KOER test, it means the EGR valve was not detected as having opened during the test. One exception to this exists: on the 2.3-liter ohc EFI (MPI) application, the code 33 means that the EGR valve did not reseat properly.

When the code 33 is received during the memory codes, it means that the computer did not see the EGR valve open the last time the car was driven or earlier. If the code 33 is not also received as a KOER code, the condition that caused the code to be generated no longer exists.

If the code 33 is received during the KOER test, it is likely no vacuum supply runs to the EGR valve. Inspect the vacuum hose that runs from the EVR to the EGR valve for restrictions, holes, and cracks. Check the vacuum hose that runs from the intake manifold to the EVR. If the vacuum hoses are okay, connect a vacuum gauge to the hose connected to the EGR valve. Repeat the KOER test. If the vacuum reading on the gauge is at least 1.5in of mercury, carefully insert a small screwdriver in one of the holes on the underside of the EGR valve. Work the EGR valve diaphragm up and down in an attempt to free any mechanical binding. Repeat the KOER test and check for the code 33. If the code 33 recurs, connect a hand-held vacuum pump to the EGR valve and apply 2in to 3in of vacuum. Does the EGR valve hold vacuum? If it does not, replace the EGR valve. If it does, replace the EVP sensor.

If vacuum does not get to the EGR valve the first time the KOER test is repeated, check for vacuum to the EVR. If no vacuum gets to the EVR, repair as necessary. If vacuum does get to the EVR, replace the EVR.

If the code 33 was received in the memory codes and not in the KOER codes, check the vacuum hose routing against the decal under the hood of the vehicle. Check the vacuum hoses for restrictions, cracks, and holes. Check the connections on the EVR. If everything looks good, clear the codes. The condition no longer exists. Make repairs to any other systems indicated in the service codes.

Code 34

The code 34 has a wide range of meanings, depending on the application. All the meanings, however, relate to the control of the EGR valve. The meanings of the code 34 are as follows:

2.3-liter ohc engine applications (except trucks): EGR flow was insufficient during the KOER test

PFE sensor–equipped vehicles: PFE sensor was defective (if received during the KOEO test) or exhaust back pressure was excessive (if received during the KOER test or memory codes)

EVP sensor–equipped vehicles: EVP voltage was above maximum limit

2.3-Liter Ohc Engine Applications (Except Trucks)

When the code 34 is received during the KOER test on 2.3-liter ohc engines, it means that insufficient exhaust gas flow was detected during the test. These engines are equipped with an EGRC valve and an EGRV valve. The EGRC is controlled by the ECA to prevent vacuum from being available to the EGR valve during warm-up, during deceleration, and at wide-open throttle. Once the EGRC allows vacuum to go to the EGR system, the EGRV is controlled by the ECA to vary the amount of vacuum available to the EGR. The ECA sends a variable duty cycle signal to the EGRV. As the duty cycle increases, the amount of vacuum available to the EGR valve increases. The code 34 is most likely caused by a problem in this system.

When the code 34 is received during the KOER test, inspect the vacuum line that runs from the intake manifold to the EGRC-EGRV system. Check the vacuum lines that run from the EGRC-EGRV system to the EGR valve.

Tee a vacuum gauge into the EGR vacuum line and repeat the KOER test. Does the vacuum increase from less than 1in of mercury to more than 5in? If it does, check the EVP sensor for proper resistance. As the plunger is slowly depressed, the resistance should decrease from 5,500 to 100 ohms. If the EVP resistance is incorrect, replace the EVP sensor; if it is correct, replace the ECA.

If the vacuum did not change according to specifications, confirm that the vacuum routing to and from the EGRC-EGRV assembly is correct. If the routing is correct, replace the EGRC-EGRV assembly.

PFE Sensor–equipped Vehicles

The likely causes of the KOEO code 34 on the PFE sensor–equipped applications are as follows:
Faulty PFE sensor

Obstructed PFE pressure feed tube

Check the PFE pressure feed tube for restrictions. If you find no restrictions, replace the PFE sensor.

The KOER code 34 means that the PFE has sensed excessive exhaust back pressure. Remove the EGO sensor (oxygen sensor) and install a fuel pressure gauge. This may require purchasing plugs and adapters from a local hardware store. Start the engine, and run it at 2500rpm. Observe the pressure gauge. If the pressure is greater than 3psi, the exhaust is restricted. If the pressure remains below 3psi, replace the PFE sensor.

If the memory code 34 is received, check the connections to the PFE electrical connector. Inspect the pressure tube to the PFE sensor. If these items are okay, no additional service for the code 34 is required at this time.

EVP Sensor–equipped Vehicles

The KOEO code 34 indicates that a connection at the EVP sensor is bad; the EGR valve is not seating properly; the EGR valve is binding or sooted up, preventing it from seating properly; or the EVP sensor is faulty.

If the code 34 is accompanied by the code 84, refer to the code 84 diagnostics first. If not, connect a hand-held vacuum pump to the EGR valve and apply 15in to 20in of vacuum. This will help to free the EGR valve if it is binding. Repeat the KOEO test. If the code 34 does not return, replace the EGR valve. If the code 34 does return, replace the EVP sensor.

The KOER code 34 is generated when the EVP sensor sends a voltage greater than 0.67 volt during the KOER test. This could be the result of a restricted EVR filter, a faulty EVR solenoid, a faulty EGR valve, or a faulty EVP sensor.

To begin testing for the KOER code 34, disconnect and plug the vacuum line to the EGR valve. Repeat the KOER test. If the cause of the code 34 was improper control of vacuum to the EGR valve, the code should not return. If it does, check the EVR filter. If the EVR filter is okay, replace the EVR sensor.

If the code 34 does not return when the EGR vacuum hose is disconnected, check the EVP resistance as the EGR valve is opened using a hand-held vacuum pump. With no vacuum applied, the resistance between the EVP signal terminal and the VREF terminal should gradually decrease from 5,500 ohms to not less than 100 ohms. If the EVP sensor meets these specifications, replace the EGR valve. If the resistance drops below 100 ohms, replace the EVP sensor.

If the memory code 34 is received, inspect the EVP connections for corrosion and loose or frayed wires. Apply a vacuum to the EGR valve with a hand-held vacuum pump. If the EGR seems to bind when the vacuum is applied, replace the EGR valve. If all of these things are okay, the condition that caused the code to be generated no longer exists. No additional service for the code 34 is required at this time.

Code 35

KOEO or KOER Code, EVP Sensor–equipped Vehicles

The KOEO or KOER code 35 indicates that the voltage from the EVP sensor to pin 27 of the ECA is greater than 4.81 volts. Begin the test by disconnecting the EVP sensor and performing the KOEO test again. If the code 35 returns, repair the short to voltage in the EVP signal wire (ECA pin 27). If the code 31 is generated in place of the code 35, replace the EVP sensor. If the code 35 is still present after replacing the EVP sensor, check the wiring again and replace the ECA.

KOEO Code, PFE Sensor–equipped Vehicles

The KOEO code indicates that the voltage from the PFE sensor to pin 27 of the ECA is greater than 4.81 volts. Begin the test by disconnecting the PFE sensor and performing the KOEO test again. If the code 35 returns, repair the short to voltage in the PFE signal wire (ECA pin 27). If the code 31 is generated in place of the code 35, replace the PFE sensor. If the code 35 is still present after replacing the PFE sensor, check the wiring again and replace the ECA.

KOER Code, PFE Sensor–equipped Vehicles

On PFE sensor–equipped vehicles, the KOER code 35 means that the PFE sensor has sensed excessive exhaust back pressure. Remove the EGO sensor (oxygen sensor) and install a fuel pressure gauge. This may require purchasing plugs and adapters from a local hardware store. Start the engine, and run it at 2500rpm. Observe the pressure gauge. If the pressure is greater than 3psi, the exhaust is restricted. If the pressure remains below 3psi, replace the PFE sensor.

KOER Code, 2.3-Liter Ohc EFI Engine Applications

For 2.3-liter ohc EFI engine applications, the KOER code 35 has nothing to do with the EGR system itself. It means the engine rpm remained below the minimum rpm required to perform the EGR test.

Memory Code

The memory code 35 for both PFE and EVP applications enters the continuous monitor mode (see the "Continuous Monitor Test" discussion in the "Supplemental EEC IV Tests" section at the end of this chapter). It indicates that the code 35 condition existed during the last time that the engine ran. If the code 35 also existed in the KOEO or KOER self-test on-demand codes, make those repairs first. If it did not exist in the on-demand codes, it indicates the problem is intermittent.

To test for an intermittent code 35 on either PFE or EVP applications, enter the continuous monitor mode. If the vehicle is equipped with a PFE sensor, connect a hand-held vacuum pump to the PFE pressure port. Apply vacuum while watching the continuous monitor test voltmeter. If the voltmeter goes to 12 volts while you are applying the vacuum, replace the PFE sensor.

If the vehicle is equipped with an EVP sensor, attach the vacuum pump to the EGR valve. Apply vacuum to the valve. If the continuous monitor voltmeter goes to 12 volts while you are applying the vacuum, replace the EVP sensor.

If the application of vacuum does not affect the continuous monitor voltmeter, continue the test by wiggling the sensor wiring harness and tapping lightly on the sensor. This tapping is intended to simulate road shock, not the shock of a 60mph collision. If wiggling the wires causes the voltmeter to rise to 12 volts, repair the wire or connection as necessary. If tapping on the sensor causes the voltmeter to rise, replace the sensor. If the voltmeter does not rise to 12 volts during this test, the problem cannot be simulated at this time. Service any other codes that are received and clear the codes.

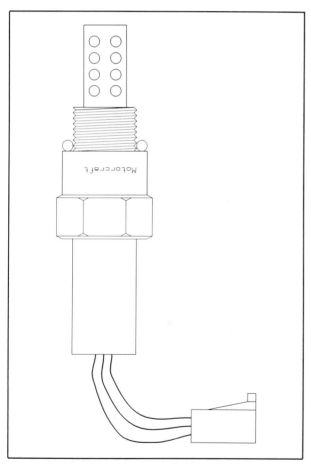

Codes related to the EGO sensor, such as 41 and 42, are common during the KOER test. If either of these codes is received, be sure the EGO sensor is hot and repeat the test. If the code persists, check the things that might affect the air-fuel ratio. Check for vacuum leaks and exhaust leaks. Check the evaporative canister and CANP solenoid. Check the fuel pressure.

Code 38

The code 38 indicates that the ITS has remained open when the throttle angle—indicated by the TP sensor—was above a point where it should have closed. Located in the ISC motor, the ITS informs the ECA of when the throttle is closed. Inspect the wiring and replace the ISC motor.

Code 39

The code 39 means the automatic transaxle, overdrive (AXOD) bypass clutch is not applying properly. This code is found only during the memory codes of the 3.0-liter EFI engine (like that used in the Taurus and Sable) and the 3.8-liter SEFI engine. Refer this code to a transmission expert or the dealer.

Code 41

If the code 41 is received during the memory codes, it indicates the EGO or HEGO sensor output voltage was stuck low for an extended time during the last forty operations of the engine. If the code 41 is received during the KOER test, it means the EGO voltage remained low throughout the KOER test.

Begin troubleshooting the code 41 by connecting a high-impedance voltmeter in parallel to the EGO sensor. Leave the EGO sensor connected. Start the engine, and run it at 2000rpm for 2 minutes. At the end of the 2 minutes, observe the voltmeter. The voltage should be switching from below 0.45 volt to above 0.45 volt several times during each 5-second interval. If the voltage remains low, disconnect the hoses between the air cleaner and the throttle assembly. Place the end of an unlit propane torch in the intake and open the propane control valve. If the voltage does not increase to above the 0.45-volt threshold, check the following:
Distributor cap
Distributor rotor

The code 41 can be caused by ignition-related problems as well as air-fuel ratio problems. Problems in the secondary ignition system can result in unburned oxygen in the exhaust. Unburned oxygen passing the EGO sensor tricks the ECA into believing the engine is running lean.

Spark plug wires
Ignition coil
Spark plugs
EGR system
Fuel pressure (check the fuel pressure against the chart that follows)
Intake leaks (also called vacuum leaks)
If you find no problems with any of these, replace the EGO or HEGO sensor.

Fuel Pressures for Passenger Cars

Engine	Idle (Psi)	Engine Off (Psi)
1.9L EFI	30–45	35–45
1.9L CFI	13–17	13–17
2.3L ohc EFI	30–45	35–45
2.3L TC EFI	30–55	35–45
2.3L HSC EFI	45–60	50–60
2.5L CFI	13–17	13–16
3.0L EFI	30–45	35–45
3.8L FWD EFI	30–45	35–45
3.8L RWD EFI	30–45	35–45
5.0L SEFI	30–45	35–45
5.0L MA SEFI	30–45	35–45
3.0L SHO SEFI	28–33	30–45
3.8L SC SEFI	30–40	35–40

Fuel Pressures for Light-Duty Trucks

Engine	Idle (Psi)	Engine Off (Psi)
2.3L EFI	30–45	35–45
2.9L EFI	30–45	35–45
3.0L EFI	30–45	35–45
4.9L EFI	45–60	50–60
5.0L EFI	30–45	35–45
5.8L EFI	30–45	35–45
7.5L EFI	30–45	35–45

Note: L means liter, TC means turbocharged, HSC means high-swirl combustion, FWD means front-wheel drive, RWD means rear-wheel drive, and MA means mass air.

Early in the testing of any EGO-related code, check the fuel pressure. All the Ford high-pressure systems provide a Schraeder valve test point.

Code 42

If the code 42 is received during the memory codes, it indicates the EGO or HEGO sensor output voltage was stuck high for an extended time during the last forty operations of the engine. If the code 42 is received during the KOER test, it means the EGO voltage remained low throughout the KOER test.

Begin troubleshooting the code 42 by connecting a high-impedance voltmeter in parallel to the EGO sensor. Leave the EGO sensor connected. Start the engine, and run it at 2000rpm for 2 minutes. At the end of the 2 minutes, observe the voltmeter. The voltage should be switching from above 0.45 volt to below 0.45 volt several times during each 5-second interval. If the voltage remains high, disconnect the hoses between the air cleaner and the throttle assembly. Create a vacuum leak. If the voltage does not decrease to below the 0.45-volt threshold, check for the following:
A saturated evaporative canister
A defective CANP valve
A defective PCV valve
Contaminated engine oil
High fuel pressure (consult the "Fuel Pressures" chart at the end of the code 41 discussion earlier in this section)

Code 43

The code 43 is generated only on the 1.9-liter engine. This code means the engine is running lean at wide-open throttle. It can be caused by low fuel pressure at wide-open throttle or clogged injectors. Connect a fuel pressure gauge to the inbound line of the fuel rail, and testdrive the car. If the fuel pressure drops at wide-open throttle, check the fuel lines for crimps and restrictions. If the fuel lines are in good condition, replace the fuel filter.

If the fuel pressure is within the specifications at wide-open throttle, have the injectors cleaned or replace them.

Code 44

When the code 44 is received during the KOER test, it indicates the thermactor air system is not working. Possible causes include these:
Blocked, leaking, or kinked vacuum lines
A defective air pump
A defective diverter valve
Defective or blocked air management solenoids

If the vacuum hoses are not damaged and are routed properly, repeat the KOEO test. After the last memory code, depress the throttle to the floor and release it. The needle will rise to 12 volts. Probe both terminals on each of the air management solenoids. These two solenoids can be located by tracing the vacuum hoses from the air management valves on the air pump. Each solenoid should have a terminal with 12 volts and a terminal with 0 volts. If neither terminal on one solenoid has 12 volts, repair the 12-volt power supply to the solenoid. If both terminals have 12 volts

The valve core of the fuel pressure test point is recessed when compared with the one used on a tire. If the proper adapter is not available, remove the valve core and connect the pressure gauge with a hose and a clamp.

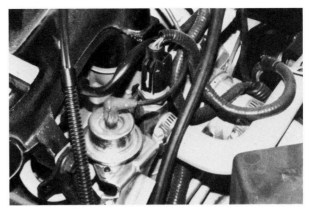

In spite of its name, if a fuel pressure problem is found, it is unlikely the pressure regulator is at fault. If the problem is low pressure, inspect the fuel system for a restriction between the fuel pump and the fuel rail. If the problem is high fuel pressure, check for a restriction between the fuel rail and the fuel tank.

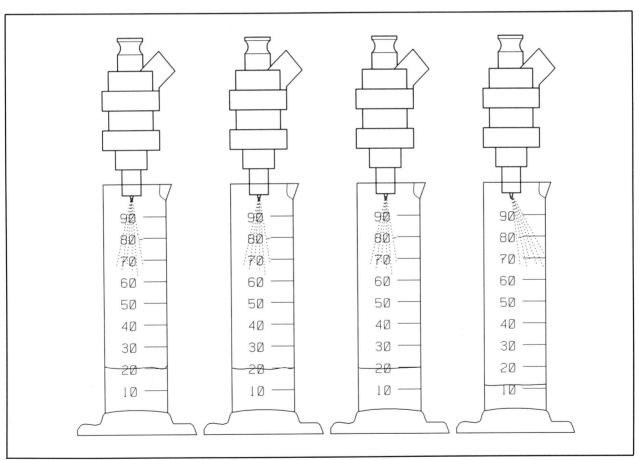

Another cause of the EGO-related code is uneven fuel flow through the injectors. Back in the old Bosch D-Jetronic days, we used to raise the injectors above the intake, place each one of them in a graduated cylinder, and crank the engine for 30 seconds while watching for a cone-shaped pattern. After cranking, we would inspect the fuel level in each of the graduated cylinders to determine if an equal amount of fuel was passing through each injector. This operation can be very difficult owing to the intake manifold configuration. A viable alternative when restricted injectors are suspected is to run a can of injector cleaner through the system. This, after all, will be the fix when a restricted injector is found anyway.

at this point, repair the wire between that solenoid and either terminal 51 or terminal 11 of the ECA, depending on the affected solenoid.

If the circuit passes the first part of the test, depress and release the throttle again. The voltmeter should drop to 0 volts. Both terminals of each air management solenoid should now have 12 volts on them. If one does not, replace the affected solenoid.

Code 45

If the KOER code 45 is received, it means that the thermactor air system is not working. Possible causes include these:
Blocked, leaking, or kinked vacuum lines
A defective air pump
A defective diverter valve
Defective or blocked AM solenoids

If the vacuum hoses are not damaged and are routed properly, repeat the KOEO test. After the last memory code, depress the throttle to the floor and release it. The needle will rise to 12 volts. Probe both terminals on each of the AM solenoids. These two solenoids can be located by tracing the vacuum hoses from the AM valves on the air pump. Each solenoid should have a terminal with 12 volts and a terminal with 0 volts. If neither terminal on one solenoid has 12 volts, repair the 12-volt power supply to the solenoid. If both terminals have 12 volts at this point, repair the wire between that solenoid and either terminal 51 or terminal 11 of the ECA, depending on the affected solenoid.

If the circuit passes the first part of the test, depress and release the throttle again. The voltmeter should drop to 0 volts. Both terminals of each AM solenoid should now have 12 volts on them. If one does not, replace the affected solenoid. (Note that this procedure is the same as the one for the KOER code 44.)

When the code 45 is received during the memory codes, check the resistance between pin 8 of the DIS module (this is the second pin from the bottom on the right side of the module) and the pin coil 3 terminal of the ignition coil pack. If the resistance is less than 5 ohms, disconnect the pin-7-to-pin-12 connector of the DIS module. Disconnect the coil pack connector. Check the resistances between pins 7, 8, 9, and 11. The resistances should be infinity ohms. If a resistance indicates a short between any two of these wires, repair the wires as necessary. If the wires test okay, replace the DIS module.

Code 46

If the KOER code 46 is received, it means that the thermactor air system is not working. Possible causes include these:
Blocked, leaking, or kinked vacuum lines
A defective air pump
A defective diverter valve
Defective or blocked AM solenoids

If the vacuum hoses are not damaged and are routed properly, repeat the KOEO test. After the last memory code, depress the throttle to the floor and release it. The needle will rise to 12 volts. Probe both terminals on each of the air management solenoids. These two solenoids can be located by tracing the vacuum hoses from the air management valves on the air pump. Each solenoid should have a terminal with 12 volts and a terminal with 0 volts. If neither terminal on one solenoid has 12 volts, repair the 12-volt power supply to the solenoid. If both terminals have 12 volts at this point, repair the wire between that solenoid and either terminal 51 or terminal 11 of the ECA, depending on the affected solenoid.

If the circuit passes the first part of the test, depress and release the throttle again. The voltmeter should drop to 0 volts. Both terminals of each AM solenoid should now have 12 volts on them. If one does not, replace the affected solenoid. (Note that this procedure is the same as the one for the KOER codes 44 and 45.)

When the code 46 is received during the memory codes, check the resistance between pin 11 of the DIS module (this is the second pin from the bottom on the right side of the module) and the pin coil 1 terminal of the ignition coil pack. If the resistance is less than 5 ohms, disconnect the pin-7-to-pin-12 connector of the DIS module. Disconnect the coil pack connector. Check the resistances between pins 7, 8, 9, and 11. The resistances should be infinity ohms. If a resistance indicates a short between any two of these wires, repair the wires as necessary. If the wires test okay, replace the DIS module.

Code 47

When the code 47 is received during the KOER test, it indicates that the VAF (vane airflow meter) was transmitting a signal that was too low during the idle portion of the test. The most likely cause of this code is a condition known as false air, which is air entering the engine without being measured by the VAF sensor. Inspect the intake system for evidence of vacuum leaks and air entering through the rubber tube that connects the VAF sensor to the throttle assembly.

When the code 47 is received during the memory codes, it relates to the 4x2-4x4 selector. Refer this problem to a transmission shop or the dealer.

Code 48

The KOER code 48 is unique to the 1.9-liter application. This code indicates that the airflow detected through the VAF sensor during the test was greater than expected. Possible causes of this code are as follows:
False air leaks, as in the code 47
Intermittent ignition or misfire

When the code 48 is received during the memory codes, check the resistance between pin 9 of the DIS module (this is the second pin from the bottom on the

FALSE AIR POSSIBILITIES

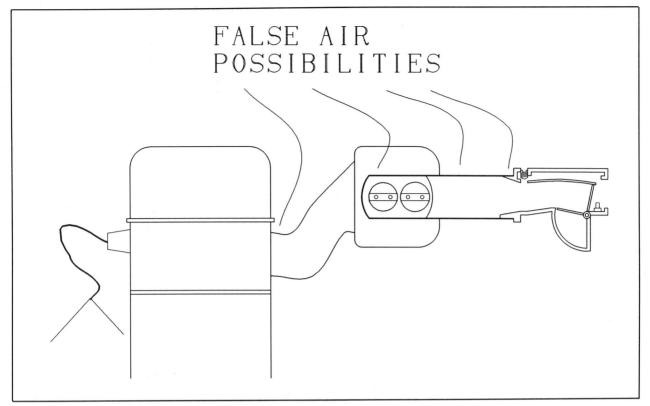

The code 47 indicates that too low a signal is being generated during the idle portion of the KOER test. The most likely cause of this code is false air, which is air entering the intake system between the VAF sensor and the intake manifold.

right side of the module) and the coil pin 2 terminal of the ignition coil pack. If the resistance is less than 5 ohms, disconnect the pin-7-to-pin-12 connector of the DIS module. Disconnect the coil pack connector. Check the resistances between pins 7, 8, 9, and 11. The resistances should be infinity ohms. If a resistance indicates a short between any two of these wires, repair the wires as necessary. If the wires test okay, replace the DIS module.

Code 49

3- and 3.8-Liter Applications

With 3.0- and 3.8-liter applications, the code 49 indicates a faulty SPOUT wire between the ECA and the DIS module. Check the resistance of pin 36 of the ECA and pin 5 of the DIS module. If the wire is good, carefully inspect the connections. If the connections are good, replace the DIS module.

5.8- and 7.5-Liter Applications

With 5.8- and 7.5-liter applications, the code 49 relates to a 1–2 shift error in the E4OD transmission. Refer this code to a transmission shop or the dealer.

Code 51

When the code 51 is received during the KOEO test, it indicates that the ECA is receiving a high voltage reading on the ECT circuit. A high voltage reading corresponds to a cold temperature reading. The presence of the code 51 means the ECA believes the temperature of the coolant to be −40 degrees Fahrenheit.

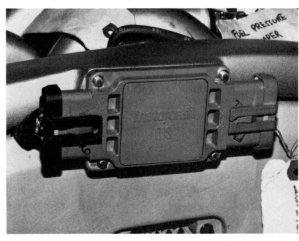

The code 49 is generated when a fault is detected in the SPOUT wire. The SPOUT wire runs between the second terminal from the bottom on the left and pin 36 of the ECA.

To locate the fault causing the code 51, disconnect the ECT harness and install a jumper wire. Repeat the KOEO test. If the code 61 is generated in place of the code 51, replace the ECT sensor.

If the code 51 returns when the KOEO test is repeated, ground the ECT signal wire (usually light green and yellow). Repeat the KOEO test. If the code 51 returns, repair the light green and yellow wire that runs between the ECT harness connector and pin 7 of the ECA. If the code 61 is logged in place of the code 51, repair the black and white wire that runs between the ECT harness connector and pin 46 of the ECA.

When the code 51 is received during the memory codes, it indicates the presence of an intermittent open circuit in the ECT circuit. Enter the continuous monitor mode (see the "Continuous Monitor Test" discussion in the "Supplemental EEC IV Tests" section at the end of this chapter). Wiggle the ECT wiring harness at both the engine and ECA ends. If a problem is indicated, repair as necessary.

When an open is detected in the ECT circuit, the code 51 is generated. This is the well-hidden location of the ECT sensor on the 3.0-liter SHO engine.

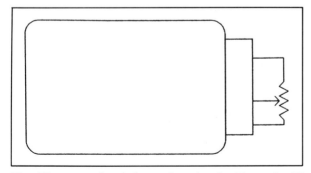

The TP sensor is a three-wire circuit. The code 53 indicates that the voltage seen on the wiper—the middle wire—was too high. This could be a short to voltage in the wiring or a defective TP sensor.

Code 52

The KOEO code 52 indicates an open circuit in the PSPS while the power steering pump is not creating pressure. Disconnect the PSPS harness and place a jumper across the terminals. Repeat the KOEO test. If the code 52 does not repeat, replace the PSPS. If the code 52 does repeat, connect the yellow and light green wire of the PSPS harness to ground and repeat the KOEO test again. If the code 52 returns, repair the yellow and light green wire. If the code 52 does not return, repair the black and white wire.

When the code 52 is received during the KOER test, it is almost always because the steering wheel was not turned. If the code 52 is received during the KOER test, repeat the test, making sure the steering wheel is turned one-half turn immediately after the engine ID code is received.

If the code 52 returns in the repeated test, inspect to see if the vehicle has a PSPS. If it has no PSPS, ignore the code 52. If it has a PSPS, disconnect the harness from the PSPS. The yellow and light green wire should have 12 volts or more. The black and white wire should have continuity to ground. Repair the wires as necessary.

If the wires test good, reconnect the harness to the PSPS. Connect a voltmeter or test light to the yellow and green wire. Start the engine and turn the steering wheel between the wheels-centered position (no load) and one-half turn in either direction. The voltage on the yellow and light green wire should cycle between 0 and 12 volts. If the voltage does not change, replace the PSPS.

Code 53

The code 53 indicates the TP sensor is exceeding the maximum expected voltage. This code can be received either during the KOEO test or during the memory codes.

If the code 53 is received during the KOEO test, disconnect the harness connector from the TP sensor. Repeat the KOER test. If the code 63 is generated, replace the TP sensor. If the code 53 returns, repair the short to voltage in the TP sensor wire.

If the code 53 is received during the memory codes as well as during the KOEO, making the KOEO repairs will eliminate the memory code problem. If code 53 is only found in the memory codes, it indicates there is an intermittent short in the TP sensor or its harness. Check the wires and terminals. If they are in good condition, ignore and clear the code.

Code 54

The code 54 indicates the ACT (Air Charge Temperature) or VAT (Vane Air Temperature) sensor voltage is exceeding its maximum voltage limit. The ACT sensor is located in the intake manifold. The VAT sensor is found only on the 2.3-liter Turbo.

When the code 54 is received during the KOEO test, it indicates that the ECA is receiving a high voltage reading on the ACT circuit. A high voltage reading corresponds to a cold temperature reading. The presence of the code 54 means the ECA believes the temperature of the air to be −40 degrees Fahrenheit.

To locate the fault causing the code 54, disconnect the ACT harness and install a jumper wire. Repeat the KOEO test. If the code 64 is generated in place of the code 54, replace the ACT sensor.

If the code 54 returns when the KOEO test is repeated, ground the ACT signal wire. Repeat the KOEO test. If the code 54 returns, repair the ACT signal wire that runs between the ACT harness connector and pin 25 of the ECA. If the code 64 is logged in place of the code 54, repair the black and white wire that runs between the ACT harness connector and pin 46 of the ECA.

When the code 54 is received during the memory codes, it indicates the presence of an intermittent open circuit in the ACT circuit. Enter the continuous monitor mode (see the "Continuous Monitor Test" discussion in the "Supplemental EEC IV Tests" section at the end of this chapter). Wiggle the ACT wiring harness at both the engine and ECA ends. If a problem is indicated, repair as necessary.

If the car is a 2.3-liter Turbo, disconnect the VAF connector and place a jumper between the VAT signal wire (the only one located at the end of the connec-

tor) and the signal return wire (the one next to the VAT signal wire). Repeat the KOEO test. If the code 54 is generated again, ground the VAT signal terminal of the VAF connector and repeat the KOEO test. If the code 54 returns, repair the open circuit between the VAT signal terminal of the VAF sensor and pin 25 of the ECA. If the code 64 is generated in place of the code 54, repair the open in the black and white signal return wire that runs from the VAF sensor to ECA terminal 46.

If the code 64 is logged when the jumper is placed from the VAF terminal for the VAT sensor to the signal return terminal, check the resistance of the VAT sensor. Connect an ohmmeter across the VAT

The circuit that causes the code 54 is the ACT sensor circuit.

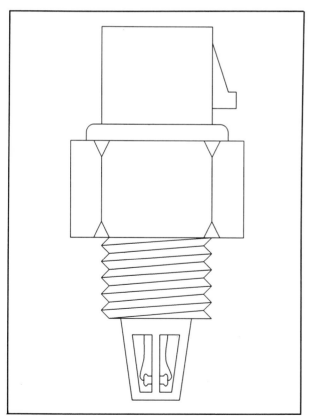

The ACT sensor is a negative temperature coefficient thermistor. As it heats up, its resistance drops.

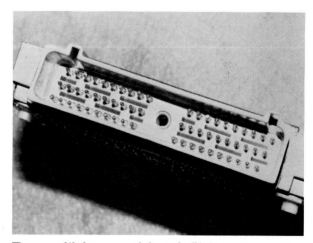

The most likely cause of the code 54 is an open circuit between the ACT sensor on the intake manifold and the ECA.

and signal return terminals of the VAF sensor. The resistance should fall on the chart below:

Vane Air Temperature Sensor Resistance

Temperature (Degrees Fahrenheit)	Resistance (Ohms)
122	830
104	1,180
86	1,700
68	2,500
50	3,770

Code 55

When the code 55 is received during the KOER test, it indicates that key power to ECA pin 5 has been lost. Inspect the red and light green wire for open circuits and shorts to ground.

Code 56

The code 56 has several meanings, depending on what type of vehicle you are working on:

1.9- and 2.3-liter Turbo applications: VAT voltage was high

Other passenger cars: MAF voltage was high

Light trucks: TOT voltage was high

1.9- and 2.3-Liter Turbo Applications

On the 1.9- and 2.3-liter Turbo applications, the code 56 can be generated only during the KOEO test. If this code is received, disconnect the VAF sensor and repeat the KOEO self-test. If the code 66 is

logged, replace the VAF sensor. If the code 56 returns, repair the short to voltage in the white and black VAF signal wire to pin 43 of the ECA.

Other Passenger Cars

Other than on the 1.9- and 2.3-liter Turbo applications, the code 56 can be logged on passenger cars only if they are using an MAF sensor. On the MAF-equipped cars, this code can be generated during the KOEO or KOER test. For both the KOEO and KOER codes, the test procedure is the same.

Disconnect the MAF sensor and repeat the KOEO test. If the code 56 returns, repair the short to voltage in the dark blue and orange wire from terminal D of the MAF sensor to pin 50 of the MAF sensor. If the code 66 is logged, replace the MAF sensor.

Light Trucks

The code 56 on light trucks is generated only on vehicles equipped with the E4OD transmission. This code relates to the TOT sensor. Refer this code to a qualified transmission specialist or dealer.

Code 57

The code 57 concerns a failure in the neutral pressure switch (NPS) of the AXOD transmission. Refer this code to a qualified transmission specialist or dealer.

Code 58

The code 58 has several meanings, which vary by application:

1.9- and 2.3-liter Turbo applications: VAT voltage was high

CFI applications: ISC motor did not make contact with throttle linkage

1.9-liter application

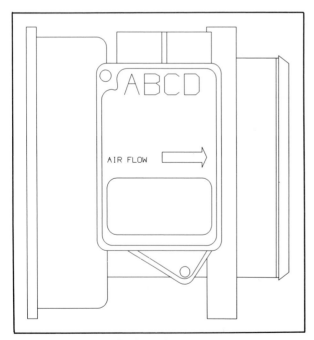

For the late-model Ford products, the codes 56 and 66 relate to the MAF sensor. The code 56 means that the voltage seen by the ECA is higher than expected. The code 66 means that the voltage seen by the ECA is lower than expected.

The MAF sensor is located in the engine airflow tube between the air filter and the throttle assembly. This is the location of the MAF sensor on the 2.3-liter. Notice the location of the ACT sensor in the air cleaner instead of its usual location in the intake manifold.

1.9- and 2.3-Liter Turbo Applications

If the code 58 is received during the KOEO test, disconnect the VAF connector and place a jumper between the VAT signal wire (the only one located at the end of the connector) and the signal return wire (the one next to the VAT signal wire). Repeat the KOEO test. If the code 58 is generated again, ground the VAT signal terminal of the VAF connector and repeat the KOEO test. If the code 58 returns, repair the open circuit between the VAT signal terminal of the VAF sensor and pin 25 of the ECA. If the code 68 is generated in place of the code 58, repair the open in the black and white signal return wire that runs from the VAF sensor to ECA terminal 46.

If the code 68 is logged when the jumper is placed from the VAF terminal for the VAT sensor to the signal return terminal, check the resistance of the VAT sensor. Connect an ohmmeter across the VAT and signal return terminals of the VAF sensor. The resistance should fall on the chart below:

Vane Air Temperature Resistance

Temperature (Degrees Fahrenheit)	Resistance (Ohms)
122	830
104	1,180
86	1,700
68	2,500
50	3,700

CFI Applications

If the code 58 is received during the KOEO or KOER test, check the four wires that run from the ISC motor to the ECA. Inspect them for open circuits, wire-to-wire shorts, and grounds. The corresponding ECA pin numbers for these wires are 41, 46, 28 (24 on the 2.5-liter), and 21. If the wires test good, replace the ISC motor.

1.9-Liter Applications

The memory code 58 can be logged only on the 1.9-liter application. Enter the continuous monitor test (refer to the "Supplemental EEC IV Tests" section at the end of this chapter). Twist the wires and tap on the sensor. Make any repairs indicated.

Code 59

The code 59 has multiple meanings. If this code is received on any application other than the 3.0-liter SHO engine, it is a transmission code and should be referred to a qualified transmission technician or the dealer. If the code is received on a 3.0-liter SHO engine, it indicates a failure in the low-speed fuel pump circuit.

If the code 59 is received during the KOEO test or during the memory codes, disconnect the sixty-pin connector from the ECA. Disconnect the ICM, which is a black box approximately 8in long and 5in wide located near the radiator. Connect an ohmmeter between ECA pin 19 and terminal 5 of the ICM connector. The resistance should be close to 0. If the

circuit is open, repair the wire. If the wire is okay, reconnect the ICM and the ECA. Check the voltage at pin 19 of the ECA and switch the key to the on position. If the voltage rises to 12 volts for 1 second, replace the ECA. If the voltage does not rise, replace the ICM.

Code 61

The code 61 indicates a low voltage on the ECT (Engine Coolant Temperature sensor) circuit.

When the code 61 is received during the KOEO test, it indicates that the ECA is receiving a low voltage reading on the ECT circuit. A low voltage reading corresponds to a hot temperature reading. The presence of the code 61 means the ECA believes the temperature of the coolant to be greater than 250 degrees Fahrenheit.

To locate the fault causing the code 61, disconnect the ECT harness. Repeat the KOEO test. If the code 51 is generated in place of the code 61, replace the ECT sensor.

If the code 61 returns when the KOEO test is repeated, repair the grounded ECT signal wire (usually light green and yellow).

When the code 61 is received during the memory codes, it indicates an intermittent short to ground in the ECT circuit. Enter the continuous monitor mode (see the "Continuous Monitor Test" discussion in the "Supplemental EEC IV Tests" section at the end of this chapter). Wiggle the ECT wiring harness at both the engine and ECA ends. If a problem is indicated, repair as necessary.

Code 62

If a code 62 is received, inspect the wiring between the ECA and the transmission. If the wiring is in good condition, take the vehicle to a transmission repair shop. This code indicates a problem in the fourth and third gear pressure switch.

Code 63

The KOEO code 63 indicates the TP signal voltage is low. Disconnect the TP sensor harness. Place a jumper wire between the VREF wire (usually orange) and the TP signal wire (usually dark green and light green). Repeat the KOEO test. If the code 63 returns, check for 5 volts at the orange VREF wire. If the VREF wire has 5 volts, repair the TP signal wire to the ECA. If the orange wire does not have 5 volts, confirm that the ignition switch was on when the voltage was tested and repair the orange wire.

If the code 53 was generated when the KOEO test was repeated, replace the TP sensor.

If the code 63 was received during the memory codes, perform the continuous monitor test (see the "Supplemental EEC IV Tests" section at the end of this chapter). Repair the wiring, connector, or sensor as required.

Code 64

The code 64 indicates the ACT (air charge temperature) or VAT (vane air temperature) sensor voltage is below its minimum limit. The ACT sensor is located in the intake manifold. The VAT sensor is found only on the 2.3-liter Turbo.

When the code 64 is received during the KOEO test, it indicates that the ECA is receiving a low voltage reading on the ACT circuit. A low voltage reading corresponds to a hot temperature reading. The presence of the code 64 means the ECA believes the temperature of the air to be 250 degrees Fahrenheit or greater.

To locate the fault causing the code 64, disconnect the ACT harness. Repeat the KOEO test. If the code 54 is generated in place of the code 64, replace the ACT sensor.

If the code 64 returns when the KOEO test is repeated, repair the short to ground in the ACT signal wire.

When the code 64 is received during the memory codes, it indicates an intermittent short to ground in the ACT circuit. Enter the continuous monitor mode (see the "Continuous Monitor Test" discussion in the "Supplemental EEC IV Tests" section at the end of this chapter). Wiggle the ACT wiring harness at both the engine and ECA ends. If a problem is indicated, repair as necessary.

If the car is a 2.3-liter Turbo, disconnect the VAF connector. Repeat the KOEO test. If the code 64 is generated again, repair the grounded VAT signal terminal of the VAF connector and repeat the KOEO test. If the code 64 returns, repair the grounded wire in the VAT signal wire. If the code 54 is generated, replace the VAF sensor.

Code 65

If the code 65 is received on a 1.9-liter application, the ECA failed to enter the closed-loop mode. Check the HEGO sensor wiring. The HEGO signal is carried by a wire connected to ECA pin 29. If the wire is in good condition, replace the EGO sensor.

If the code 65 is received on any other application, refer it to a qualified transmission specialist or dealer.

Code 66

Code 66 may have three different meanings, depending on the application.
1.9- and 2.3-liter applications: VAF sensor below minimum test voltage
MAF-equipped applications: MAF below minimum test voltage
E4OD transmission applications: TOT below minimum test voltage

1.9- and 2.3-Liter Applications

When the code 66 is received during the KOEO test on a 1.9- or 2.3-liter application, disconnect the VAF connector and place a jumper wire between the orange wire and the white and black wire (of the four wires in the connector, these are the middle wires). Repeat the KOEO test. If the code 56 is logged in place of the code 66, replace the VAF sensor.

If the code 66 remains, check for 5 volts at the orange wire in the VAF connector (make sure the ignition switch is turned on). If you find 5 volts, repair the VAF signal wire for an open or a short to ground. If you do not find 5 volts, repair the orange VREF wire for an open or a short to ground.

If the code 66 is in the memory codes, perform the continuous monitor test (see the "Supplemental EEC IV Tests" section at the end of this chapter). Repair as indicated.

MAF-equipped Applications

For MAF applications, disconnect the MAF connector and confirm that 12 volts is measured between terminals A and B. Disconnect the sixty-pin terminal from the ECA. Inspect the connectors for damaged wires and pushed or corroded pins. Check the resistance from MAF terminal D and pin 50 of the ECA; it should be less than 5 ohms. Check the resistance from MAF terminal C to ECA pin 9; it should be less than 5 ohms. If these resistances are okay, check the resistance of each wire to ground; it should be infinite. Repair any of these wires as indicated through the test.

If the wires test good, reconnect the ECA and the MAF sensor. Start the engine and allow it to idle. Check the voltage on ECA pin 50. If the voltage is between 0.2 and 1.5 volts, replace the ECA. If the voltage is not within these specs, replace the MAF sensor.

E4OD Transmission Applications

For light-duty trucks equipped with the E4OD transmission, refer this code to a qualified transmission specialist or the dealer.

Code 67

Code 67 may have four different meanings, depending on the application.
Light-duty trucks with the E4OD transmission: Manual lever position (MLP) was out of range; air conditioner input was high
AXOD-equipped 3.8-liter applications: NPS failed to close
Standard transmission applications: Clutch switch circuit failed
All other applications: NDS was open or air conditioner input was open

Light-Duty Trucks with the E4OD Transmission

If the code 67 is received, confirm that the air conditioner was turned off during the KOEO test. If the air conditioner was turned off, refer this code to a qualified transmission specialist or the dealer.

AXOD-equipped 3.8-Liter Applications

Refer the code 67 to a qualified transmission specialist or the dealer.

Standard Transmission Applications

If the code 67 is received, confirm that the air conditioner was turned off during the KOEO test. If the air conditioner was turned off, refer this code to a qualified transmission specialist or the dealer.

All Other Applications

If the code 67 is received, confirm that the air conditioner and heater control is in the off position and the transmission is in park or neutral. Check the voltage at ECA pin 30. If the voltage is greater than 1 volt, inspect the wiring and connections between the NDS and pin 30 of the ECA. If the wiring and connections are in good condition, replace the NDS. If the voltage is less than 1 volt and the vehicle is not equipped with air conditioning, replace the ECA.

If the vehicle is equipped with air conditioning, check the voltage at pin 10 of the ECA. If the voltage is greater than 1 volt, trace and repair the short to voltage in the air conditioner clutch circuit. If the voltage is less than 1 volt, replace the processor.

Code 68

Like many other codes, the code 68 has several possible meanings, which depend on the application:

1.9-liter EFI applications: VAT voltage was low

1.9- and 2.5-liter CFI applications: ITS was closed (if received during the KOEO test) or ITS was open (if received during the KOER test)

3.8-liter AXOD applications

1.9-Liter EFI Applications

When the code 68 is received during the KOEO test, it indicates that the ECA is receiving a low voltage reading on the ACT circuit. A low voltage reading corresponds to a hot temperature reading. The presence of the code 68 means the ECA believes the temperature of the air to be 250 degrees Fahrenheit or greater.

To locate the fault causing the code 68, disconnect the ACT harness. Repeat the KOEO test. If the code 58 is generated in place of the code 68, replace the ACT sensor.

If the code 68 returns when the KOEO test is repeated, repair the short to ground in the ACT signal wire.

When the code 68 is received during the memory codes, it indicates an intermittent short to ground in the ACT circuit. Enter the continuous monitor mode (see the "Continuous Monitor Test" discussion in the "Supplemental EEC IV Tests" section at the end of this chapter). Wiggle the ACT wiring harness at both the engine and ECA ends. If a problem is indicated, repair as necessary.

1.9- and 2.5-Liter CFI Applications

The KOEO code 68 indicates the ITS was closed throughout the KOEO test. If the code 68 is received during the KOER test, it indicates the ITS remained open throughout the KOER test.

To begin troubleshooting, check the four wires that run from the ISC motor to the ECA. Inspect them for open circuits, wire-to-wire shorts, and grounds. The corresponding ECA pin numbers for these wires are 41, 46, 28 (24 on the 2.5-liter applications), and 21. If the wires test good, replace the ISC motor.

The memory code 68 can be logged only on the 1.9-liter application. Enter the continuous monitor test (refer to the "Supplemental EEC IV Tests" section at the end of this chapter). Twist the wires and tap on the sensor, which is located inside the ISC motor. Make any repairs indicated.

3.8-Liter AXOD Applications

Refer the code 68 to a qualified transmission specialist or the dealer.

Code 69

Refer the code 69 to a qualified transmission specialist or the dealer.

Code 71

Code 71 is a very rare code. It can indicate three different problems, depending on the application.

1.9-liter EFI (1989 only) and 2.3-liter Turbo applications: Software reinitialization was detected

CFI applications: ITS was closed on preposition

3.8-liter AXOD applications: Cluster control assembly circuit failed

1.9-Liter EFI (1989 only) and 2.3-Liter Turbo Applications

When the code 71 is received during the KOER test, it indicates that key power to ECA pin 5 has been lost. Inspect the red and light green wire for open circuits and shorts to ground.

CFI Applications

If the code 71 is received, to begin troubleshooting, check the four wires that run from the ISC motor to the ECA. Inspect them for open circuits, wire-to-wire shorts, and grounds. The corresponding ECA pin numbers for these wires are 41, 46, 28 (24 on the 2.5-liter), and 21. If the wires test good, replace the ISC motor.

3.8-Liter AXOD Applications

Refer the code 71 to the dealer.

Code 72

The most common reason for receiving a code 72 is a problem in the vacuum hose to the MAP sensor. However, a few applications have another meaning for this code.

SHO and 3.8-liter SC applications: Power interrupt was detected

3.8-liter AXOD applications, memory code

All other applications, KOER code: Insufficient MAP change was detected during goose test

SHO and 3.8-Liter SC Applications

If the code 72 is received, initiate the continuous monitor mode (see the "Continuous Monitor Test" discussion in the "Supplemental EEC IV Tests" section at the end of this chapter). Check for an intermittent open circuit to the ICM ground (ICM

When the code 72 is received, inspect the vacuum hose to the MAP sensor for leaks and restrictions. If the vacuum hose is good, connect a hand-held vacuum pump to the MAP sensor. Apply approximately 18in of vacuum to the MAP sensor. Does the MAP sensor hold vacuum? If it does not, replace it. If it does, tee a vacuum gauge and repeat the KOER test. If the vacuum on the gauge drops when the throttle is snapped, replace the MAP sensor. If the vacuum does not drop, check the vacuum hose against vacuum routing chart under the hood of the vehicle. Repair as necessary.

terminal 15). Also check the VPWR wire (ICM terminal 24) and VBAT (ICM terminals 3 and 4) for intermittent opens, shorts, or grounds.

3.8-Liter AXOD Applications, Memory Code
    Refer the code 72 to the dealer.

All Other Applications, KOER Code
    The KOER code 72 indicates that during the KOER test, the frequency being generated did not rise when the throttle was snapped. Inspect the vacuum hose to the MAP sensor for leaks and restrictions. If the vacuum hose is good, connect a hand-held vacuum pump to the MAP sensor. Apply approximately 18in of vacuum to the MAP sensor. Does the MAP sensor hold vacuum? If it does not, replace the MAP sensor. If it does hold vacuum, tee a vacuum gauge and repeat the KOER test. If the vacuum on the gauge drops when the throttle is snapped, replace the MAP sensor. If the vacuum does not drop, check the vacuum hose against the vacuum routing chart under the hood of the vehicle. Repair as necessary.

Code 73

When the code 73 is received during the KOER test, repeat the KOER test. This time, ensure that the throttle is snapped to wide open. If the code 73 repeats, replace the TP sensor.

Code 74

The code 74 during the KOER test indicates the ECA did not see the BOO signal cycle high. If the brake pedal was not depressed during the KOER test, repeat the test, depressing and releasing the brake pedal immediately after the engine ID codes.
    If the code 74 returns, connect a voltmeter to ECA pin 2. With the ignition switch on, depress and release the brake pedal. If the voltage cycles high and low, replace the ECA. If the voltage does not cycle high and low, repair the BOO circuit as necessary.

Code 75

If the code 75 is received, connect a voltmeter to ECA pin 2. With the ignition switch on, depress and release the brake pedal. If the voltage cycles high and low, replace the ECA. If the voltage does not cycle high and low, repair the BOO circuit as necessary.

Code 77

If the code 77 is received, the operator did not do the goose test. Repeat the KOER test. Within 10 seconds of the dynamic response code, push the accelerator to the floor and release it. If the code 77 returns, replace the ECA.

Code 79

If the code 79 is received, confirm that the air conditioner and heater control is in the off position and the transmission is in park or neutral. Check the voltage at ECA pin 30. If the voltage is greater than 1 volt, inspect the wiring and connections between the NDS and pin 30 of the ECA. If the wiring and connections are all right, replace the NDS. If the voltage is less than 1 volt and the vehicle is not equipped with air conditioning, replace the ECA.
    If the vehicle is equipped with air conditioning, check the voltage at pin 10 of the ECA. If the voltage is greater than 1 volt, trace and repair the short to voltage in the air conditioner clutch circuit. If the voltage is less than 1 volt, replace the processor.

Code 81

The code 81 relates to the failure of ECA pin 11 or ECA pin 51 to drop low when the engine is not running. Pins 11 and 51 are the control circuits for the AM control circuit. Trace the vacuum hoses from the air pump control valves to locate the AM solenoids. Each of the solenoids should have 12 volts on one terminal only. If neither terminal has 12 volts, repair the open circuit between the AM solenoids and pins 37 and 57 of the ECA. If both terminals have 12 volts, repair the open circuit between the AM solenoids and ECA pin 11 or ECA pin 51.

Code 82
3.8-Liter SC Applications
    The code 82 relates to the supercharger bypass solenoid (SBS). When this code is received, it indicates the voltage at pin 38 remained high during the KOEO test.
    Disconnect the SBS and test the resistance of the solenoid windings. If the resistance is between 50 and 100 ohms, turn the ignition switch on and check for 12 volts at one of the SBS harness terminals only. If you

find 12 volts, check for continuity between the other terminal of the SBS harness and pin 38 of the ECA. If you find less than 5 ohms of resistance, ensure that the wire is not grounded. Repair as necessary.

If the resistance is not between 50 and 100 ohms, replace the SBS. If all the above test within specifications, replace the ECA.

All Other Applications

The code 82 relates to the failure of ECA pin 11 or ECA pin 51 to drop low when the engine is not running. Pins 11 and 51 are the control circuits for the AM control circuit. Trace the vacuum hoses from the air pump control valves to locate the AM solenoids. Each of the solenoids should have 12 volts on one terminal only. If neither terminal has 12 volts, repair the open circuit between the AM solenoids and pins 37 and 57 of the ECA. If both terminals have 12 volts, repair the open circuit between the AM solenoids and ECA pin 11 or ECA pin 51.

Code 83

2.3-Liter Ohc EFI Applications

The code 83 relates to the failure of ECA pin 33 or ECA pin 52 to drop low when the engine is not running. Pins 33 and 52 are the control circuits for the EGR. Trace the vacuum hoses from the EGR valve to locate the EGRV and EGRC solenoids. Each of the solenoids should have 12 volts on one terminal only. If neither terminal has 12 volts, repair the open circuit between the AM solenoids and pin 37 of the ECA. If both terminals have 12 volts, repair the open circuit between the EGRV and EGRC solenoids and ECA pin 33 or ECA pin 52.

3.0-Liter SHO Applications

When the code 83 is logged, it means the voltage output for the fuel pump control circuit of the ICM did not change during the KOEO test. Check the resistance between ECA pin 41 and ICM terminal 11. If the resistance is less than 5 ohms, measure the resistance from the ICM terminal to ground; this resistance should be infinity. If the wire resistances are incorrect, repair as necessary. Check the resistance between ICM terminals 11 and 24. If the resistance is greater than 100 ohms or less than 65 ohms, replace the ICM. If the wire resistances are correct, replace the ECA.

Code 84

EGR control problems will often generate a code 84.

2.3-liter ohc EFI applications: EGRV circuit failed
All other applications: EVR circuit failed

2.3-Liter Ohc EFI Applications

The code 84 relates to the failure of ECA pin 33 or ECA pin 52 to drop low when the engine is not running. Pins 33 and 52 are the control circuits for the EGR. Trace the vacuum hoses from the EGR valve to

The code 83 means the voltage controlling the solenoids that control the EGR did not change during the engine-running test. Check the wiring for these solenoids.

locate the EGRV and EGRC solenoids. Each of the solenoids should have 12 volts on one terminal only. If neither terminal has 12 volts, repair the open circuit between the AM solenoids and pin 37 of the ECA. If both terminals have 12 volts, repair the open circuit between the EGRV and EGRC solenoids and ECA pin 33 or ECA pin 52.

All Other Applications

If the code 84 is received, measure the resistance of the EVR. If the resistance is not between 30 and 70 ohms, replace the EVR solenoid. If the resistance is between 30 and 70 ohms, with the key on, check for 12 volts to one of the EVR harness terminals only. Repair the wire if necessary. If you find 12 volts, check the resistances between the EVR terminal that did not have 12 volts and both pin 33 (pin 52 for the 1.9-liter CFI) and ground. The resistances should be less than 5 ohms to pin 33 (or pin 52) and infinite ohms to ground. Repair the wires as necessary. If the wires and the EVR test good, replace the ECA.

Code 85

KOEO code: CANP circuit failed
Memory code, 1.9-liter EFI applications only: Fuel pressure was high

KOEO Code

If the code 85 is received, measure the resistance of the CANP solenoid. If the resistance is not between 40 and 90 ohms, replace the CANP solenoid. If the resistance is between 40 and 90 ohms, with the key on, check for 12 volts to one of the CANP harness terminals only. Repair the wire if necessary. If the resistance is 12 volts, check the resistances between the CANP terminal that did not have 12 volts and both pin 21 and ground. You should find less than 5 ohms to pin 21 and infinite ohms to ground. Repair the wires as necessary. If the wires and the CANP solenoid test good, replace the ECA.

Memory Code, 1.9-Liter EFI Applications Only

The memory code 85 relates to high fuel pressure. If the code 42 is also received, service that code first. If no code 42 is received, check and repair the fuel pressure as necessary. High fuel pressure is caused by either a defective fuel pressure regulator or a restricted return line.

Code 86

KOEO Code, 2.3- and 2.9-Liter EFI and 3.0-Liter EFI Light Trucks

Refer the code 86 to a qualified transmission specialist or the dealer.

Memory Code, 1.9 EFI Applications Only

Use the same procedure given for the code 85.

Code 87

2.5-Liter CFI, 3.0-Liter EFI, 3.0-Liter SHO SEFI, and 3.8-Liter AXOD SEFI Applications

When the code 87 is logged, it means the voltage output for the fuel pump control circuit of the ICM did not change during the KOEO test. Check the resistance between ECA pin 22 and ICM terminal 18. If the resistance is less than 5 ohms, measure the resistance from the ICM terminal to ground; this resistance should be infinity. If the wire resistances are incorrect, repair as necessary. Check the resistance between ICM terminals 18 and 24. If the resistance is greater than 100 ohms or less than 65 ohms, replace the ICM. If the wire resistances are correct, replace the ECA.

If the code 87 was a memory code, use the continuous monitor (Wiggle) test to isolate the source of the problem (see the "Supplemental EEC IV Tests" section at the end of this chapter).

All Other Applications

Begin troubleshooting the code 87 by confirming that the inertia switch has not been tripped. Press the button on the top of the switch to reset the switch. After confirming that the inertia switch has not been tripped, check for 12 volts at the fuel pump relay. If you do not find 12 volts, replace the inertia switch. If you do find 12 volts, check the wire from the fuel pump relay to pin 22 of the ECA. The resistance should be less than 5 ohms and the wire should not be shorted-to-power or shorted-to-ground. If the wire tests good, replace the fuel pump relay. If the code 87 persists, replace the ECA.

Code 88

Code 88 will have different meanings, depending on the application.
2.3-liter ohc EFI light-duty trucks: Dual-plug inhibit (DPI) failed
All other applications: Electric cooling fan failed

2.3-Liter Ohc EFI Light-Duty Trucks

When the memory code 88 is received on the 2.3-liter ohc EFI light-duty truck, begin testing by disconnecting the terminal-1-to-terminal-6 connector (the one on the left) of the DIS module. Disconnect the harness from the ECA. Inspect both harnesses for pushed-back pins, corrosion, and damaged wires. If the harnesses and terminals are in good condition, check the resistance between terminal 6 of the DIS module and pin 32 of the ECA. If the resistance is less than 5 ohms, check the wire for a short to ground or power. If the wire is good, replace the DIS module. If the resistance is greater than 5 ohms or grounded or shorted-to-power, repair the wire as necessary.

All Other Applications

For all other applications, when the code 88 is received, it indicates a problem with the ICM control of the electric cooling fan. Disconnect the ECA, and disconnect the ICM connector. Test the resistance from ECA harness pin 52 and ground. If the resistance is less than 10,000 ohms, repair the short to ground. If the resistance is greater than 10,000 ohms, reconnect the ICM. Leave the ECA disconnected. Turn the ignition switch on. If the fan runs, replace the ECA. If the fan does not run, replace the ICM.

Code 89

Refer the code 89 to a qualified transmission specialist or the dealer.

Code 91

E4OD Applications

Refer the code 91 to a qualified transmission specialist or the dealer.

All Other Applications

If the code 91 is received during the memory codes, it indicates the left EGO or HEGO sensor output voltage was stuck low for an extended time during the last forty operations of the engine. If this code is received during the KOER test, it means the EGO voltage remained low throughout the KOER test.

Begin troubleshooting the code 91 by connecting a high-impedance voltmeter in parallel to the EGO sensor. Leave the EGO sensor connected. Start the engine and run it at 2000rpm for 2 minutes. At the end of the 2 minutes, observe the voltmeter. The voltage should be switching from below 0.45 volt to above 0.45 volt several times during each 5-second interval. If the voltage remains low, disconnect the hoses between the air cleaner and the throttle assembly. Place the end of an unlit propane torch in the intake and open the propane control valve. If the voltage does not increase to above the 0.45-volt threshold, check the following:
Distributor cap
Distributor rotor
Spark plug wires
Ignition coil
Spark plugs
EGR system

Fuel pressure (check the fuel pressure against the chart that follows)

Intake leaks (also called vacuum leaks)

If you find no problems with any of these, replace the EGO or HEGO sensor.

Fuel Pressures for Passenger Cars

Engine	Idle (Psi)	Engine Off (Psi)
1.9L EFI	30–45	35–45
1.9L CFI	13–17	13–17
2.3L ohc EFI	30–45	35–45
2.3L TC EFI	30–55	35–45
2.3L HSC EFI	45–60	50–60
2.5L CFI	13–17	13–16
3.0L EFI	30–45	35–45
3.8L FWD EFI	30–45	35–45
3.8L RWD EFI	30–45	35–45
5.0L SEFI	30–45	35–45
5.0L MA SEFI	30–45	35–45
3.0L SHO SEFI	28–33	30–45
3.8L SC SEFI	30–40	35–40

Fuel Pressures for Light-Duty Trucks

Engine	Idle (Psi)	Engine Off (Psi)
2.3L EFI	30–45	35–45
2.9L EFI	30–45	35–45
3.0L EFI	30–45	35–45
4.9L EFI	45–60	50–60
5.0L EFI	30–45	35–45
5.8L EFI	30–45	35–45
7.5L EFI	30–45	35–45

Code 92

E4OD-equipped Vehicles

Refer the code 92 to a qualified transmission specialist or the dealer.

All Other Applications

If the code 92 is received during the memory codes, it indicates the left EGO or HEGO sensor output voltage was stuck high for an extended time during the last forty operations of the engine. If this code is received during the KOER test, it means the EGO voltage remained low throughout the KOER test.

Begin troubleshooting the code 92 by connecting a high-impedance voltmeter in parallel to the EGO sensor. Leave the EGO sensor connected. Start the engine and run it at 2000rpm for 2 minutes. At the end of the 2 minutes, observe the voltmeter. The voltage should be switching from above 0.45 volt to below 0.45 volt several times during each 5-second interval. If the voltage remains high, disconnect the hoses between the air cleaner and the throttle assembly. Create a vacuum leak. If the voltage does not decrease to below the 0.45-volt threshold, check for the following:

All the Ford high-pressure systems provide a Schraeder valve test point. Unfortunately, when the fuel pressure needs to be tested on a low-pressure CFI system, the pressure gauge will have to be teed into the inbound fuel line to the CFI throttle body assembly.

A saturated evaporative canister

A defective CANP valve

A defective PCV valve

Contaminated engine oil

High fuel pressure (consult the "Fuel Pressures" chart at the end of the code 91 discussion earlier in this section)

Code 93

CFI Applications

The code 93 indicates that the TP (throttle position) sensor voltage is low at full ISC motor extension. Inspect the throttle control linkage for binding or damage. If the linkage is in good condition, replace the ISC motor.

All Other Applications

Refer the code 93 to a qualified transmission specialist or the dealer.

Code 94

E4OD Applications

Refer the code 94 to a qualified transmission specialist or the dealer.

All Other Applications

When the code 94 is received during the KOER test, it indicates the side of the thermactor air system with cylinders 5 to 8 is not working. Possible causes include the following:

Blocked, leaking, or kinked vacuum lines
A defective air pump
A defective diverter valve
Defective or blocked air management solenoids

If the vacuum hoses are not damaged and are routed properly, repeat the KOEO test. After the last memory code, depress the throttle to the floor and release it. The needle will rise to 12 volts. Probe both terminals on each of the air management solenoids. These two solenoids can be located by tracing the vacuum hoses from the air management valves on the air pump. Each solenoid should have a terminal with 12 volts and a terminal with 0 volts. If neither terminal on one solenoid has 12 volts, repair the 12-volt power supply to the solenoid. If both terminals have 12 volts at this point, repair the wire between that solenoid and either ECA terminal 51 or ECA terminal 11, depending on the affected solenoid.

If the circuit passes the first part of the test, depress and release the throttle again. The voltmeter should drop to 0 volts. Both terminals of each AM solenoid should now have 12 volts on them. If one does not, replace the affected solenoid.

Code 95

ICM-equipped Vehicles

If the code 95 is received during the KOEO test, begin troubleshooting it by confirming that the inertia switch has not been tripped. Press the button on the top of the switch to reset the switch. After confirming that the inertia switch has not been tripped, check the resistance across the two terminals of the inertia switch. If the resistance is greater than 5 ohms, replace the inertia switch. If the resistance is less than 5 ohms, turn the ignition switch off and listen carefully for the fuel pump. If the fuel pump is running, disconnect the ICM. If the fuel pump continues to run, repair the short to power in the wire that runs from ICM terminal 5 to ECA pin 19. If the fuel pump does not continue to run, replace the ICM.

If the fuel pump was not running with the key off, check the resistance of the wire running from ICM terminal 5 to ECA pin 19. If the resistance is greater than 5 ohms, repair the wire. If the resistance is less than 5 ohms, check the ICM ground. If the ground is good, replace the ECA.

If the code 95 is received during the memory codes, start the engine, tap on the ICM, and wiggle and twist the wiring harness. If the engine stumbles or dies when the ICM is tapped, replace the ICM. If the engine stumbles or dies when the wiring is wiggled and twisted, repair the intermittent open in the wiring or connector.

Non-ICM-equipped Vehicles

If the code 95 is received, confirm that the inertia switch has not been tripped. Check the resistance across the terminals of the inertia switch. If the resistance is greater than 5 ohms, replace the inertia switch. If the resistance is less than 5 ohms, turn the ignition switch off and listen for the fuel pump. If the fuel pump continues to run when the key is off, disconnect the fuel pump relay. Check for a short to voltage in the wire that runs from the fuel pump relay to the pump. If the fuel pump shuts off when the fuel pump relay is disconnected, replace the fuel pump relay.

If the fuel pump does not run when the key is off, disconnect the ECA harness connector and measure the resistance between ECA pin 8 (pin 50 if the vehicle is a 3.8-liter SEFI RWD) and the fuel pump relay. If the resistance is less than 5 ohms, check the resistance between pin 8 (pin 50) and the battery's negative terminal. If the resistance is less than 10 ohms, replace the ECA. If the measured resistances are incorrect, repair the wires as necessary.

If the code 95 is received during the memory codes, start the engine, tap on the fuel pump relay, and wiggle and twist the wiring harness. If the engine stumbles or dies when the fuel pump relay is tapped, replace the fuel pump relay. If the engine stumbles or dies when the wiring is wiggled and twisted, repair the intermittent open in the wiring or connector.

Code 96

ICM-equipped Vehicles

If the code 96 is received during the KOEO test or the memory codes, disconnect the sixty-pin connector from the ECA. Disconnect the ICM (integrated controller module) which is a black box approximately 8in long and 5in wide located near the radiator. Connect an ohmmeter between ECA pin 19 and terminal 5 of the ICM connector. The resistance should be close to 0. If the circuit is open, repair the wire. If the wire is okay, reconnect the ICM and the ECA. Check the voltage at pin 19 of the ECA and switch the key to the on position. If the voltage rises to 12 volts for 1 second, replace the ECA. If the voltage does not rise, replace the ICM.

Non-ICM-equipped Vehicles

If the code 96 is received during both the KOEO test and the memory codes, check for 12 volts to the fuel pump relay. With the ignition switch turned off, one terminal of the fuel pump relay should have 12 volts. If none of them do, repair the open circuit between the fuel pump relay and the battery. If one terminal does have 12 volts, connect a voltmeter between the wire running from the relay to the pump and ground. Cycle the ignition switch several times. If the voltage does not go to 12 volts each time, replace the fuel pump relay. If the voltage does go to 12 volts each time, replace the ECA.

Code 97

Refer the code 97 to a qualified transmission specialist or the dealer.

Code 98

E4OD-equipped Vehicles

Refer the code 98 to a qualified transmission specialist or the dealer.

All Other Applications

If the code 98 is received during the KOER test in place of the engine ID code, abort the KOER test and make the repairs indicated in the KOEO test.

Code 99

E4OD-equipped Vehicles

Refer the code 99 to a qualified transmission specialist or the dealer.

All Other Applications

Repeat the KOEO test. If the code 99 returns, replace the ECA.

Two-Digit Codes Summary

Code	Meaning
11	System pass was completed
12	Rpm did not reach upper test limit
13	Rpm did not reach lower test limit
	DC motor did not move
	DC motor did not follow dashpot
14	PIP circuit failed
15	Power to keep-alive memory was interrupted
	ROM test failed
16	Rpm were above self-test limit
	Rpm were too low to perform test
17	Rpm were below self-test limit
18	Tach signal to ECA was lost
	SPOUT circuit was open
19	Rpm were erratic during test
	EEC power supply failed
	CID sensor input failed
21	ECT was out of range
22	MAP or BP was out of range
23	TP was out of range
24	ACT was out of range
	VAT was out of range
25	KS did not detect detonation during KOER test
26	VAF was out of range
	MAF was out of range
	TOT was out of range
28	VAT was out of range
	Primary tach signal was lost, dual-plug applications, right side
29	VSS failed to deliver signal to ECA
31	PFE voltage was low
	EVP voltage was low
32	EGR valve was not seated
	EVP voltage was low
33	EGR valve did not open
	EVP was out of range
34	EGR flow was insufficient
	PFE sensor was defective or exhaust back pressure was excessive
	EVP voltage was above maximum limit
35	EVP voltage was high
	PFE voltage was high
	Rpm were too low for EGR test
38	ITS circuit was open
39	AXOD bypass clutch did not apply properly
41	EGO or HEGO was lean
42	EGO or HEGO was rich
43	EGO or HEGO was lean at wide-open throttle
44	Air pump system was inoperative on side with cylinders 1 to 4
45	DIS coil pack 3 failed
	Air pump air was always ahead of EGO or HEGO sensor
46	DIS coil pack 1 failed
	Air pump air was not bypassed during self-test
47	Low airflow was indicated at base idle
	4x4 switch did not close
48	High airflow was indicated at base idle
	DIS coil pack 2 failed
49	SPOUT wire between ECA and DIS module was faulty
	1–2 shift error occurred
51	ECT voltage was high
52	PSPS circuit was open
	PSPS circuit did not change
53	TP voltage was high
54	ACT voltage was high
	VAT voltage was high
55	Key power to ECA was open
56	VAF voltage was high
	MAF voltage was high
	TOT voltage was high
57	AXOD NPS was open
58	VAT voltage was high
	ISC motor did not make contact with throttle linkage
59	AXOD 4–3 pressure switch failed
	Fuel pump circuit failed
61	ECT voltage was low
62	AXOD 4–3 or 3–2 pressure switch failed
63	TP voltage was low
64	ACT voltage was low
	VAT voltage was low
65	ECA failed to enter closed-loop mode
	Overdrive cancel switch did not change state
66	VAF sensor below minimum test voltage
	MAF below minimum test voltage
	TOT below minimum test voltage
67	MLP was out of range; air conditioner input was high
	NPS failed to close
	Clutch switch circuit failed
	NDS was open or air conditioner input was open

Code	Meaning
68	VAT voltage was low
	ITS was closed or open
69	AXOD 3–4 or 3–2 switch failed
	3–4 shift error occurred
71	Software reinitialization was detected
	ITS was closed on preposition
	Cluster control assembly circuit failed
72	Power interrupt was detected
	Insufficient MAP change was detected during goose test
73	Insufficient TP change was detected during goose test
74	BOO circuit was always open, did not change during test
75	BOO was always high
76	Insufficient VAF change was detected during goose test
77	Technician did not do goose test
79	Air conditioner was on during test
81	Insufficient Intake Air Control (IAC) output was detected during test
	AM circuit failed
82	SC bypass circuit failed
	AM circuit failed
83	EGRC circuit failed
	High-speed fan circuit failed
	Low-speed fuel pump relay circuit failed
84	EGRV circuit failed
	EVR circuit failed
85	CANP circuit failed
86	Fuel pressure was high
	3–4 shift circuit failed
	Fuel pressure was low
87	Fuel pump primary circuit failed
88	DPI failed
	Electric cooling fan failed
89	Converter clutch circuit failed
	AXOD lockup solenoid circuit failed
91	Left EGO or HEGO was always lean
	Shift solenoid 1 circuit failed
	Left EGO or HEGO did not switch
92	Left EGO or HEGO was always rich
	Shift solenoid 2 circuit failed
93	TP sensor input was low
94	Thermactor air was inoperative, right bank
	Converter clutch circuit failed
95	Fuel pump secondary circuit failed
96	Fuel pump secondary circuit failed
	High-speed fuel pump circuit failed
97	Overdrive cancel indicator circuit failed
98	Hard fault failure occurred
	Electronic pressure control circuit failed
99	EEC system did not learn to control idle
	Electronic pressure control circuit failed

EEC IV Three-Digit Test Codes

Some 1991 and later applications produce a three-digit code. When dealing with three-digit appli-cations, cross-reference the test procedure by using the following chart:

Ford Three-Digit Codes Summary

Code	Meaning
111	System pass was completed
112	ACT sensor circuit was below minimum voltage (250 degrees Fahrenheit or greater was indicated)
113	ACT sensor circuit was above maximum voltage (− 40 degrees Fahrenheit or lower was indicated)
114	ACT sensor circuit was higher or lower than expected during KOEO or KOER test
115	ECT was higher or lower than expected during KOEO or KOER test
117	ECT sensor circuit was below minimum voltage (250 degrees Fahrenheit or greater was indicated)
118	ECT sensor circuit was above maximum voltage (− 40 degrees Fahrenheit or lower was indicated)
121	Closed-throttle voltage was higher or lower than expected during KOEO or KOER test
	TP sensor voltage was higher or lower than expected
122	TP sensor circuit was below minimum voltage
123	TP sensor voltage was above maximum
	TP sensor voltage was higher than expected
	TP sensor voltage was lower than expected
126	MAP or BP sensor was higher or lower than expected
128	MAP sensor vacuum hose was damaged or disconnected
129	Insufficient MAP or MAF change was detected during dynamic response test
	Oxygen sensor switch was lacking during KOER, indicating lean (bank 2)
	Oxygen sensor switch was lacking during KOER, indicating rich (bank 2)
	MAF sensor circuit was below minimum voltage
	MAF sensor circuit was above maximum voltage
	MAF was higher or lower than expected during KOEO or KOER
167	Insufficient TP sensor change was detected during dynamic response
171	Fuel system was at adaptive limits; oxygen sensor was unable to switch (bank 1)
172	Oxygen sensor switches were lacking, indicating lean (bank 1)
173	Oxygen sensor switches were lacking, indicating rich (bank 1)
	Fuel system was at adaptive limits; oxygen sensor was unable to switch (bank 2)
	Oxygen sensor switches were lacking,

indicating lean (bank 2)

Oxygen sensor switches were lacking, indicating rich (bank 2)

179 Fuel system was at lean adaptive limit at part throttle; system was rich (bank 1)

181 Fuel system was at rich adaptive limit at part throttle; system was lean (bank 1)

182 Fuel system was at lean adaptive limit at idle; system was rich (bank 1)

183 Fuel system was at rich adaptive limit at idle; system was lean (bank 1)

MAF was higher than expected

MAF was lower than expected

Injector pulse width was higher than expected (with BP sensor)

Injector pulse width was higher or MAF was lower than expected (without BP sensor)

Injector pulse width was lower than expected (with BP sensor)

Injector pulse width was lower or MAF was higher than expected (without BP sensor)

Fuel system was at lean adaptive limit at part throttle; system was rich (bank 2)

Fuel system was at rich adaptive limit at part throttle; system was lean (bank 2)

Fuel system was at lean adaptive limit at idle; system was rich (bank 2)

Fuel system was at rich adaptive limit at idle; system was lean (bank 2)

211 PIP circuit failed

212 IDM input to ECA was lost; SPOUT circuit was grounded

213 SPOUT circuit was open

CID circuit failed

EEC processor detected coil 1 primary circuit failure (DIS and EDIS—electronic version)

EEC processor detected coil 2 primary circuit failure (DIS, EDIS)

EEC processor detected coil 3 primary circuit failure (DIS, EDIS)

IDM signal was lost, left side (dual-plug DIS)

Spark timing defaulted to 10 degrees (SPOUT circuit was open)

Spark timing error occurred

IDM signal was lost, right side (dual-plug DIS)

DPI control failed (dual-plug DIS)

EEC processor detected coil 1, 2, 3, or 4 primary circuit failure (dual-plug DIS)

225 Knock was not sensed during dynamic response test

IDM signal was not received (EDIS)

Crankshaft position sensor error occurred (EDIS)

EEC processor detected coil 1, 2, 3, or 4 primary circuit failure (EDIS)

Spark signal pulse width error occurred (EDIS)

EEC processor detected coil 4 primary circuit failure (DIS, EDIS)

Crankshaft position sensor signal was not sensed with the engine off (EDIS)

EDIS to EEC processor IDM pulse width transmission error occurred

ECA was operating in DIS failure mode

Secondary circuit failed, coil 1, 2, 3, or 4 (EDIS)

311 Thermactor air system was inoperative during KOER (bank 1 with dual HEGO)

312 Thermactor air was misdirected during KOER

313 Thermactor air was not bypassed during KOER

Thermactor air system was inoperative during KOER (bank 2 with dual HEGO)

EGR (EPT—EGR Pressure Transducer) circuit voltage was lower than expected (PFE)

327 EGR (EVP, EPT) circuit was below minimum voltage (PFE)

328 EGR (EVP) closed-valve voltage was lower than expected

332 Insufficient EGR flow was detected (PFE)

334 EGR (EVP) closed-valve voltage was higher than expected

EGR (EPT) sensor voltage was higher or lower than expected during KOEO (PFE)

Exhaust pressure was high; EGR (EPT) circuit voltage was higher than expected (PFE)

337 EGR (EVP, EPT, PFE) circuit was above maximum voltage

Octane adjust service pin was in use

411 Rpm could not be controlled during KOER low-rpm check

412 Rpm could not be controlled during KOER high-rpm check

452 Insufficient input from VSS was detected

511 EEC processor ROM test failed

512 EEC processor keep-alive memory (KAM) test failed

513 EEC processor internal voltage failed

519 PSPS circuit was open

521 PSPS did not change state

522 Vehicle was not in park or neutral during KOEO

Vehicle was in gear or air conditioner was on

528 Clutch switch circuit failed

Data communication link (DCL) or EEC processor circuit failed

DCL or electronic instrument cluster (EIC) circuit failed

BOO circuit failed or was not actuated during KOER

Code	Meaning
531	Insufficient rpm change occurred during KOER dynamic response test
	Cylinder balance test was invalid owing to throttle movement during test
	Cylinder balance test was invalid owing to CID sensor circuit failure
539	Air conditioner or defroster was on during KOEO
542	Fuel pump circuit was open, EEC processor to motor ground
543	Fuel pump circuit was open, battery to EEC processor
	Inlet air control (IAC) circuit failed
552	Air management 1 (AM1) circuit failed
553	Air management 2 (AM2) circuit failed
	SBS circuit failed
556	Fuel pump relay primary circuit failed
558	EVR circuit failed
	Auxiliary electro-drive fan (AEDF) circuit failed
	HEDF circuit failed
	EDF circuit failed
565	CANP circuit failed
	3–4 shift solenoid circuit failed
569	Auxiliary canister purge (AUX-CANP) circuit failed
	EDF did not respond
	1–2 shift error occurred
	2–3 shift error occurred
	3–4 shift error occurred
	Shift solenoid 1 (SS1) circuit failed
	Shift solenoid 2 (SS2) circuit failed
	Electronic pressure control (EPC) circuit failed
	EPC driver was open in EEC processor
	Coast clutch solenoid (CCS) circuit failed
	Computer controlled clutch (CCC) solenoid circuit failed
	Excessive converter clutch slippage occurred
629	CCC failed (CCC, CCO, LUS, and modulated lockup solenoid [MLUS])
	Overdrive cancel indicator light (OCIL) circuit failed
	Overdrive cancel switch (OCS) circuit did not change states during KOER
	4x4 switch was closed during KOEO
	MLP voltage was higher or lower than expected
	TOT was higher or lower than expected during KOEO or KOER
	TOT sensor circuit was above maximum voltage (− 40 degrees Fahrenheit was indicated)
	TOT sensor circuit was below minimum voltage (240 degrees Fahrenheit was indicated)
	Input from turbine speed sensor (TSS) was insufficient
	Shift solenoid 3 (SS3) circuit failed
	Incorrect gear ratio was obtained for first gear
	Incorrect gear ratio was obtained for second gear
	Incorrect gear ratio was obtained for third gear
	Incorrect gear ratio was obtained for fourth gear
	EPC circuit failed
	MLUS circuit failed
	MLP sensor did not indicate park during KOEO
998	Hard fault was present, FMEM mode

Supplemental EEC IV Tests

The ECA is capable of performing four tests other than the STAR, or quick, test used to acquire trouble codes. Each of these is designed to meet a specific diagnostic need.

Continuous monitor test
Output state test
Computed timing test
SEFI test

Continuous Monitor (wiggle) Test

The continuous monitor test is often referred to by its more popular and descriptive name: wiggle test. It is designed to locate the source of memory codes that result from intermittent shorts, opens, and grounds. The Ford EEC IV system is unique in its ability to locate intermittent problems that are not present when the technician is working on the vehicle.

Begin by clearing the memory codes. This is done by entering the KOEO test. When the first KOEO code is received, disconnect the STI wire (the jumper wire you placed between the large test connector and the single wire test connector) and shut off the ignition switch. The memory codes are now cleared.

To enter the wiggle test, connect the voltmeter and jumper wires as described for the retrieval of trouble codes. Perform the KOEO or KOER test. Immediately after the last code is received, disconnect and immediately reconnect the STI wire.

At this point, the voltmeter should read 0 volts. Pull, twist, and wiggle the wires and wiring harness attached to the actuator or sensor in question. Tap on the device. Gently twist the device. All the time you are doing this, watch the voltmeter. If the needle rises to 12 volts during a given action, that action has created an open, short, or ground. Repair or replace the device or wire you were manipulating as the needle moved. At the same time, a code relating to the defective wire will be put into memory. Repeat the KOEO test. Observe the memory codes. Make the indicated repairs according to the two- and three-digit code charts given earlier in this chapter.

Output State Test

The output state test is performed when a symptom or code indicates that one of the actuators may not be working. It is entered by initiating the KOEO test. When the last of the memory codes is received, press the throttle to the floor and release it. When the throttle is released, several of the actuators—EVR, EGRC, and EGRV, to name a few—will be energized by the ECA. When the throttle is depressed and released again, these actuators will deenergize.

The state of the actuators—energized or deenergized—can be monitored with the voltmeter used for the KOEO test. When the voltmeter is reading 12 volts, it means the actuators are energized. When the voltmeter is reading 0 volts, it means the actuators are deenergized.

When led to the output state test by a code or symptom, use a test light to test the control of the actuator by the ECA. One of the two terminals of the actuator should have 12 volts regardless of the state of the actuator. The second terminal should have 12 volts when the voltmeter is reading 0 volts, and 0 volts when the voltmeter is reading 12 volts.

If neither terminal has 12 volts, inspect the wiring and fuses for an open power supply to the actuator.

If one terminal has 12 volts but the other always has 0, regardless of state, inspect that wire for a short to ground. If the wire is in good condition, the actuator has an open circuit in the solenoid windings. Replace the actuator.

If both terminals always have 12 volts, check for an open in the wire between the actuator and the ECA. If the wire is good, check the connections at the actuator and the ECA. If the connections are also good, replace the ECA.

Computed Timing Test

The computed timing test is used to test the ECA's ability to control the ignition timing accurately. To enter the computed timing test, connect a timing light and run the KOER test. After the last code is received, check the timing. At this point, the ECA should have advanced the timing to initial plus 20 degrees, plus or minus 3 degrees.

If the computed timing is incorrect, check the initial timing. The initial timing spec should be printed on the EPA decal under the hood of the vehicle. If the initial timing is correct, check the continuity of the yellow and light green SPOUT wire. If the SPOUT wire is in good condition, replace the ignition module and repeat the computed timing test. If the repeated computed timing test is incorrect, replace the ECA.

SEFI Test

The SEFI test is available only on Sequential Electronic Fuel Injection applications. After completing the KOER test, lightly tap the throttle; a 2- to 3-degree throttle movement is all that is required. After a rather lengthy pause, the ECA will begin shutting off one injector at a time and measuring the rpm drop. If the rpm drop from any of the cylinders is not enough, a single-digit code will be pulsed. The number of pulses relates to the number of the cylinder that is weak. If nine pulses are received, it means all cylinders are in good condition.

Sequential Electronic Fuel Injection Test Codes versus Cylinders

Code	90	10	20	30	40	50	60	70	80	77
Cylinder number	Pass	1	2	3	4	5	6	7	8	Repeat test
ECA pin number	Pass	58	59	12	13	14	15	42	52	Repeat test

Remember that a weak cylinder can be caused by many things other than an injector problem. Check the following:

Ignition coil
Distributor cap
Distributor rotor
Spark plugs (these may be fouled)
Spark plug wires
CANP solenoid
PCV valves
DIS
EGR
Air filter
Engine oil (fuel may have contaminated this)
Power ground (this may be poor)
Fuel pressure (check the fuel pressure against the chart that follows)
Vacuum leaks
Cold engine

Fuel Pressures for Passenger Cars

Engine	Idle (Psi)	Engine Off (Psi)
1.9L EFI	30–45	35–45
1.9L CFI	13–17	13–17
2.3L ohc EFI	30–45	35–45
2.3L TC EFI	30–55	35–45
2.3L HSC EFI	45–60	50–60
2.5L CFI	13–17	13–16
3.0L EFI	30–45	35–45
3.8L FWD EFI	30–45	35–45
3.8L RWD EFI	30–45	35–45
5.0L SEFI	30–45	35–45
5.0L MA SEFI	30–45	35–45
3.0L SHO SEFI	28–33	30–45
3.8L SC SEFI	30–40	35–40

Fuel Pressures for Light-Duty Trucks

Engine	Idle (Psi)	Engine Off (Psi)
2.3L EFI	30–45	35–45
2.9L EFI	30–45	35–45
3.0L EFI	30–45	35–45
4.9L EFI	45–60	50–60
5.0L EFI	30–45	35–45
5.8L EFI	30–45	35–45
7.5L EFI	30–45	35–45

If all of these are good, check the injector resistance against the following chart:

Injector Resistance

Trucks	Resistance (Ohms)
2.3L EFI	13.5–18
2.9L EFI	13.5–18
3.0L EFI	15–18
4.9L EFI	13.5–18
5.0L EFI	13.5–18
5.8L EFI	13.5–18
7.5L EFI	13.5–19

Injector Resistance

Application	Resistance (Ohms)
1.9L EFI	2–2.7
1.9L CFI	1–2
2.3L ohc EFI	15–19
2.3L TC EFI	2–3
2.3L HSC EFI	13.5–16
2.5L CFI	1–2
3.0L EFI	15–18
3.0L SHO SEFI	13.5–16
3.8L AXOD SEFI	13.5–16
3.8L RWD SEFI	13.5–16
3.8L SC SEFI	13.5–16
5.0L SEFI	13.5–19
5.0L MA SEFI	13.5–19

9

Troubleshooting by Symptom

Ford fuel injection systems, especially the EEC IV system, feature excellent self-diagnostic systems. Sometimes, however, the symptom you are trying to eliminate occurs for too short a time or at the wrong time for the onboard diagnostics to log a code. Therefore, part of many troubleshooting procedures will be a logically sequenced manual test of most of the engine systems. The procedures outlined in this chapter can be used either before the onboard diagnostics, in conjunction with the onboard diagnostics, or after the onboard diagnostics have failed to locate the source of the problem.

Items to Be Tested
Engine condition
Ignition condition

Visual Inspection
Coolant level and leaks
Hoses, coolant and vacuum
Battery and cable condition
Alternator and accessory drive belts
Electrical and electronic connections
Cleanliness
Wire and hose routing
Age and condition of tune-up parts
Test fuel pressure
Pull trouble codes and set aside

The first step in good troubleshooting is a thorough visual inspection.

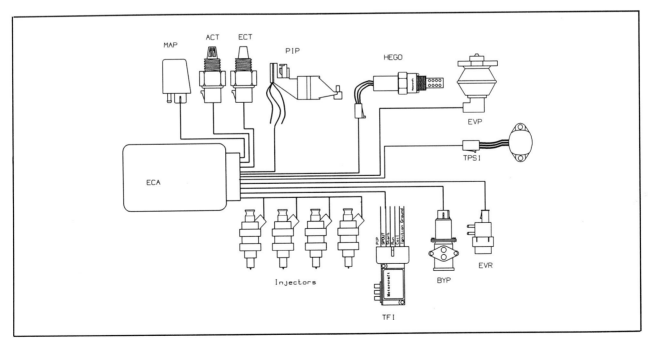

These are the fuel injection components that are most often at fault when a drivability problem occurs.

Fuel pressure
Engine coolant temperature sensor
Throttle position sensor
Manifold absolute pressure or barometric pressure
    sensor
Mass airflow sensor (where appropriate)
Vane airflow sensor (where appropriate)
Vane air temperature sensor (where appropriate)
Air charge temperature sensor
EGR valve position sensor
Pressure feedback EGR sensor

Engine Condition

Compression

The first step in troubleshooting any drivability problem is to confirm that the engine is mechanically sound. Begin by checking the compression. While performing the compression test, make sure to disable the ignition system and hold the throttle wide open. One easy and effective way to disable the ignition system is to disconnect the six-wire connector on the distributor-type TFI system, or the right side six-wire connector on the DIS module. The results of the compression test should indicate that all cylinders are within 10 to 15 percent of one another.

Cylinder Leakage

A good, and some feel superior, alternative to the compression test is the cylinder leakage test. A cylinder leakage tester can be obtained from any major automotive tool distributor.

To perform a cylinder leakage test, remove the spark plugs, bring cylinder 1 up to top dead center, and connect the cylinder leakage tester. Connect the shop air to the cylinder leakage tester. The leakage tester measures the pressure difference between the shop air entering the cylinder and the amount of pressure retained in the cylinder. Cylinder leakage should be less than 20 percent on all cylinders. Although different manufacturers show limits as low as 5 percent, in most cases, the failure of the cylinder to seal to a level greater than 20 percent will not significantly affect drivability.

Vacuum Leaks

Very small vacuum leaks can present themselves as major drivability problems. Locating vacuum leaks can be tricky, and many inside tricks of the auto repair industry are used to do so.

One old trick is to spray carburetor cleaner around the intake system. The idea is that the carburetor cleaner will be sucked into the combustion chamber, causing a change in engine speed or smoothness. Although this is a good idea, the use of such highly volatile chemicals has two problems. First, carburetor cleaner is highly flammable. Second, when the carburetor cleaner is sprayed, it is lighter than air. As a result, it does not always end up where you think you are spraying.

An alternative to the carburetor cleaner is propane. Use a standard, unlit propane torch, running it along the intake system. When a vacuum leak is found, the engine will smooth out or the rpm will increase.

In the late 1980s and early 1990s, electronics entered the science of detecting vacuum leaks. Several manufacturers now market an electronic ear designed to hear the very narrow frequency band of vacuum leaks.

Ignition Condition
Distributor-Type Ignition

To test for spark, insert a screwdriver into the spark end of a plug wire and hold it about 1/4in from a good ground. Crank the engine and check for spark.

Many drivability problems can be diagnosed by raising the hood and looking closely at vacuum hoses, coolant hoses, secondary ignition components, and loose electrical and electronic connections.

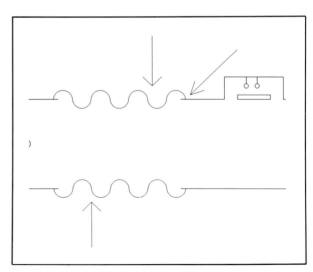

False air enters the intake system between the VAF sensor and the intake manifold. Visually check the intake system, especially hose connections for possible leaks.

If a spark occurs, remove one of the spark plugs; insert it into the plug wire; place the plug on a good ground, such as the intake manifold; and crank the engine. If the spark plug sparks and does not appear worn, proceed to the fuel pump testing discussion in the "Symptom: Engine Cranks but Won't Start" section later in this chapter.

If no spark comes from the spark plug wire, probe the negative terminal of the ignition coil with a test light. If you are not sure which side of the coil is negative, first insert the test light on one side, then crank the engine, and then insert the light on the other side. One side of the coil should have a relatively steady supply of switched ignition voltage, and the other side should flash on and off as the engine is cranked. If neither has power, then you have an open wire in the voltage supply to the coil. If both sides have steady power, then the problem is the primary ignition's control of the coil. In the old days, the first thing to look at would have been the points. Today, we have to look at what replaces the points: the pickup coil, the ignition module, and the connecting wiring.

The variable reluctance transducer is the standard type of pickup coil that Ford has used since the debut of electronic ignition in 1975. This pickup produces an AC signal. To test it, disconnect the connector at the pickup and connect an AC voltmeter. With the introduction of the EEC IV fuel injection system, Ford switched to the Hall effect sensor. It consists of a permanent magnet that sits opposite a transistor that is extrasensitive to magnetic fields. A set of ferrous metal blades rotates through the gap between the magnet and the transistor, causing the magnetic field to be alternately interrupted and not interrupted. The result is a pulse directly proportional to the speed of rotation. This pulse can be detected by connecting a tachometer to the blue PIP wire at the ignition module. This applies whether the system is a distributor type or distributorless. When the engine is cranked, the tachometer should read something other than 0. If it reads 0, replace the PIP Hall effect sensor.

You can replace the TFI ignition module with a known good unit, but you have no accurate way to test it without special equipment. A trick of the trade will confirm that a module is probably good but will not determine if it is bad.

Remove the ignition module from the distributor but leave it connected to the six-wire harness. Remove the coil wire from the distributor cap. Notice the three terminals on the top of the module. Momentarily apply 12 volts to the terminal located closest to the six-wire connector.

If the pickup produces a tachometer reading at the PIP terminal—or the PIP OUT terminal, in the case of the DIS systems—the problem is wiring or the ignition module.

Distributorless Ignition

The DIS was developed for the 1988 model year. Like the distributor applications, if no high-voltage spark occurs, the fault could lie in the pickup coil or the ignition module. It could also lie in the engine position sensors.

The DIS uses Hall effect sensors to monitor the positions of the camshaft and crankshaft. On the 2.3-liter Rangers, the cam sensor is located in the

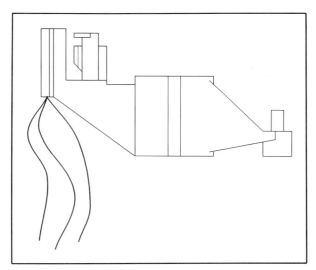

Intermittent problems with the PIP sensor can cause stalling, hesitation, and intermittent no-starts. Sometimes an educated guess is the only way to solve a problem. An intermittent PIP problem can exist for a long time and never set a code. If no other cause can be found for these symptoms, replace the PIP sensor.

An intermittent problem with the TFI module can cause the same sporadic symptoms as a defective PIP sensor. If the PIP replacement does not cure the problem, replace the TFI module. The upper module is the early type, which had a relatively high failure rate. The lower module seems to be more dependable; it is the later style.

On the 3.0-liter SHO engine, the PIP sensor is located behind the crankshaft pulley.

crankshaft. On all other applications, the cam sensor is located on the camshaft.

To check the crankshaft (PIP) sensor, probe the middle wire at the PIP sensor connector. This wire runs to terminal 4 of the DIS module. With the ignition on, the reading should be either 5 volts or more or 0 volts. Whichever it is, carefully rotate the crankshaft. Within one-half revolution of the crankshaft, the voltage should change from low (less than 1 volt) to high (greater than 5 volts).

If the voltage was high and remains high, check the continuity of the wire from the PIP sensor to the module. If the wire is good, with no shorts or opens, replace the PIP sensor. If the voltage was low and remained low, check for 12 volts to any of the terminals. If you find 12 volts, inspect the ground. If the ground is good, replace the sensor. If you do not find 12 volts at the sensor, repair the 12-volt power supply wire as needed.

To check the camshaft (CID) sensor, probe the middle wire at the CID sensor connector. This wire runs to terminal 2 of the DIS module. With the ignition on, the reading should be either 5 volts or more or 0

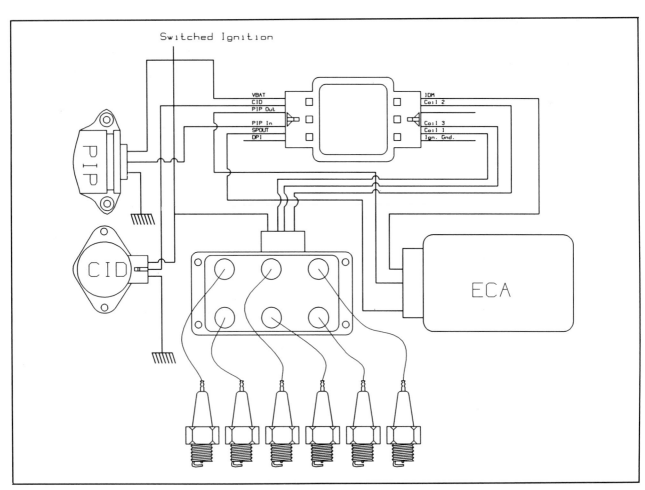

This is the schematic for the DIS as used on the V-6 applications.

volts. Whichever it is, carefully rotate the crankshaft. Within one revolution of the crankshaft, the voltage should change from low (less than 1 volt) to high (greater than 5 volts).

If the voltage was high and remains high, check the continuity of the wire from the CID to the module. If the wire is good, with no shorts or opens, replace the CID sensor. If the voltage was low and remained low, check for 12 volts to any of the terminals. If you find 12 volts, inspect the ground. If the ground is good, replace the sensor. If you do not find 12 volts at the sensor, repair the 12-volt power supply wire as needed.

If the voltage at terminal 4 of the ignition module switches high and low as the crankshaft is rotated, the crank sensor is good.

If the voltage at terminal 2 of the ignition module switches high and low as the crankshaft is rotated, the cam sensor is good.

You should find 12 volts on the wire connected to terminal 1 of the ignition module.

You should find continuity to ground through ignition module terminal 7.

If all the above are true and none of the coils are producing a spark, then replace the ignition module. If even one of the coils produces a spark, the problem is most likely a defective coil pack.

Quick Check Tips

1. If no spark occurs but the injector pulses, then the lack of spark is a result of a secondary ignition problem such as a bad coil, distributor cap, or rotor. If no spark occurs and the injector does not pulse, then the problem is likely a primary ignition problem.

2. A quick and easy test for pulses from DIS cam and crank sensors is to connect a dwell meter to terminals 2 and 4 of the ignition module. If the sensors are good, the tachometer will read greater than 0. If the sensor being tested is bad, the reading will be 0.

Fuel Pressure

The next step in troubleshooting a drivability problem is to check the fuel pressure. Almost all EFI (MPI) applications provide a Schraeder valve for connecting a fuel pressure gauge. For applications that do not provide a Schraeder valve and for all CFI applications, it is necessary to tee the fuel pressure gauge in the line that runs between the fuel filter and the fuel pressure regulator.

Position the fuel pressure gauge where it can be easily and safely seen from the driver's seat. Compare the readings against those in the following chart. If the fuel pressure is correct with the engine idling, rev the engine. Does the fuel pressure increase? It should on EFI applications; it should not on CFI applications. If the fuel pressure is correct with the car not moving, drive the car while observing the fuel pressure. If the pressure drops as the symptom being diagnosed occurs, the problem is inadequate fuel volume. Check the fuel filters—do not forget the one

Although fuel pressure is controlled by the fuel pressure regulator, when the pressure is incorrect, it is most often the result of filter and other restriction problems.

in the tank. Look for kinked or restricted lines. If all of these are in good condition, replace the fuel pump.

Fuel Pressures for Passenger Cars

Engine	Idle (Psi)	Engine Off (Psi)
1.9L EFI	30–45	35–45
1.9L CFI	13–17	13–17
2.3L OHC EFI	30–45	35–45
2.3L TC EFI	30–55	35–45
2.3L HSC EFI	45–60	50–60
2.5L CFI	13–17	13–16
3.0L EFI	30–45	35–45
3.8L FWD EFI	30–45	35–45
3.8L RWD EFI	30–45	35–45
5.0L SEFI	30–45	35–45
5.0L MA SEFI	30–45	35–45
3.0L SHO SEFI	28–33	30–45
3.8L SC SEFI	30–40	35–40

Fuel Pressures for Light-Duty Trucks

Engine	Idle (Psi)	Engine Off (Psi)
2.3L EFI	30–45	35–45
2.9L EFI	30–45	35–45
3.0L EFI	30–45	35–45
4.9L EFI	45–60	50–60
5.0L EFI	30–45	35–45
5.8L EFI	30–45	35–45
7.5L EFI	30–45	35–45

Sensors

If the fuel pressure is correct, the next thing to check is the output signals of the various sensors.

Engine Coolant Temperature Sensor

The ECT sensor performs many of the duties the choke used to perform on a carburetor. If the ECT sends a high voltage to the ECA, it means the coolant temperature is very low—as low as −40 degrees Fahrenheit. If the ECT sends a low voltage to the ECA, it means the temperature of the engine is extremely high—higher than 250 degrees Fahrenheit.

If an inaccurate temperature reading is received by the ECA, it will make improper decisions about air-fuel ratio, ignition timing, and even transmission control. Any one of these problems can cause rich running, poor fuel economy, fouled spark plugs, and starting problems.

Three things need to be tested concerning the coolant temperature sensor. The first is the voltage on the ECT signal wire (light green and yellow) with the harness connected to the ECT sensor. Probe the ECT signal wire. If the voltage is 5 volts or greater or if the voltage is 0 volts, it indicates a short, ground, or open in the ECT circuit. Perform the KOEO test to diagnose and repair. If the voltage is between 0 and 5 volts, it means that the circuit wiring is in good condition.

The second step is to check the sensor resistance. Disconnect the ECT harness. Connect an ohmmeter across the terminals of the ECT sensor. Compare the resistance specs with those in the following chart:

Engine Coolant Temperature Sensor Voltage and Resistance

Temperature (Degrees Fahrenheit)	Temperature (Degrees Celsius)	Voltage (Volts)	Resistance (Ohms)
248	120	0.27	1,180
230	110	0.35	1,550
212	100	0.46	2,070
194	90	0.6	2,800
176	80	0.78	3,840
158	70	1.02	5,370
140	60	1.33	7,700
122	50	1.7	10,970
104	40	2.13	16,150
86	30	2.6	24,270
68	20	3.07	37,300
50	10	3.51	58,750

If the resistance of the sensor is incorrect, replace it. If the resistance is correct, reconnect the ECT harness. Connect an analog voltmeter to the ECT signal wire. Tap on the sensor, wiggle the wires, and gently twist the connection. If the voltage remains constant, the ECT circuit has no problems. If the voltage fluctuates, perform the continuous monitor test and make the indicated repairs.

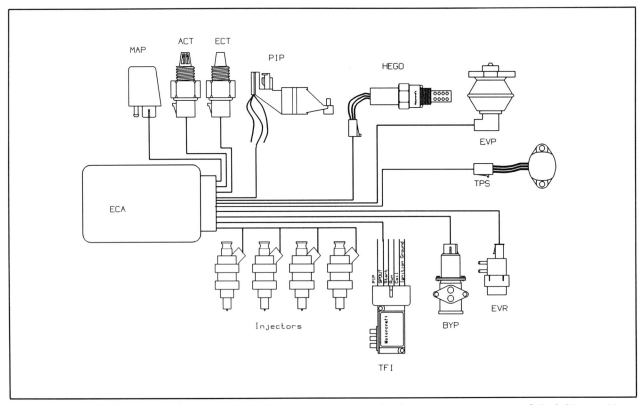

Checking the individual components of a fuel injection system might seem to be a large task, but in reality, relatively few components cause drivability problems severe enough to be noticed by the average driver.

Throttle Position Sensor

The TP sensor replaces the carburetor's accelerator pump. When it is defective, the most noticeable symptom will be a stumble or hesitation. Three things are tested concerning the TP sensor: closed-throttle voltage, wide-open-throttle voltage, and transition voltages.

Begin testing the TP sensor by connecting a voltmeter to the TP signal wire (usually dark green and light green). Open and close the throttle. The voltage should increase and decrease from about 0.5 volt to 4.5 volts. If the voltage does not change in this manner, perform the KOEO test.

Using a digital voltmeter connected to the ECT signal wire, compare the closed-throttle readings and wide-open-throttle readings to those on the following chart:

Throttle Position Sensor Readings

Application	Degrees Opening	Closed Volts	Minimum Volts	Maximum Volts
1.9L EFI	4–13	0.8–1.2	0.24	4.84
1.9L CFI	0–12 off	0.49–1.15	0.39	4.84
	2.5–14 run	0.71–1.25		
2.3L ohc EFI	0–13.5	0.59–1.22	0.2	4.84
2.3L TC EFI	2.5–15	0.71–1.3	0.2	4.84
2.3L HSC EFI	3–13.5	0.73–1.22	0.2	4.84
2.5L HSC CFI	1–15 off	0.66–1.3	0.39	4.84
	3.5–25	0.76–1.78		
3.0L EFI	0–13.5	0.59–1.22	0.34	4.84
3.0L SHO	0–4.5	0.38–0.82	0.23	4.89
3.8L FWD and RWD	3–13.5	0.73–1.22	0.39	4.84
3.8L and 5.0L SEFI				
3.8L SC MA	0–13.5	0.49–1.22	0.39	4.84
5.0L MA SEFI				

Truck	Degrees Opening	Closed Volts	Minimum Volts	Maximum Volts
2.3L DIS EFI	0–13.5	0.59–1.22	0.34	4.84
2.9L EFI	0–13.5	0.59–1.22	0.34	4.84
3.0L EFI	0–13.5	0.59–1.22	0.34	4.84
4.9L EFI	3–13.5	0.73–1.22	0.2	4.84
5.0L EFI	3–13.5	0.73–1.22	0.2	4.84
5.8L EFI	3–13.5	0.73–1.22	0.2	4.84
7.5L EFI	3–13.5	0.73–1.22	0.2	4.84
5.8L and 7.5L EFI E4OD	3–13.5	0.73–1.22	0.34	4.84

If these readings are correct, connect an analog meter to the TP signal wire and slowly open the throttle. The voltage should rise smoothly from the closed-throttle voltage to the wide-open-throttle voltage. If the voltmeter hesitates or drops during the throttle movement, replace the TP sensor.

Vane Air Temperature Sensor Specifications

The vane air temperature sensor measures the density of the air entering the engine. This measurement is important for precise control of the air-fuel ratio. A deficit in this sensor or circuit can cause the engine to run either rich or lean. Check this sensor when experiencing symptoms such as hesitation, stalling, or poor fuel economy. Compare your readings to the chart.

Temperature (Degrees Fahrenheit)	Temperature (Degrees Celsius)	Voltage (Volts)	Resistance (Kohms)
248	120	0.38	0.11
230	110	0.46	0.14
212	100	0.56	0.19
194	90	0.76	0.25
176	80	0.95	0.33
158	70	1.19	0.44
140	60	1.49	0.6
122	50	1.84	0.83
104	40	2.23	1.18
86	30	2.65	1.7
68	20	3.07	2.5
50	10	3.46	3.77

Air Charge Temperature Sensor Specifications

Like the vane air temperature sensor, the ACT measures the density of the air entering the engine. This measurement is important for precise control of the air-fuel ratio. A deficit in this sensor or circuit can cause the engine to run either rich or lean. Check this sensor when experiencing symptoms such as hesitation, stalling, or poor fuel economy. Compare your readings to the chart below.

Temperature (Degrees Fahrenheit)	Temperature (Degrees Celsius)	Voltage (Volts)	Resistance (Kohms)
248	120	0.27	1.18
230	110	0.35	1.55
212	100	0.46	2.07
194	90	0.6	2.8
176	80	0.78	3.84
158	70	1.02	5.37
140	60	1.33	7.7
122	50	1.7	10.97
104	40	2.13	16.15
86	30	2.6	24.27
68	20	3.07	37.3
50	10	3.51	58.75

Mass Air Flow Sensor

The MAF sensor is one of the primary sensors in the calculation of the load variable. The load variable is calculated by the ECA on applications that do not use a MAP sensor. As with the MAP sensor, a fault in the MAF sensor or MAF circuit can cause a stumble or hesitation.

With the engine warmed up and idling, gently tap on the MAF sensor. If the engine rpm drop noticeably or if the engine dies, replace the MAF sensor.

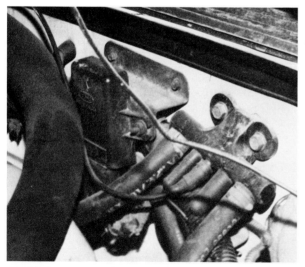

The MAP sensor produces a variable frequency signal.

If the "tap test" is passed, refer to the MAF troubleshooting procedure listed under codes 26, 56, or 66 in chapter 8.

The MAF puts out a variable voltage. As the engine speed and load on the engine change, the voltage put out by the MAF changes. This chart can be used to confirm the MAF output of the vehicle you are working on is correct. Connect a voltmeter between pin 50 of the ECA and ground.

MAF Output Voltage

Engine Condition	MAF Signal Voltage (Volts)
Idle	0.8
20mph	1.1
40mph	1.7
60mph	2.1

The EGR valve position sensor almost never causes a drivability problem. However, the voltage reading of the EVP can indicate if the EGR itself is opening and closing properly.

EGR Valve Position Sensor Specifications

EGR Valve Opening (Percent)	Voltage (Volts)
0	0.4
10	0.75
20	1.1
30	1.45
40	1.8
50	2.15
60	2.5
70	2.85
80	3.2
90	3.55
100	3.9

Manifold Absolute Pressure Sensor

The MAP sensor replaces the vacuum advance and the power valve of older technologies. It measures the load on the engine. As the engine load increases, the frequency output from the MAP sensor also increases. This increase in frequency should follow the increase in load in a direct fashion. If for some reason the change in MAP frequency should hesitate or falter, then the engine will stumble or die.

Connect a frequency counter or tachometer to the center wire of the MAP sensor where it connects to the ECA. Position the tachometer where it can be viewed safely while driving—or, ideally, take along an observer. The tachometer reading should increase as you accelerate. The voltage should change as the engine load changes. Have your observer watch the tachometer carefully as the car stumbles or dies. Does the frequency drop all the way to 0? If it does, inspect the wires thoroughly. With the tachometer still connected, tug gently on the wires to the MAP sensor. Wiggle the wires and connectors. If the frequency does not drop when you wiggle the wires but did peg low as you drove the car, then replace the MAP sensor. If the frequency does fluctuate as you wiggle the wires, repair the damaged wire.

Normally if the MAP sensor passes the quick test, the MAP sensor is in good condition. Intermittent or momentary defects cannot always be detected by the ECA diagnostic system. If you are experiencing a stumbling, hesitation, or stalling problem, use a hand-held vacuum pump and compare your reading to this chart.

MAP Frequencies

Vacuum (In)	Frequency (Hertz)
30	80
27	88
24	95
21	102
18	109
15	117
12	125
9	133
6	141
3	150
0	159

The chart below cannot really be used for diagnostics unless you are blessed with a flow bench. However, it does illustrate how the output voltage should increase as the airflow increases.

Vane Airflow Sensor Specifications

Airflow (Cubic Meters per Hour)	Voltage Output (Volts)
9	0.8
16	1.35
26	1.85
40	2.25
60	2.65
100	3.15
160	3.6
240	4.
380	4.5

If the PFE (Pressure Feedback EGR) passes the quick test, there is no need to do further testing. This chart, however, shows how the voltage should change as the pressure changes in the tube that runs from the exhaust system to the EGR.

Pressure Feedback EGR Specifications

Pressure (Psi)	Vacuum (In-Hg)	Voltage (Volts)
1.82		4.75
1.36		4.38
0.91		4.0
0.46		3.63
0	0	3.25
	5	1.22
	7.4	0.25

Note: In-hg means inches-mercury.

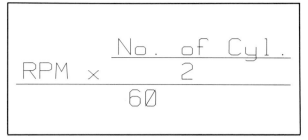

$$RPM \times \frac{No.\ of\ Cyl.}{2}$$
$$\overline{60}$$

The MAP sensor signal can be checked with a tachometer. Convert the rpm readings to frequency by using this formula.

Symptom: Engine Cranks But Won't Start

Five things are necessary to get an internal-combustion gasoline engine to start:
Sufficient engine cranking speed (which is necessary to create compression)
Compression
Air
Spark
Fuel

The following is a logical procedure in testing for a no-start condition.

Engine Cranking Speed Testing

One quick and easy—although not very scientific—way of checking engine cranking speed is by sound. This is especially effective if you are working on your own car or a model with which you are very familiar. The use of a tachometer for this test is good, since not only will it tell you what the cranking speed of the engine is, but if you do not get a tachometer reading, that will tell you the primary ignition is not working. Traditionally, the tachometer is connected to the negative side of the coil. If you are working on a distributorless engine, connect your digital tachometer to the PIP wire at terminal 3 of the DIS module.

Compression Testing

Compression is a function of engine cranking speed and proper cylinder sealing. As with checking engine cranking speed, the skilled technician can often tell by the sound of the engine whether or not compression is sufficient for it to start. If the quality of compression is at all in doubt, a proper compression test should be done. Low compression on one or two cylinders usually is not enough to keep the engine from starting; a no-start condition would require that several of the cylinders have low compression. Low compression in all cylinders might be caused by a jumped timing chain or stripped timing gears. If the compression is good in some cylinders but not in others, the most likely cause is a blown head gasket, worn rings, or bad valves.

Air Testing

To a large extent, the ability of the engine to bring air into the combustion chamber is dependent on the same things that give the engine compression. These things are the intake system design, the condition of the exhaust system, the condition of the air filter, the BYP air control valve, and the throttle plates.

Testing this system involves a visual inspection. Check the condition of the air filter. If it appears dirty or restricted, replace it. On multipoint fuel injected applications that use a Mass Air Flow sensor, it is especially important to check the air tube that connects the MAF sensor to the throttle assembly for evidence of false air. Inspect that the idle air control valve and throttle plates are not coked. Also inspect the throttle for free movement.

On the opposite side of the combustion chamber from the intake system is the exhaust. For the intake to be able to pull air in, the exhaust must be capable of letting air out. Have someone crank the engine while you hold your hand over the tailpipe. You should feel noticeable pressure against your hand. If you are unsure whether or not the pressure is sufficient, compare it to the amount being pushed out the exhaust while cranking a car that will start.

Spark Testing

For troubleshooting the ignition system, refer to chapter 4.

Fuel Pump Testing

When the key is turned to the run position but the engine is not cranked, the fuel pump will run for about 2 seconds, then shut off. If you can hear the fuel pump run for this 2 seconds, then you know that the fuel pump relay and the ECA's control of the relay are operative.

Connect a fuel pressure gauge to the Schraeder valve on the fuel rail of the multiport fuel injection (MPFI) applications. No such valve is provided on the newer CFI applications. It will be necessary to tee the gauge into the inbound fuel line. Crank the engine for several seconds. The fuel pressure gauge should indicate more than 30psi but less than 45psi for MPFI applications and between 9psi and 15psi for CFI applications. Note that V-6 and V-8 CFI applications will have fuel pressure similar to that of the MPFI system. This pressure should hold for several minutes to hours, slowly bleeding off. If the pressure drops off quickly, then the fuel pump check valve, fuel pressure regulator, or an injector is leaking.

If the pressure is low, run a volume test before and after the fuel filter. Disconnect the fuel filter on the outbound side. Using an approved fuel container, install a hose on the outbound end of the fuel filter and crank the engine for about 15 seconds. The pump should flow a minimum of a pint. If the flow is less, remove the filter and repeat the test. Install a new filter if the flow is good before the filter but reduced after the filter.

If the pressure is low but the flow is adequate, replace the fuel pressure regulator.

If the fuel pressure is correct, check to see if the injectors are opening. This can be done in several good ways, but the best way is to use a stethoscope. If a mechanics-style stethoscope is not available, a piece of 1/2in heater hose held near the ear and next to the injector will do almost as well. Listen for the injectors to open and close while the engine is being cranked. If the injectors are not clicking and no spark occurs, repair the ignition system first. If spark occurs but the injectors do not click while cranking, check for voltage at the pink and black wire, which supplies voltage for the injectors. If voltage is present, connect a tachometer to the negative side of the injectors. Cranking the engine should show some sort of a reading. We do not care what the reading is as long as it is not 0. If no reading is shown, connect a dwell meter set on the four-cylinder scale to the PIP input to the ECA. Crank the engine. The dwell meter should read about 45 degrees Fahrenheit. If the reading remains high or low (90 or 0 degrees Fahrenheit), check the continuity in the blue wire from the ignition module to the ECA. On engines equipped with DIS, it is also necessary for the ECA to receive a signal from the cam sensor. Connect a dwell meter to the CID wire that runs from the ignition module to the ECA. Although the reading on this wire might be erratic, we can consider it okay if it is anything other than 0 or 90 degrees Fahrenheit.

If you find a wire carrying 12 volts to the injectors, if a pulse occurs on the PIP wire, if the wires are good, and if a pulse occurs on the CID wire on the DIS, check for continuity from the injectors to the appropriate ECA terminal.

Symptom: Engine Dies or Stumbles on Tip-in Acceleration

Back in the days of carburetors, an engine's dying or stumbling on tip-in acceleration would have pointed toward a bad accelerator pump, an interruption in primary ignition as the breaker plate moved from application of vacuum advance, a low float level, or secondary ignition problems. The same general areas should be addressed on GM fuel-injected cars. For this symptom, the items to check are as follows:
Spark plugs and plug wires
Distributor cap and rotor (where applicable)
Fuel pressure at idle and on acceleration
MAP or MAF signal (the modern equivalent of vacuum advance)
TP signal (the modern equivalent of the accelerator pump)
Miscellaneous items

Spark Plug and Plug Wire Testing

For testing procedures concerning plugs and plug wires, refer to chapter 4.

Distributor Cap and Rotor Testing

For testing procedures concerning the distributor cap and rotor, refer to chapter 4.

Fuel Pressure Testing

Attach the fuel pressure gauge on the MPFI applications to the Schraeder valve. Tee the gauge into the inbound line to the throttle body on CFI applications. Start the engine. Allow it to run for a few seconds, then check the fuel pressure. For MPFI applications, it should be higher than 30psi; for CFI applications, it should be higher than 12psi.

If the fuel pressure is low, rev up the engine while watching the fuel pressure gauge. The MPFI systems should have an immediate increase of about 5psi to 10psi in fuel pressure when the throttle is cracked open. Although the CFI systems should have no increase in fuel pressure, they also should have no loss of fuel pressure.

If the fuel pressure performs properly under these conditions, it does not rule out the possibility that a loss of fuel pressure is at fault. Running the engine and snapping the throttle does not create nearly the fuel demands that actual acceleration creates. Secure the fuel pressure gauge in a safe place where it can be seen while driving the car. Take the car out for a test drive and watch for a noticeable decrease in fuel pressure as the hesitation or stalling occurs. If the problem is stalling, be sure to notice if the decrease in fuel pressure occurs before or after the engine dies. It is normal for the fuel pressure to drop after the engine dies.

If the fuel pressure fails to increase on MPFI applications, or if it drops, the problem is insufficient supply volume. Check or replace the fuel filter. Also inspect the lines for kinking, damage, or restriction.

MAP or MAF Signal Testing

Test the MAP or MAF signal according to the methods described in the "Items to Be Tested" section earlier in this chapter.

TP Sensor Testing

Test the TP sensor according to the methods described in the "Items to Be Tested" section earlier in this chapter.

Miscellaneous Testing

Other things that can cause a hesitation or stalling on tip-in acceleration and methods for checking them are as follows:

Water contamination in the fuel: Disconnect the outbound line of the fuel filter and prepare to capture a small quantity of fuel in a clear plastic container. Cycle the ignition switch on and off several times to energize the fuel pump. Allow the captured fuel to sit in the container undisturbed for about 30 minutes. If a high concentration of water is in the gasoline, it will settle to the bottom of the container. The corrective action is to drain the tank and refill it using a water-purging additive, which can be obtained at your local auto parts store.

False air—especially between the MAF sensor and throttle assembly, where applicable: Perform a careful visual inspection of the corrugated rubber tube connecting the MAF sensor to the throttle assembly.

Alternator output voltage lower than 9 volts or greater than 16 volts: Connect a voltmeter to the output terminal of the alternator, start the engine, and check the voltage at both idle and part throttle.

A bad ground on the ignition ground (IGN GND) wire of the ignition module: Visually inspect the IGN GND wire for both tightness and lack of corrosion.

A prematurely opening or leaking EGR: Disconnect the vacuum hose from the EGR valve and plug it. Testdrive the car. If the symptom is gone, inspect the vacuum hose for proper routing. If the routing is correct, replace the EGR solenoid. If the problem persists, remove the EGR valve and inspect to see that it is sealing properly when no vacuum is applied.

A prematurely opening or leaking CANP valve: With a pair of self-clamping pliers, clamp off the CANP hose and testdrive the car. If the symptom is relieved, replace the CANP solenoid.

Symptom: Engine Cuts Out and Misses at Idle or at Low Engine Speeds

The engine's cutting out and missing at idle or at low engine speeds implies that one or two cylinders are not supplying the same amount of power as the rest. The offending cylinder can be isolated as described in chapter 4 or by using a pair of "sissy pliers" (nonconductive pliers designed for removing spark plug wires with the engine running) to locate the weak cylinder. The cylinder or cylinders that do not produce an rpm drop when the wire is removed are the offending parties.

After locating the bad cylinder, the following items must be checked:
Plug wires
Spark plugs
Compression
Fuel pressure
Injector wiring
Injector balance
Water contamination in the fuel
Valve action and timing

Plug Wire Testing

Basically, two tests are performed on the spark plug wires: the rainy day test and the resistance test. To perform the rainy day test, fill a spray bottle with water, start the engine, and allow it to warm up. Spray the plug wires with a fine water mist. When you spray a wire with leaking secondary insulation, the misfire will get worse.

For the resistance test, shut off the engine and then remove, test, and reinstall one plug wire at a time. Using an ohmmeter set on the 100,000-ohm-or-greater scale, check the resistance of each wire you remove. If any resistances are above 30,000 ohms, replace the appropriate wires.

Spark Plug Testing

Without a good ignition oscilloscope, the best way to test the spark plugs is to swap the plug on the weak cylinder with a plug from a good cylinder. If the bad cylinder moves, then the spark plug was at fault and should be replaced.

Compression Testing

Refer to chapter 4 for a thorough discussion of compression testing.

Fuel Pressure Testing

Test the fuel pressure as described in the "Symptom: Engine Dies or Stumbles on Tip-in Acceleration" section earlier in this chapter.

Refer to the "Fuel pressures" chart in the code 41 discussion in chapter 8 for the correct pressure for the car you are working on.

Injector Wiring Testing: MPFI and CFI Applications

Testing the injector wiring harness electronically can be difficult on some applications. A practical alternative is to use a mechanics stethoscope, touching each injector and listening for the distinctive click of its opening and closing. Should any of the injectors fail to click, exchange it with one of the good ones. If the nonclicking injector moves, you have a bad injector. If it does not move, then inspect and repair the bad wiring harness.

Injector Flow Testing

CFI Applications

Throttle body injection should be checked for a good spray pattern. A poor spray pattern can cause a weak cylinder in the same way a bad injector wiring harness can. Since the injector spray pattern on CFI application can be seen while the engine is running, connect a timing light to the engine and hold it so that it shines on the injector spray. Since the timing light and the injector or injectors are both synchronized to primary ignition, the spray will appear to stop in midair for close inspection. The spray should be cone shaped and spraying straight down from the center of the injector.

MPFI Applications

MPFI applications are a little tougher to deal with on the issue of injector flow testing. Back in the old Bosch D-Jetronic days, we used to raise the injectors above the intake, place each one of them in a graduated cylinder, and crank the engine for 30 seconds while watching for a cone-shaped pattern.

After cranking, we would inspect the fuel levels in each of the graduated cylinders to determine if an equal amount of fuel was passing through each injector. MPFI engine design does not facilitate this type of flow testing.

An alternative method of performing the injector flow test requires a special tool known as an EFI tester. This device costs between $100 and $300 and can be obtained through any of the "tool truck" dealers. It pulses the injector between one and five hundred times when activated.

Connect a fuel pressure gauge to the MPFI fuel rail. Connect the battery leads of the EFI tester to the battery and injector 1. Cycle the key once or twice to pressurize the fuel system to between 16psi and 19psi. If the pressure is too high, bleed it down to the proper range before testing the injector. Set the tester for one hundred pulses of 5 milliseconds and press the button. The pressure indicated on the fuel pressure gauge will drop. Record the amount of pressure loss.

Repeat this procedure with each injector, recording the pressure drops. Retest any injector that has a large variation from the others. Any injector that shows more than a 1.5psi difference in pressure drop, either higher or lower than the rest, is restricted, leaking, or not closing properly. Clean the injectors with one of the injector cleaning systems that are available (these systems cost about $100 and up) or simply replace the offending injector or injectors.

Water Contamination Testing

Use the procedure described in the "Symptom: Engine Dies or Stumbles on Tip-in Acceleration" section earlier in this chapter.

Valve Action Testing

The compression test checked for valves that did not seal properly. If you have not found the cause of the miss by now, it is time to remove the valve cover or covers and measure the pushrod lift. If the movement of the pushrods varies from one cylinder to another, then the camshaft and lifters need to be replaced. (Note that exhaust and intake valve may have different lifts, but all the intakes and all the exhausts should be the same.)

Symptom: Delayed or Extended Start

With a delayed or extended start, the engine cranks okay, and it eventually does start, but the cranking time is several seconds rather than the start-up being almost immediate. Possible causes are the following:

Improper driver's starting procedure
Sticking or binding TP sensor sending a high voltage to the ECA
High resistance in the coolant sensor circuit

Incorrect fuel pressure
Stuck-open EGR valve
Deteriorated secondary ignition
Drainage of fuel in the fuel rail back into the tank
through the pump check valve or through the
system pressure regulator
Leaking injectors

Starting Procedure

MPFI and low-pressure CFI systems are designed to start the engine with the foot off the accelerator. The exception to this is some of the V-6 and V-8 applications from the mid-1980s. These used a fast-idle cam controlled by a bimetal spring similar to the fast-idle arrangement on a carburetor. Pressing the accelerator once on these releases the fast-idle cam for an easy start. On all other applications, pressing the accelerator just a little while cranking the engine greatly increases the amount of fuel passing through the injectors. This could flood the engine. Pressing the accelerator even farther will put the ECA into the clear-flood mode. Clear-flood virtually shuts down the injectors and will make an engine that is not flooded difficult to start.

The correct starting procedure is to crank the engine with your foot off the gas pedal until the engine starts.

Throttle Position Sensor Testing

Check the TP output voltage (the dark green and light green wire). If the closed-throttle voltage is above 1 volt, either adjust or replace the TP sensor. *Note:* Some nonadjustable TP sensors (sensors with no adjustment slots) may be as high as 1.2 volts and be acceptable.

Coolant Sensor Testing

Back probe the yellow wire at the coolant temperature sensor. The voltage should be less than 4.8 volts but greater than 0.2 volt. If the starting problem is primarily a cold-start one, then use an ohmmeter to measure the resistance of the sensor with the engine cold. If the starting problem is primarily a hot-start one, then measure the coolant sensor resistance with the engine near operating temperature and compare your readings against those in the chart below:

Engine Coolant Temperature Sensor Voltage

Temperature (Degrees Fahrenheit)	Temperature (Degrees Celsius)	Voltage (Volts)	Resistance (Ohms)
248	120	0.27	1,180
230	110	0.35	1,550
212	100	0.46	2,070
194	90	0.6	2,800
176	80	0.78	3,840
158	70	1.02	5,370
140	60	1.33	7,700
122	50	1.7	10,970
104	40	2.13	16,150
86	30	2.6	24,270
68	20	3.07	37,300
50	10	3.51	58,750

Fuel Pressure Testing

Test the fuel pressure as described in the "Symptom: Engine Dies or Stumbles on Tip-in Acceleration" section earlier in this chapter.

Exhaust Gas Recirculation Testing

Remove and visually inspect the EGR valve to ensure that the pintle is seating properly.

Secondary Ignition Testing

Inspect the cap, rotor, spark plugs, plug wires, and coil wire as described in chapter 4 and in the "Symptom: Engine Cuts Out and Misses at Idle or at Low Engine Speeds" section earlier in this chapter.

Fuel Rail Drainage Testing

If fuel is not held in the fuel rail between operations of the vehicle, then it is necessary for the pump to fill and pressurize the fuel system before the car will start and run. The fuel can drain back into the tank through two components: the fuel pump check valve and the system pressure regulator.

Fuel Pump Check Valve

Connect a fuel pressure gauge. Start the engine and allow it to run for a few minutes. Shut the engine off, and monitor the residual pressure for 30 minutes or so. During this time, the residual pressure should drop very slowly and not reach 0. It is normal and acceptable for the pressure to drop to 0 in a matter of hours.

If the pressure drops, repressurize the fuel system and clamp off the outbound line from the tank. If the fuel pressure remains up, replace the fuel pump; it has a bad check valve.

System Pressure Regulator

If the pressure drops when the outbound line from the fuel tank is clamped off, repressurize the system and clamp off the return line to the tank. If the pressure does not drop now, replace the pressure regulator. If the pressure continues to drop, test the injectors for leakage.

Injector Leakage Testing

If clamping off the outbound and return lines from the gas tank did not stop a loss of fuel pressure, the only place the fuel could be leaking is through the injectors and into the intake manifold. Remove the fuel rail assembly from the intake manifold and reconnect it to the fuel lines so that the injectors are visible and the fuel rail can still be pressurized by the fuel pump. Pressurize the fuel rail and observe the tips of the injectors. Any injector that forms a drop of fuel heavy enough to fall off and then begins to form another one can be considered leaking.

If a leaking injector is found—including the cold-start injector on applications having one—using an injector cleaning system may help, or you might simply replace the bad injector.

Symptom: Lack of Power

If the car does not have the expected or usual amount of power, check for the following:

Dirty air filter
Restricted fuel filter
Contaminated fuel
Low fuel pressure
ECA grounds
EGR failure to close
Restricted exhaust
Incorrectly adjusted throttle linkage
Alternator voltage lower than 9 volts or higher than 16 volts
Low compression
Incorrect valve timing
Worn camshaft
Problems in the secondary ignition

All of these possible causes of the symptom have been discussed earlier in this chapter in sections concerning other symptoms, except for dirty air filter, ECA grounds, restricted exhaust, and incorrectly adjusted throttle linkage.

Air Filter Testing

The test for a dirty air filter is probably the easiest of all diagnostic tasks. Remove the air filter from the air cleaner and inspect it. If the air filter is dirty, replace it. If in doubt, replace it.

Electronic Control Assembly Grounds Inspection

The ECA is grounded to the engine block. A bad connection at the ground can cause any number of different drivability symptoms, including a lack of power. Inspect all ground connections on the engine block. On some applications, these grounds are well hidden and pose a real challenge to finding and inspecting. Also check the ground cable from the battery to the engine.

Exhaust Testing

A restricted exhaust can reduce the engine's ability to breathe as much as a dirty air filter can. The only effective way to test for excessive exhaust back pressure is with a back pressure gauge. This can be purchased through automotive tool dealers. It can also be made by taking your EGO sensor down to the local hardware store and purchasing whatever pipe fittings are necessary to adapt a carburetor-style fuel pressure gauge to the hole where the EGO sensor installs.

Install the exhaust back pressure gauge into the EGO sensor hole. Start the engine and allow it to idle. With the engine at normal operating temperature, the gauge reading should not exceed 1.25psi.

Now raise the engine rpm to over 2000, hold it there, and observe the gauge. If the reading is over 3psi, the exhaust has excessive back pressure.

Often, even among knowledgeable, professional mechanics, the most common component to condemn for excessive back pressure is the catalytic converter. Although this is a likely suspect, it is by no means the only component to be at fault. Also inspect the mufflers and exhaust pipes. Remember, many of the exhaust components, including the catalytic converter, carry a five-year, fifty thousand-mile warranty—and even more in some jurisdictions.

Throttle Linkage Testing

Remove whatever is necessary to view the throttle plates in the throttle assembly. Have someone fully depress the throttle while you inspect to see that the throttle plates fully open. If they do not, adjust the throttle linkage as necessary. Also look for any obstruction to the full movement of the throttle, such as the carpet or floor mat being bunched up under the accelerator pedal.

Symptom: Hunting Idle

A hunting idle is distinguished from a miss in that the idle speed varies in slow surges over a wide rpm range. Possible causes of this symptom include the following:

Bad motor mounts
Sticking or binding throttle linkage
Sticking or binding TP sensor
Incorrect or fluctuating alternator output voltage
Misadjusted or defective park-neutral switch (also known as neutral safety switch) circuit
Defective or incorrect PCV valve
Vacuum leak
Defective or erratic evaporative control system
Erratic PSPS input
An ECA ground
EGR valve failure to seat properly
Inconsistent fuel pressure
Uneven compression
Problems with the air conditioner (if the problem only occurs with the air conditioner on)
Erratic idle air control system

Only the diagnostic methods not discussed under other symptoms earlier in this chapter are discussed in this section.

Motor Mount Testing

If the motor mounts are broken, this will allow the engine to move as it runs. This movement could put stress on the throttle cable or linkage, pulling the throttle open and closed. Checking the motor mounts is done by prying on them with a large pry bar. If you are able to unseat the engine off of its mounts as you do this, the mounts are bad and should be replaced.

Park-Neutral Switch Circuit Testing

Back probe the pin 30 wire at the neutral safety switch, which is usually located near the base of the steering column where it goes through the firewall. In park or neutral, this wire should carry 0 volts. In all other gears, it should carry 12 volts.

If the voltage fluctuates as the engine surges, adjust the park-neutral switch. If adjustment does not eliminate the voltage fluctuation, replace the switch.

If 0 volts is measured both in park or neutral and in other gears, disconnect the park-neutral connector and test for 12 volts on the pin 30 wire. If 12 volts is measured, replace the park-neutral switch.

Should the voltage on the pin 30 wire be 0 when the park-neutral connector is disconnected, then trace the wire back to the ECA. You should find 12 volts on pin 30 at the ECA with the park-neutral connector disconnected. If you find 12 volts at the ECA, repair the open circuit in the pin 30 wire. If you do not find 12 volts at the ECA, inspect the wire for a grounded condition.

If the pin 30 wire is not grounded, then the ECA is defective.

Note: Before replacing the ECA, always double- and triple-check your test results. Also, your local dealer may be able to replace the ECA at little or no charge under an emission warranty. Check with the service manager before purchasing a new ECA.

Positive Crankcase Ventilation Valve Testing

With the engine idling, remove the PCV valve from its normal position in the valve cover or intake manifold. Leave the PCV valve connected to its vacuum hose. Place your thumb over the end of the valve; if the surging idle ceases, replace the PCV valve.

Power Steering Pressure Switch Testing

Back probe the pin 24 wire at the Power Steering Pressure Switch (PSPS) with a voltmeter. It should carry 12 volts with the engine idling and no load on the power steering system. If the voltage fluctuates between 12 and 0 volts as the idle surges, check the power steering fluid level. If the level is correct, replace the PSPS. If the new PSPS behaves the same way, replace the power steering pump.

Turn the steering wheel to full lock either direction. The voltage should drop to 0 volts and remain there without fluctuating as long as the steering is held at full lock.

If the pin 24 wire has 0 volts on it with no load on the steering, remove the connector from the PSPS. If the voltage goes to 12 volts, replace the PSPS. If the new PSPS behaves the same way, then replace the power steering pump.

If the pin 24 wire has 0 volts on it when removed from the PSPS, then trace the wire back to the PSPS. At the ECA, if the wire has 12 volts, repair the open circuit in the pin 24 wire.

If the wire has 0 volts at the ECA with the PSPS harness disconnected, then inspect the pin 24 wire for a ground. If the wire is not grounded, replace the ECA.

Although the ECA can be at fault for drivability problems, it almost never is. Before replacing the ECA, double-check your test results and all the other possibilities for causes of the problem.

Symptom: Surge at Cruise Speeds

A surge at cruise speeds involves variations in engine power and load even when the throttle is held in a steady position. Possible causes are as follows:
Normal operation of the automatic transmission converter clutch or the ACC
Vacuum leak
Restricted fuel filter or lines
Erratic fuel pressure
Secondary ignition
All of these topics are covered earlier in this chapter.

Symptom: Dieseling or Running-On

Dieseling or running-on is when the engine continues to run or chug even after the ignition switch has been shut off. Only one thing can cause this to happen: fuel getting into the intake system from somewhere. Sources of this fuel are listed below:
Leaking injectors
Defective CANP system
Severe contamination of the crankcase with fuel
Leakage of the fuel pressure regulator into the vacuum hose
The first problem is covered earlier in this chapter.

Canister Purge System Testing

If the CANP valve is allowing fuel vapors to leak into the intake manifold as the engine is shut off, it will supply the fuel necessary to cause the engine to diesel. Crimp the CANP hose (the largest one running from the CANP valve to the intake manifold), and then run and shut off the engine several times. If the dieseling is gone, replace the CANP valve.

Crankcase Contamination Testing

If the crankcase is severely contaminated with fuel vapors, these vapors can get into the intake as the engine is shut off and cause the engine to diesel.

Remove the PCV valve from the valve cover or intake manifold, and then run and shut off the engine several times. If the dieseling is gone, change the oil.

Fuel Pressure Regulator Leakage Testing

On rare occasions, the diaphragm in the fuel pressure regulator will get a slight tear, allowing fuel to be sucked into the intake manifold. This of course applies only to the systems that raise fuel pressure as the intake manifold pressure increases (MPFI systems).

The required repair is the replacement of the fuel pressure regulator.

Symptom: Exhaust Odors

In some cases, owing to a wide range in the quality of fuel, exhaust odor is unavoidable. This is because all fossil fuels contain sulfur. The quantity of sulfur in each gallon of gasoline varies depending on where the fuel originated and where it was refined. The first thing that should be done to get rid of a rotten-egg smell is to try several different brands of gas. If the problem persists regardless of brand, then the problem is likely that the engine is running rich. Check for the following:
Fuel pressure problems
CANP system problems
Leaking injectors
Vacuum leak
Ruptured diaphragm in the fuel pressure regulator
Problems related to the codes 41 and 42, as
    discussed in Chapter 8.

Symptom: Backfire

A backfire occurs when fuel ignites in either the intake or the exhaust. Proper diagnosis requires a feel for whether the backfire occurred in the intake or the exhaust. Check for the following:
Secondary ignition
Vacuum leaks
Exhaust leaks
Valve timing problems
Air pump system problems
The first four items were covered earlier in this chapter.

Air Pump System Testing

Some of the cars that use an air pump system will be programmed to pump air into the exhaust manifold or catalytic converter under normal cruise conditions. The air will divert to the atmosphere on deceleration. Clamp off the hose that runs from the diverter valve to the pipe running down to the exhaust. Road test the car. If the backfire is gone, replace the diverter valve.

Symptom: Detonation, Knocking, or Pinging

If you were to take a couple of marbles, drop them in a coffee can, and give the can a good shake, then you would come close to simulating the sound of detonation. Generally speaking, this condition is caused by excessive heat in the combustion chamber. The possible problems are as follows:
Overheating engine
Failure of EGR valve to open
Inoperative detonation sensor system
Poor fuel quality

Engine Temperature Testing

Although the engine temperature gauge or warning light is designed to alert the driver if the engine is overheating, this system monitors only one point in the cooling system. Other places in the engine can be hotter than the one where the engine temperature warning sensor is located. A visual check of the following should eliminate the possibility of overheating being the cause of detonation:
Low coolant level
Restricted airflow through the radiator
Defective radiator electric cooling fan
Defective or loose belt on belt-driven cooling fan

Exhaust Gas Recirculation Valve Testing

The function of the EGR valve is to cool the combustion process to reduce the emissions of oxides of nitrogen. A by-product of this function is to reduce combustion temperatures so that detonation will not occur. If the EGR valve fails to open, the excess combustion temperatures will cause detonation.

Begin testing this system by ensuring that with the key on and the engine off, 12 volts is passing through both wires connected to the EGR control solenoid.

If 12 volts is passing through both wires, start the engine and ground the control wire. When you open the throttle, the EGR valve should also now open. The engine will die; either way, the EGR valve is working.

If the EGR valve fails to open, check for vacuum to and from the EGRC solenoid. If you find no vacuum into the control solenoid with the throttle cracked open, check for correct vacuum hose routing as shown on the vehicle's underhood decal. If you find vacuum in but no vacuum out, replace the EGRC solenoid.

If you find vacuum to the EGRC solenoid and to the EGR but the EGR valve does not open, replace the EGR valve.

Detonation Sensor System Testing

If the detonation sensor circuit is inoperative, the code 25 will be set during the KOER test. Follow the code 25 diagnostic routine described in chapter 8.

Fuel Quality Testing

Detonation can also result from poor fuel quality today, just as in the days of the big iron land rockets of the 1960s. This symptom might be eliminated by simply changing fuels.

Symptom: Poor Fuel Economy

If poor fuel economy is a concern, check for the following:
Poor tune-up condition
Air conditioner compressor failure to cycle off
Vacuum leaks
Poor engine condition
High fuel pressure
Restricted exhaust
Poor driving habits

Old Tech, New Tech

If many readers were working on a 1972 model Chevrolet, they would have no problem troubleshooting a drivability problem based on the symptom. Those of you who fit into this category may find this chart helpful in troubleshooting based on symptom. If a problem can be caused by an old tech component, there is a new tech equivalent that can cause the same symptom.

Old Tech	New Tech
Accelerator pump	TP sensor
	Rise in fuel pressure on acceleration
	MAP sensor
Choke	ECT sensor
	ACT sensor
Power valve	MAP sensor
Vacuum advance	MAP sensor
Thermal vacuum switches	ECT sensor
Mechanical advance	PIP signal to the ECA
Float level	Fuel pressure
Idle mixture screws	EGO sensor
Carburetor jet size	EGO sensor

ECA Pin Usage

1.9-Liter EFI

Pin Number	Color	Use	Abbreviation
1	Y	Keep-alive power	KAPWR
4	DG/Y	Ignition diagnostic monitor	IDM
7	LG/Y	Engine coolant temperature sensor	ECT
8	PK/BK	Fuel pump monitor	FPM
10	BK/Y	Air conditioner compressor clutch	ACC
16	BK/O	Ignition ground	IGN GND

The best place to test for proper readings from the sensors is at the 60-pin connector of the ECA. Unfortunately, most applications place the ECA terminal in a location that is almost impossible to find.

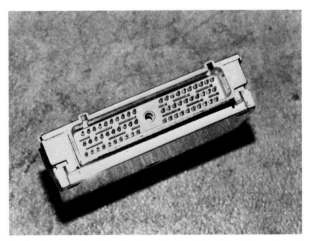

By testing at the 60-pin terminal, all parts of the circuit are tested except the connection between the 60-pin harness and the ECA.

To make testing the input signals to the ECA easier, Ford provides its dealers with a breakout box. This box connects in series between the 60-pin harness and the ECA. The model shown here is made by OTC and is available to the general public.

Pin Number	Color	Use	Abbreviation
17	T/LB	Self-test output and shift indicator	STO/SIL
20	BK	Case ground	CSE GND
21	O/BK	Idle speed control (bypass air)	ISC/BPA
22	T/LG	Fuel pump	FP
25	LG/P	Vane air temperature	VAT
26	O/W	Reference voltage	VREF
29	DG/P	Heated exhaust gas oxygen sensor	HEGO
30	GY/O	Neutral drive/ clutch engage switch	NDS/CES
32	GY/Y	Canister purge solenoid	CANP
35	Y	Exhaust gas recirculation shutoff	EGR S/O
36	Y/LG	Spark out (timing control)	SPOUT
37	R	Vehicle power	VPWR
40	BK/LG	Power ground	PWR GND
43	W/BK	Vane airflow	VAF
45	LG/BK	Barometric pressure	BP
46	BK/W	Signal return	SIG RTN
47	DG/LG	Throttle position sensor	TP
48	W/R	Self-test input	STI
49	O	Heated exhaust gas oxygen sensor	HEGO
53	T/R	Check-engine light	CEL
54	O/LB	Wide-open-throttle A/C cutoff	WAC
56	DB	Profile ignition pickup	PIP
57	R	Vehicle power	VPWR
58	T/R	Injector bank 1	INJ 1
59	T/O	Injector bank 2	INJ 2
60	BK/LG	Power ground	PWR GND

2.5-Liter CFI

Pin Number	Color	Use	Abbreviation
1	Y	Keep-alive power	KAPWR
2	R/LG	Brake on-off	BOO
3	DG/W	Vehicle speed sensor positive	VSS +
4	DG/Y	Ignition diagnostic monitor	IDM
5	R/LG	Key power	KPWR
6	O/Y	Vehicle speed sensor negative	VSS −
7	LG/Y	Engine coolant temperature sensor	ECT
8	PK/BK	Fuel pump monitor	FPM
10	PK/LB	A/C compressor clutch	ACC

Pin Number	Color	Use	Abbreviation
13	O/Y	Vehicle speed control solenoid positive	SOL +
16	BK/O	Ignition ground	IGN GND
17	T/R	Self-test output and "Check Engine"	STO/MIL
20	BK	Case ground	CSE GND
21	Y/BK	Idle speed control (bypass air)	ISC/BPA
22	T/LG	Fuel pump	FP
23	Y/LG	Power steering pressure switch	PSPS
24	W/R	Idle tracking switch	ITS
25	LG/P	Air charge temperature	ACT
26	O/W	Reference voltage	VREF
27	BR/LG	EGR valve position	EVP
29	DG/P	Heated exhaust gas oxygen sensor	HEGO
30	LB/Y	Neutral drive switch	NDS
31	GY/Y	Canister purge solenoid	CANP
33	DG	EGR vacuum regulator	EVR
34	LB/PK	Data output link	DOL
35	W/PK	Speed control vent	SCVNT
36	Y/LG	Spark out (timing control)	SPOUT
37	R	Vehicle power	VPWR
39	O	Speed control command switch ground	SCCS GND
40	BK/LG	Power ground	PWR GND
41	W	Idle speed control negative	ISC −
42	GY/BK	Speed control vacuum	SCVAC
45	LG/BK	Manifold absolute pressure	MAP
46	BK/W	Signal return	SIG RTN
47	DG/LG	Throttle position sensor	TP
48	W/BK	Self-test input	STI
49	O	Heated exhaust gas oxygen sensor ground	HEGOG
50	LB/BK	Speed control command switch	SCCS
52	PK	High electro-drive fan	HEDF
54	R	Wide-open-throttle A/C cutoff	WAC
55	T/O	Low electro-drive fan	EDF
56	DB	Profile ignition pickup	PIP
57	R	Vehicle power	VPWR
58	T/R	Injector	INJ 1
60	BK/LG	Power ground	PWR GND

2.5-Liter (Manual Transaxle) MTX CFI

Pin Number	Color	Use	Abbreviation
1	Y	Keep-alive power	KAPWR
2	R/LG	Brake on-off	BOO
3	DG/W	Vehicle speed sensor positive	VSS +
4	DG/Y	Ignition diagnostic monitor	IDM
5	R/LG	Key power	KPWR
6	O/Y	Vehicle speed sensor negative	VSS −
7	LG/Y	Engine coolant temperature sensor	ECT
8	PK/BK	Fuel pump monitor	FPM
10	PK/LB	A/C compressor clutch	ACC
13	O/Y	Vehicle speed control solenoid positive	SOL +
16	BK/O	Ignition ground	IGN GND
17	T/R	Self-test output and "Check Engine"	STO/MIL
20	BK	Case ground	CSE GND
21	Y/BK	Idle speed control (bypass air)	ISC/BPA
22	T/LG	Fuel pump	FP
23	Y/LG	Power steering pressure switch	PSPS
24	W/R	Idle tracking switch	ITS
25	LG/P	Air charge temperature	ACT
26	O/W	Reference voltage	VREF
27	BR/LG	EGR valve position	EVP
29	DG/P	Heated exhaust gas oxygen sensor	HEGO
30	P/Y	Clutch engage switch	CES
31	GY/Y	Canister purge solenoid	CANP
33	DG	EGR vacuum regulator	EVR
35	W/PK	Speed control vent	SCVNT
36	Y/LG	Spark out (timing control)	SPOUT
37	R	Vehicle power	VPWR
39	O	Speed control command switch ground	SCCS GND
40	BK/LG	Power ground	PWR GND
41	W	Idle speed control negative	ISC −
42	GY/BK	Speed control vacuum	SCVAC
45	LG/BK	Manifold absolute pressure	MAP
46	BK/W	Signal return	SIG RTN
47	DG/LG	Throttle position sensor	TP
48	W/BK	Self-test input	STI
49	O	Heated exhaust gas oxygen sensor ground	HEGOG
50	LB/BK	Speed control command switch	SCCS
53	P	Shift indicator light	SIL
54	R	Wide-open-throttle A/C cutoff	WAC
55	T/O	Electro-drive fan	EDF
56	DB	Profile ignition pickup	PIP
57	R	Vehicle power	VPWR
58	T/R	Injector	INJ 1
60	BK/LG	Power ground	PWR GND

3.0-Liter EFI

Pin Number	Color	Use	Abbreviation
1	Y	Keep-alive power	KAPWR
2	R/LG	Brake on-off	BOO
3	DG/W	Vehicle speed sensor positive	VSS +
4	DG/Y	Ignition diagnostic monitor	IDM
	R/LB	Ignition diagnostic monitor (Calif.)	
6	O/Y	Vehicle speed sensor negative	VSS −
7	LG/Y	Engine coolant temperature sensor	ECT
8	PK/BK	Fuel pump monitor	FPM
10	PK/LB	A/C compressor clutch	ACC
13	O/Y	Vehicle speed control solenoid positive	SOL +
16	BK/O	Ignition ground	IGN GND
17	T/R	Self-test output and "Check Engine"	STO/MIL
18	DG/P	Transmission 4–3 switch	THS 4–3
19	O/Y	Transmission 3–2 switch	THS 3–2
20	BK	Case ground	CSE GND
21	O/BK	Idle speed control (bypass air)	ISC/BPA
22	T/LG	Fuel pump	FP
23	Y/R	Knock sensor	KS
24	Y/G	Power steering pressure switch	PSPS
25	LG/P	Air charge temperature	ACT
26	O/W	Reference voltage	VREF
27	BR/LG	Pressure feedback EGR (Calif.)	PFE

Pin Number	Color	Use	Abbreviation
28	T/O	Data communication link positive (Calif.)	DATA +
29	DG/P	Heated exhaust gas oxygen sensor	HEGO
30	P/Y	Neutral pressure switch	NPS
31	GY/Y	Canister purge solenoid	CANP
33	DG	EGR vacuum regulator	EVR
34	LB/PK	Data output link	DOL
35	W/PK	Speed control vent	SCVNT
36	Y/LG	Spark out (timing control)	SPOUT
37	R	Vehicle power	VPWR
39	O	Speed control command switch ground	SCCS GND
40	BK/LG	Power ground	PWR GND
42	GY/BK	Speed control vacuum	SCVAC
45	LG/BK	Manifold absolute pressure	MAP
46	BK/W	Signal return	SIG RTN
47	DG/LG	Throttle position sensor	TP
48	W/BK	Self-test input	STI
49	O	Heated exhaust gas oxygen sensor ground	HEGOG
50	LB/BK	Speed control command switch	SCCS
52	PK	High electro-drive fan	HEDF
53	T/LB	Locking upshift solenoid (transmission)	LUS
54	R	Wide-open-throttle A/C cutoff	WAC
55	T/O	Electro-drive fan	EDF
56	DB	Profile ignition pickup	PIP
57	R	Vehicle power	VPWR
58	T/R	Injector bank 1	INJ 1
59	T/O	Injector bank 2	INJ 2
60	BK/LG	Power ground	PWR GND

3.0-Liter SHO SEFI

Pin Number	Color	Use	Abbreviation
1	Y	Keep-alive power	KAPWR
2	Y/LG	Power steering pressure switch	PSPS
3	DG/W	Vehicle speed sensor positive	VSS +
4	DG/Y	Ignition diagnostic monitor	IDM
5	R/LG	Brake on-off	BOO
6	O/Y	Vehicle speed sensor negative	VSS −
7	LG/Y	Engine coolant temperature sensor	ECT
9	T/LB	Mass airflow signal return	MAF RTN
10	PK/LB	A/C compressor clutch	ACC
11	O/Y	Vehicle speed control solenoid positive	SOL +
12	BR/Y	Injector 3	INJ 3
13	BR/LB	Injector 4	INJ 4
14	T/LB	Injector 5	INJ 5
15	LG	Injector 6	INJ 6
16	BK/O	Ignition ground	IGN GND
17	T/R	Self-test output and "Check Engine"	STO/MIL
18	PK	Octane adjust	OCT ADJ
19	PK/BK	Fuel pump monitor	FPM
20	BK	Case ground	CSE GND
21	O/BK	Idle speed control (bypass air)	ISC/BPA
22	T/LG	Fuel pump	FP
23	Y/R	Knock sensor	KS
24	DG	Cylinder identification sensor	CID
25	LG/P	Air charge temperature	ACT
26	O/W	Reference voltage	VREF
27	BR/LG	Pressure feedback EGR	PFE
28	LB/BK	Speed control command switch	SCCS
29	DG/P	Heated exhaust gas oxygen sensor	HEGO
30	P/Y	Clutch engage switch	CES
31	GY/Y	Canister purge solenoid	CANP
32	LG/P	Inlet air control solenoid	IAC
33	DG	EGR vacuum regulator	EVR
35	W/PK	Speed control vent	SCVNT
36	Y/LG	Spark out (timing control)	SPOUT
37	R	Vehicle power	VPWR
39	O	Speed control command switch ground	SCCS GND
40	BK/LG	Power ground	PWR GND
41	LB/O	High fuel pump relay	HFP

43	DB/LG	Heated exhaust gas oxygen 2	HEGO 2
45	LG/BK	Barometric pressure sensor	BP
46	BK/W	Signal return	SIG RTN
47	DG/LG	Throttle position sensor	TP
48	W/BK	Self-test input	STI
49	O	Heated exhaust gas oxygen sensor ground	HEGOG
50	DB/O	Mass airflow sensor	MAF
51	GY/BK	Speed control vacuum solenoid	SCVAC
54	R	Wide-open-throttle A/C cutoff	WAC
55	T/O	Electro-drive fan	EDF
56	DB	Profile ignition pickup	PIP
57	R	Vehicle power	VPWR
58	T	Injector 1	INJ 1
59	W	Injector 2	INJ 2
60	BK/LG	Power ground	PWR GND

3.8-Liter AXOD SEFI

Pin Number	Color	Use	Abbreviation
1	Y	Keep-alive power	KAPWR
2	Y/LG	Power steering pressure switch	PSPS
3	DG/W	Vehicle speed sensor positive	VSS +
4	DG/Y	Ignition diagnostic monitor	IDM
5	R/LG	Brake on-off	BOO
6	O/Y	Vehicle speed sensor negative	VSS −
7	LG/Y	Engine coolant temperature sensor	ECT
8	BK/LB	Data communication link negative	DATA −
9	GY/W	Transmission temperature switch	TTS
10	PK/LB	A/C compressor clutch	ACC
11	O/Y	Vehicle speed control solenoid positive	SOL +
12	BR/Y	Injector 3	INJ 3
13	BR/LB	Injector 4	INJ 4
14	T/LB	Injector 5	INJ 5
15	LG	Injector 6	INJ 6
16	BK/O	Ignition ground	IGN GND
17	T/R	Self-test output and "Check Engine"	STO/MIL
18	DG/P	Transmission 4/3 switch	THS 4-3
19	O/Y	Transmission 3/2 switch	THS 3-2
20	BK	Case ground	CSE GND
21	O/BK	Idle speed control (bypass air)	ISC/BPA
22	T/LG	Fuel pump	FP
25	LG/P	Air charge temperature	ACT
26	O/W	Reference voltage	VREF
27	BR/LG	Pressure feedback EGR	PFE
28	LB/BK	Speed control command switch	SCCS
29	DB/LG	Heated exhaust gas oxygen sensor 1	HEGO 1
30	P/Y	Neutral pressure switch	NPS
31	GY/Y	Canister purge solenoid	CANP
32	LG	Air suspension control (Lincoln only)	ACL
33	DG	EGR vacuum regulator	EVR
34	LB/PK	Data output link (except Lincoln)	DOL
35	W/PK	Speed control vent	SCVNT
36	Y/LG	Spark out (timing control)	SPOUT
37	R	Vehicle power	VPWR
39	O	Speed control command switch ground	SCCS GND
40	BK/LG	Power ground	PWR GND
41	PK	High electro-drive cooling fan	HEDF
43	DB/LG	Heated exhaust gas oxygen 2	HEGO 2
44	T/O	Data communication link positive	DATA +
	O/BK	Data communication link positive (Lincoln only)	
45	LG/BK	Manifold absolute pressure	MAP
46	BK/W	Signal return	SIG RTN
47	DG/LG	Throttle position sensor	TP
48	W/BK	Self-test input	STI
49	O	Heated exhaust gas oxygen sensor ground	HEGOG
50	PK/BK	Fuel pump monitor	FPM
51	GY/BK	Speed control vacuum solenoid	SCVAC

Pin Number	Color	Use	Abbreviation
53	T/LB	Locking upshift solenoid (transmission)	LUS
54	R	Wide-open-throttle A/C cutoff	WAC
55	T/O	Electro-drive fan	EDF
56	DB	Profile ignition pickup	PIP
57	R	Vehicle power	VPWR
58	T	Injector 1	INJ 1
59	W	Injector 2	INJ 2
60	BK/LG	Power ground	PWR GND

3.8-Liter RWD SEFI

Pin Number	Color	Use	Abbreviation
1	Y	Keep-alive power	KAPWR
3	DG/W	Vehicle speed sensor positive	VSS +
4	DG/Y	Ignition diagnostic monitor	IDM
5	LG	Brake on-off	BOO
6	BK/W	Vehicle speed sensor negative	VSS −
7	LG/Y	Engine coolant temperature sensor	ECT
8	O/BK	Data communication link negative	DATA −
10	PK/LB	A/C compressor clutch	ACC
11	O/Y	Vehicle speed control solenoid positive	SOL +
12	BR/Y	Injector 3	INJ 3
13	BR/LB	Injector 4	INJ 4
14	T/LB	Injector 5	INJ 5
15	LG	Injector 6	INJ 6
16	BK/O	Ignition ground	IGN GND
17	Y/BK	Self-test output and "Check Engine"	STO/MIL
20	BK	Case ground	CSE GND
21	R/LG	Idle speed control (bypass air)	ISC/BPA
22	T/LG	Fuel pump	FP
25	LG/P	Air charge temperature	ACT
26	O/W	Reference voltage	VREF
27	BR/LG	Pressure feedback EGR	PFE
28	LB/BK	Speed control command switch	SCCS
29	T/O	Heated exhaust gas oxygen sensor R	HEGO R
30	R/LB	Neutral drive switch	NDS
31	GY/Y	Canister purge solenoid	CANP
33	DG	EGR vacuum regulator	EVR
34	LB/PK	Data output link	DOL
35	W/PK	Speed control vent	SCVNT
36	Y/LG	Spark out (timing control)	SPOUT
37	R	Vehicle power	VPWR
39	O	Speed control command switch ground	SCGND
40	BK/LG	Power ground	PWR GND
43	T/R	Heated exhaust gas oxygen L	HEGO L
44	O/BK	Data communication link positive	DATA +
45	DB/LG	Manifold absolute pressure	MAP
46	BK/W	Signal return	SIG RTN
47	DG/LG	Throttle position sensor	TP
48	W/R	Self-test input	STI
49	O	Heated exhaust gas oxygen sensor ground	HEGOG
50	PK/BK	Fuel pump monitor	FPM
51	GY/BK	Speed control vacuum solenoid	SCVAC
54	O/LB	Wide-open-throttle A/C cutoff	WAC
56	DB	Profile ignition pickup	PIP
57	R	Vehicle power	VPWR
58	T	Injector 1	INJ 1
59	W	Injector 2	INJ 2
60	BK/LG	Power ground	PWR GND

3.8-Liter SC SEFI

Pin Number	Color	Use	Abbreviation
1	Y	Keep-alive power	KAPWR
2	Y	A/C pressure cutoff switch	APCS
3	DG/W	Vehicle speed sensor positive	VSS +
4	DG/Y	Ignition diagnostic monitor	IDM
5	LG	Brake on-off	BOO
6	BK/W	Vehicle speed sensor negative	VSS −
7	LG/Y	Engine coolant temperature sensor	ECT
9	T/LB	Mass airflow signal return	MAFRTN
10	PK/LB	A/C compressor clutch	ACC

11	O/Y	Vehicle speed control solenoid positive	SOL+
12	BR/Y	Injector 3	INJ 3
13	BR/LB	Injector 4	INJ 4
14	T/LB	Injector 5	INJ 5
15	LG	Injector 6	INJ 6
16	LB	Ignition ground	IGN GND
17	Y/BK	Self-test output and "Check Engine"	STO/MIL
18	BK/W	Octane adjust	OCTADJ
19	PK/BK	Fuel pump monitor	FPM
20	BK	Case ground	CSE GND
21	R/LG	Idle speed control (bypass air)	ISC/BPA
22	T/LG	Fuel pump	FP
23	Y/R	Knock sensor	KS
24	DG	Cylinder identification sensor	CID
25	LG/P	Air charge temperature	ACT
26	O/W	Reference voltage	VREF
27	BR/LG	Pressure feedback EGR	PFE
28	LB/BK	Speed control command switch	SCCS
29	T/O	Heated exhaust gas oxygen sensor 1	HEGO 1
30	O/W	Neutral drive switch	NDS
31	GY/Y	Canister purge solenoid	CANP
32	O/W	Air suspension control	ACL
33	Y	EGR vacuum regulator	EVR
35	W/PK	Speed control vent	SCVNT
36	Y/LG	Spark out (timing control)	SPOUT
37	R	Vehicle power	VPWR
38	LG/P	Supercharger bypass solenoid	SBS
39	BK	Speed control command switch ground	SCGND
40	BK/LG	Power ground	PWR GND
41	PK	High electro-drive cooling fan	HEDF
43	T/R	Heated exhaust gas oxygen 2	HEGO 2
45	DB/LG	Barometric pressure sensor	BP
46	BK/W	Signal return	SIG RTN
47	DG/LG	Throttle position sensor	TP
48	W/R	Self-test input	STI
49	O	Heated exhaust gas oxygen sensor ground	HEGOG

50	DB/O	Mass airflow sensor	MAF
51	GY/BK	Speed control vacuum solenoid	SCVAC
53	P	Shift indicator light	SIL
54	R	Wide-open-throttle A/C cutoff	WAC
55	T/O	Electro-drive fan	EDF
56	DB	Profile ignition pickup	PIP
57	R	Vehicle power	VPWR
58	T	Injector 1	INJ 1
59	W	Injector 2	INJ 2
60	BK/LG	Power ground	PWR GND

5.0-Liter SEFI, All But Mark VII

Pin Number	Color	Use	Abbreviation
1	Y	Keep-alive power	KAPWR
2	LG	Brake on-off	BOO
3	DG/W	Vehicle speed sensor positive	VSS+
4	DG/Y	Ignition diagnostic monitor	IDM
6	BK/W	Vehicle speed sensor negative	VSS−
7	LG/Y	Engine coolant temperature sensor	ECT
10	PK/LB	A/C compressor clutch	ACCS
11	LG/BK	Air management solenoid 2	AM2
12	BR/Y	Injector 3	INJ 3
13	BR/LB	Injector 4	INJ 4
14	T/LB	Injector 5	INJ 5
15	LG	Injector 6	INJ 6
16	BK/O	Ignition ground	IGN GND
17	T/R	Self-test output and "Check Engine"	STO/MIL
20	BK	Case ground	CSE GND
21	W/LB	Idle speed control (bypass air)	ISC/BPA
22	T/LG	Fuel pump	FP
25	LG/P	Air charge temperature	ACT
26	O/W	Reference voltage	VREF
27	BR/LG	EGR valve position sensor	EVP
29	DG/P	Heated exhaust gas oxygen sensor R	HEGO R
30	R/LB	Neutral drive switch	NDS
31	GY/Y	Canister purge solenoid	CANP
33	DG	EGR vacuum regulator	EVR
34	LB/PK	Data output link	DOL
35	W/PK	Speed control vent	SCVNT
36	Y/LG	Spark out (timing control)	SPOUT

137

Pin Number	Color	Use	Abbreviation
37	R	Vehicle power	VPWR
38	LG	Speed control vacuum	SCVAC
39	GY/BK	Speed control command switch ground	SCGND
40	BK/LG	Power ground	PWR GND
41	O/Y	Vehicle speed control solenoid positive	SOL+
42	T/O	Injector 7	INJ 7
43	DL/LG	Heated exhaust gas oxygen L	HEGO L
45	LG/BK	Manifold absolute pressure	MAP
46	BK/W	Signal return	SIG RTN
47	DG/LG	Throttle position sensor	TP
48	W/BK	Self-test input	STI
49	O	Heated exhaust gas oxygen sensor ground	HEGOG
50	LB/BK	Fuel pump monitor	FPM
51	W/R	Air management 1	AM1
52	LB	Injector 8	INJ 8
54	O/LB	Wide-open-throttle A/C cutoff	WAC
56	DB	Profile ignition pickup	PIP
57	R	Vehicle power	VPWR
58	T	Injector 1	INJ 1
59	W	Injector 2	INJ 2
60	BK/LG	Power ground	PWR GND

5.0-Liter SEFI Lincoln Mark VII

Pin Number	Color	Use	Abbreviation
1	BK/O	Keep-alive power	KAPWR
2	LG	Brake on-off	BOO
3	DG/W	Vehicle speed sensor positive	VSS+
4	DG/Y	Ignition diagnostic monitor	IDM
6	P/LB	Vehicle speed sensor negative	VSS−
7	LG/Y	Engine coolant temperature sensor	ECT
10	LG/P	A/C compressor clutch	ACCS
11	LG/BK	Air management solenoid 2	AM2
12	BR/Y	Injector 3	INJ 3
13	BR/LB	Injector 4	INJ 4
14	T/LB	Injector 5	INJ 5
15	LG	Injector 6	INJ 6
16	BK/O	Ignition ground	IGN GND
17	Y/BK	Self-test output and "Check Engine"	STO/MIL
20	BK	Case ground	CSE GND
21	W/LB	Idle speed control (bypass air)	ISC/BPA
22	T/LG	Fuel pump	FP
25	LG/P	Air charge temperature	ACT
26	O/W	Reference voltage	VREF
27	BR/LG	EGR valve position sensor	EVP
29	DG/P	Heated exhaust gas oxygen sensor R	HEGO R
30	R/LB	Neutral drive switch	NDS
31	GY/Y	Canister purge solenoid	CANP
33	DG	EGR vacuum regulator	EVR
34	LB/PK	Data output link	DOL
35	W/PK	Speed control vent	SCVNT
36	Y/LG	Spark out (timing control)	SPOUT
37	R	Vehicle power	VPWR
38	GY/BK	Speed control vacuum	SCVAC
39	GY/BK	Speed control command switch ground	SCGND
40	BK/LG	Power ground	PWR GND
41	O/Y	Vehicle speed control solenoid positive	SOL+
42	T/O	Injector 7	INJ 7
43	DL/LG	Heated exhaust gas oxygen L	HEGO L
45	DB/LG	Manifold absolute pressure	MAP
46	BK/W	Signal return	SIG RTN
47	DG/LG	Throttle position sensor	TP
48	W/R	Self-test input	STI
49	O	Heated exhaust gas oxygen sensor ground	HEGOG
50	LB/BK	Fuel pump monitor	FPM
51	W/R	Air management solenoid 1	AM1
52	LB	Injector 8	INJ 8
54	O/LB	Wide-open-throttle A/C cutoff	WAC
56	DB	Profile ignition pickup	PIP
57	R	Vehicle power	VPWR
58	T	Injector 1	INJ 1
59	W	Injector 2	INJ 2
60	BK/LG	Power ground	PWR GND

5.0-Liter MA SEFI

Pin Number	Color	Use	Abbreviation
1	BK/O	Keep-alive power	KAPWR
3	DG/W	Vehicle speed sensor positive	VSS +
4	DG/Y	Ignition diagnostic monitor	IDM
6	O/Y	Vehicle speed sensor negative	VSS −
7	LG/Y	Engine coolant temperature sensor	ECT
9	T/LB	Mass airflow signal return	MAFRTN
10	PK/LB	A/C compressor clutch	ACC
12	BR/Y	Injector 3	INJ 3
13	BR/LB	Injector 4	INJ 4
14	T/LB	Injector 5	INJ 5
15	LG	Injector 6	INJ 6
16	BK/O	Ignition ground	IGN GND
17	T	Self-test output and shift indicator light	STO/SIL
19	PK/BK	Fuel pump monitor	FPM
20	BK	Case ground	CSE GND
21	R/LB	Idle speed control (bypass air)	ISC/BPA
22	T/LG	Fuel pump	FP
25	LG/P	Air charge temperature	ACT
26	O/W	Reference voltage	VREF
27	BR/LG	Pressure feedback EGR	PFE
29	DG/P	Heated exhaust gas oxygen sensor R	HEGO R
30	W/PK	Neutral drive switch (automatic)	NDS
	LB/Y	Neutral gear switch (manual)	NGS
31	GY/Y	Canister purge solenoid	CANP
32	LG/BK	Air management solenoid 2	AM2
33	DG	EGR vacuum regulator	EVR
36	Y/LG	Spark out (timing control)	SPOUT
37	R	Vehicle power	VPWR
38	W/R	Air management solenoid 1	AM1
40	BK/W	Power ground	PWR GND
42	T/O	Fuel injector 7	INJ 7
43	DB/LG	Heated exhaust gas oxygen L	HEGO L
45	LG/BK	Barometric pressure sensor	BP
46	BK/W	Signal return	SIG RTN
47	DG/LG	Throttle position sensor	TP
48	T/R	Self-test input	STI
49	O	Heated exhaust gas oxygen sensor ground	HEGOG
50	DB/O	Mass airflow sensor	MAF
52	L/B	Fuel injector 8	INJ 8
54	O/LB	Wide-open-throttle A/C cutoff	WAC
56	DB	Profile ignition pickup	PIP
57	R	Vehicle power	VPWR
58	T	Injector 1	INJ 1
59	W	Injector 2	INJ 2
60	BK/LG	Power ground	PWR GND

2.3-Liter EFI

Pin Number	Color	Use	Abbreviation
1	Y/BK	Keep-alive power	KAPWR
2	LG	Brake on-off	BOO
3	DG/W	Vehicle speed sensor positive	VSS +
4	LG/P	Ignition diagnostic monitor	IDM
6	BK/W	Vehicle speed sensor negative	VSS −
7	LG/Y	Engine coolant temperature sensor	ECT
8	O/LB	Fuel pump monitor	FPM
10	T/Y	A/C compressor clutch	ACC
16	BK/O	Ignition ground	IGN GND
17	T/R	Self-test output and "Check Engine"	STO/MIL
18	W/R	Octane adjust switch	OCT ADJ
20	BK	Case ground	CSE GND
21	GY/W	Idle speed control (bypass air)	ISC/BPA
22	T/LG	Fuel pump	FP
24	DG/W	Power steering pressure switch	PSPS
25	Y/R	Air charge temperature	ACT
26	O/W	Reference voltage	VREF
27	BR/LG	EGR valve position sensor	EVP
29	DG/P	Heated exhaust gas oxygen sensor	HEGO
30	GY/O	Neutral drive switch (automatic)	NDS
	W/BK	Neutral gear switch, clutch engage switch	NGS CES
32	GY/O	Dual-plug inhibit	DPI

Pin Number	Color	Use	Abbreviation
33	DG	EGR vacuum regulator	EVR
36	Y/LG	Spark out (timing control)	SPOUT
37	R	Vehicle power	VPWR
40	BK/LG	Power ground	PWR GND
43	LG/P	A/C demand	ACD
45	DB/LG	Manifold absolute pressure	MAP
46	BK/W	Signal return	SIG RTN
47	DG/LG	Throttle position sensor	TP
48	W/R	Self-test input	STI
49	O	Heated exhaust gas oxygen sensor ground	HEGOG
52	T/LB	Shift solenoid 3/4	SS 3/4
53	W	Converter clutch override	CCO
	W	Case ground (manual only)	CSE GND
54	R	Wide-open-throttle air conditioner cutoff	WAC
56	DB	Profile ignition pickup	PIP
57	R	Vehicle power	VPWR
58	LG/W	Injector bank 1	INJ 1
59	T/R	Injector bank 2	INJ 2
60	BK/LG	Power ground	PWR GND

2.9-Liter EFI

Pin Number	Color	Use	Abbreviation
1	Y/BK	Keep-alive power	KAPWR
2	LG	Brake on-off	BOO
3	DG/W	Vehicle speed sensor positive	VSS +
4	DG/Y	Ignition diagnostic monitor	IDM
6	BK/W	Vehicle speed sensor negative	VSS −
7	LG/Y	Engine coolant temperature sensor	ECT
8	O/LB	Fuel pump monitor	FPM
10	T/Y	A/C compressor clutch	ACC
16	BK/O	Ignition ground	IGN GND
17	T/R	Self-test output and "Check Engine"	STO/MIL
20	BK	Case ground	CSE GND
21	GY/W	Idle speed control (bypass air)	ISC/BPA
22	T/LG	Fuel pump	FP
25	LG/P	Air charge temperature	ACT
26	O/W	Reference voltage	VREF

Pin Number	Color	Use	Abbreviation
29	DG/P	Heated exhaust gas oxygen sensor	HEGO
30	W/BK	Neutral drive switch (automatic)	NDS
	W/BK	Neutral gear switch, clutch engage switch	NGS CES
36	Y/LG	Spark out (timing control)	SPOUT
37	R	Vehicle power	VPWR
40	BK/LG	Power ground	PWR GND
45	DB/LG	Manifold absolute pressure	MAP
46	BK/W	Signal return	SIG RTN
47	DG/LG	Throttle position sensor	TP
48	W/R	Self-test input	STI
49	O	Heated exhaust gas oxygen sensor ground	HEGOG
52	T/LB	Shift solenoid 3/4	SS 3/4
53	W	Converter clutch override	CCO
54	R	Wide-open-throttle A/C cutoff	WAC
56	DB	Profile ignition pickup	PIP
57	R	Vehicle power	VPWR
58	LG/W	Injector bank 1	INJ 1
59	T/R	Injector bank 2	INJ 2
60	BK/LG	Power ground	PWR GND

3.0-Liter EFI

Pin Number	Color	Use	Abbreviation
1	Y	Keep-alive power	KAPWR
2	R/LG	Brake on-off	BOO
3	DG/W	Vehicle speed sensor positive	VSS +
4	DG/Y	Ignition diagnostic monitor	IDM
6	BK/Y	Vehicle speed sensor negative	VSS −
7	LG/Y	Engine coolant temperature sensor	ECT
8	O/LB	Fuel pump monitor	FPM
10	BK/Y	A/C compressor clutch	ACC
16	BK/O	Ignition ground	IGN GND
17	T/R	Self-test output and "Check Engine"	STO/MIL
20	BK	Case ground	CSE GND
21	O/BK	Idle speed control (bypass air)	ISC/BPA
22	T/LG	Fuel pump	FP
25	LG/P	Air charge temperature	ACT

26	O/W	Reference voltage	VREF
29	DG/P	Heated exhaust gas oxygen sensor	HEGO
30	LB/BK	Neutral drive switch (automatic)	NDS
	W/BK	Neutral gear switch, clutch engage switch	NGS CES
31	GY/Y	Canister purge solenoid	CANP
34	LB/PK	Data output link	DOL
36	Y/LG	Spark out (timing control)	SPOUT
37	R	Vehicle power	VPWR
40	BK/LG	Power ground	PWR GND
45	DB/LG	Manifold absolute pressure	MAP
46	BK/W	Signal return	SIG RTN
47	DG/LG	Throttle position sensor	TP
48	W/R	Self-test input	STI
49	O	Heated exhaust gas oxygen sensor ground	HEGOG
52	T/LB	Shift solenoid 3/4	SS 3/4
53	W	Converter clutch override	CCO
54	R	Wide-open-throttle A/C cutoff	WAC
56	DB	Profile ignition pickup	PIP
57	R	Vehicle power	VPWR
58	T/O	Injector bank 1	INJ 1
59	T/R	Injector bank 2	INJ 2
60	BK/LG	Power ground	PWR GND

4.9-Liter F-Series and Bronco

Pin Number	Color	Use	Abbreviation
1	Y	Keep-alive power	KAPWR
3	DG/W	Vehicle speed sensor positive	VSS +
4	DG/Y	Ignition diagnostic monitor	IDM
6	BK	Vehicle speed sensor negative	VSS −
7	LG/Y	Engine coolant temperature sensor	ECT
8	BR	Fuel pump monitor	FPM
10	BK/Y	A/C compressor clutch	ACC
16	BK/O	Ignition ground	IGN GND
17	PK/LG	Self-test output and "Check Engine"	STO/MIL
20	BK	Case ground	CSE GND
21	GY/W	Idle speed control (bypass air)	ISC/BPA
22	T/LG	Fuel pump	FP

25	Y/R	Air charge temperature	ACT
26	O/W	Reference voltage	VREF
27	BR/LG	EGR valve position sensor	EVP
29	DG/P	Heated exhaust gas oxygen sensor	HEGO
30	GY/Y	Neutral drive switch (automatic)	NDS
33	DG	EGR vacuum regulator solenoid	EVR
36	Y/LG	Spark out (timing control)	SPOUT
37	R	Vehicle power	VPWR
40	BK/LG	Power ground	PWR GND
43	LG/P	Air conditioner demand	ACD
45	DB/LG	Manifold absolute pressure	MAP
46	BK/W	Signal return	SIG RTN
47	DG/LG	Throttle position sensor	TP
48	W/R	Self-test input	STI
49	O	Heated exhaust gas oxygen sensor ground	HEGOG
51	W/R	Air management solenoid 1	AM1
56	DB	Profile ignition pickup	PIP
57	R	Vehicle power	VPWR
58	T/O	Injector bank 1	INJ 1
59	T/R	Injector bank 2	INJ 2
60	BK/LG	Power ground	PWR GND

4.9-Liter E-Series

Pin Number	Color	Use	Abbreviation
1	BK/O	Keep-alive power	KAPWR
3	DG/W	Vehicle speed sensor positive	VSS +
4	DG/Y	Ignition diagnostic monitor	IDM
6	O/Y	Vehicle speed sensor negative	VSS −
7	LG/Y	Engine coolant temperature sensor	ECT
8	OL/B	Fuel pump monitor	FPM
10	BK/Y	A/C compressor clutch	ACC
11	W/BK	Air management solenoid 2	AM2
16	BK/O	Ignition ground	IGN GND
17	T/R	Self-test output and "Check Engine"	STO/MIL
20	BK	Case ground	CSE GND

Pin Number	Color	Use	Abbreviation
21	GY/W	Idle speed control (bypass air)	ISC/BPA
22	T/LG	Fuel pump	FP
23	LG/BK	Knock sensor	KS
25	Y/R	Air charge temperature	ACT
26	O/W	Reference voltage	VREF
27	BR/LG	EGR valve position sensor	EVP
29	DG/P	Heated exhaust gas oxygen sensor	HEGO
30	LB/W	Neutral drive switch (automatic)	NDS
	LB/Y	Clutch engage switch (manual)	CES
33	DG	EGR vacuum regulator solenoid	EVR
36	Y/LG	Spark out (timing control)	SPOUT
37	R	Vehicle power	VPWR
40	BK/LG	Power ground	PWR GND
43	LG/P	A/C demand	ACD
45	DB/LG	Manifold absolute pressure	MAP
46	BK/W	Signal return	SIG RTN
47	DG/LG	Throttle position sensor	TP
48	W/R	Self-test input	STI
49	O	Heated exhaust gas oxygen sensor ground	HEGOG
51	W/R	Air management solenoid 1	AM1
56	DB	Profile ignition pickup	PIP
57	R	Vehicle power	VPWR
58	T/O	Injector bank 1	INJ 1
59	T/R	Injector bank 2	INJ 2
60	BK/LG	Power ground	PWR GND

Pin Number	Color	Use	Abbreviation
11	W/BK	Air management solenoid 2	AM2
16	BK/O	Ignition ground	IGN GND
17	PK/LG	Self-test output and "Check Engine"	STO/MIL
20	BK	Case ground	CSE GND
21	GY/W	Idle speed control (bypass air)	ISC/BPA
22	T/LG	Fuel pump	FP
25	Y/R	Air charge temperature	ACT
26	O/W	Reference voltage	VREF
27	BR/LG	EGR valve position sensor	EVP
29	DG/P	Heated exhaust gas oxygen sensor	HEGO
30	GY/Y	Neutral drive switch (automatic)	NDS
33	DG	EGR vacuum regulator solenoid	EVR
36	Y/LG	Spark out (timing control)	SPOUT
37	R	Vehicle power	VPWR
40	BK/LG	Power ground	PWR GND
45	DB/LG	Manifold absolute pressure	MAP
46	BK/W	Signal return	SIG RTN
47	DG/LG	Throttle position sensor	TP
48	W/R	Self-test input	STI
49	O	Heated exhaust gas oxygen sensor ground	HEGOG
51	W/R	Air management solenoid 1	AM1
56	DB	Profile ignition pickup	PIP
57	R	Vehicle power	VPWR
58	T/O	Injector bank 1	INJ 1
59	T/R	Injector bank 2	INJ 2
60	BK/LG	Power ground	PWR GND

5.0-Liter F-Series and Bronco

Pin Number	Color	Use	Abbreviation
1	Y	Keep-alive power	KAPWR
3	DG/W	Vehicle speed sensor positive	VSS +
4	DG/Y	Ignition diagnostic monitor	IDM
6	BK	Vehicle speed sensor negative	VSS −
7	LG/Y	Engine coolant temperature sensor	ECT
8	BR	Fuel pump monitor	FPM
10	BK/Y	A/C compressor clutch	ACC

5.0-Liter E-Series

Pin Number	Color	Use	Abbreviation
1	BK/O	Keep-alive power	KAPWR
3	DG/W	Vehicle speed sensor positive	VSS +
4	DG/Y	Ignition diagnostic monitor	IDM
6	O/Y	Vehicle speed sensor negative	VSS −
7	LG/Y	Engine coolant temperature sensor	ECT
8	O/LB	Fuel pump monitor	FPM
10	BK/Y	A/C compressor clutch	ACC

Pin Number	Color	Use	Abbreviation
11	W/BK	Air management solenoid 2	AM2
16	BK/O	Ignition ground	IGN GND
17	T/R	Self-test output and "Check Engine"	STO/MIL
20	BK	Case ground	CSE GND
21	GY/W	Idle speed control (bypass air)	ISC/BPA
22	T/LG	Fuel pump	FP
23	LG/BK	Knock sensor	KS
24	Y/LG	Power steering pressure switch	PSPS
25	Y/R	Air charge temperature	ACT
26	O/W	Reference voltage	VREF
27	BR/LG	EGR valve position sensor	EVP
29	DG/P	Heated exhaust gas oxygen sensor	HEGO
30	LB/W	Neutral drive switch (automatic)	NDS
33	DG	EGR vacuum regulator solenoid	EVR
36	Y/LG	Spark out (timing control)	SPOUT
37	R	Vehicle power	VPWR
40	BK/LG	Power ground	PWR GND
45	DB/LG	Manifold absolute pressure	MAP
46	BK/W	Signal return	SIG RTN
47	DG/LG	Throttle position sensor	TP
48	W/R	Self-test input	STI
49	O	Heated exhaust gas oxygen sensor ground	HEGOG
51	W/R	Air management solenoid 1	AM1
56	DB	Profile ignition pickup	PIP
57	R	Vehicle power	VPWR
58	T/O	Injector bank 1	INJ 1
59	T/R	Injector bank 2	INJ 2
60	BK/LG	Power ground	PWR GND

5.8-Liter EFI F-Series and Bronco

Pin Number	Color	Use	Abbreviation
1	Y	Keep-alive power	KAPWR
2	LG	Brake on-off	BOO
3	DG/W	Vehicle speed sensor positive	VSS +
4	DG/Y	Ignition diagnostic monitor	IDM
6	BK	Vehicle speed sensor negative	VSS −
7	LG/Y	Engine coolant temperature sensor	ECT
8	BR	Fuel pump monitor	FPM
10	BK/Y	A/C compressor clutch	ACC
11	W/BK	Air management solenoid 2	AM2
12	LB/BK	4x4 switch (E4OD only)	4x4L
16	BK/O	Ignition ground	IGN GND
17	PK/LG	Self-test output and "Check Engine"	STO/MIL
20	BK	Case ground	CSE GND
21	GY/W	Idle speed control (bypass air)	ISC/BPA
22	T/LG	Fuel pump	FP
25	Y/R	Air charge temperature	ACT
26	O/W	Reference voltage	VREF
27	BR/LG	EGR valve position sensor	EVP
29	DG/P	Heated exhaust gas oxygen sensor	HEGO
30	GY/Y	Neutral drive switch (automatic)	NDS
	LB/W	Neutral gear switch, clutch engage switch	NGS CES
31	GY/Y	Canister purge solenoid	CANP
32	LG/W	Overdrive cancel indicator light (E4OD)	OCIL
33	DG	EGR vacuum regulator	EVR
36	Y/LG	Spark out (timing control)	SPOUT
37	R	Vehicle power	VPWR
38	LB/Y	Electronic pressure control solenoid (E4OD)	EPC
40	BK/LG	Power ground	PWR GND
41	T/LB	Overdrive cancel switch (E4OD only)	OCS
42	O/BK	Transmission oil temperature sensor	TOT
45	DB/LG	Manifold absolute pressure	MAP
46	BK/W	Signal return	SIG RTN
47	DG/LG	Throttle position sensor	TP
48	W/R	Self-test input	STI
49	O	Heated exhaust gas oxygen sensor ground	HEGOG

Pin Number	Color	Use	Abbreviation
51	W/R	Air management solenoid 1	AM1
52	O/Y	Shift solenoid 3/4	SS 3/4
53	P/Y	Converter clutch override	CCO
56	DB	Profile ignition pickup	PIP
57	R	Vehicle power	VPWR
58	T/O	Injector bank 1	INJ 1
59	T/R	Injector bank 2	INJ 2
60	BK/LG	Power ground	PWR GND

5.8-Liter EFI E-Series

Pin Number	Color	Use	Abbreviation
1	Y	Keep-alive power	KAPWR
2	LG	Brake on-off	BOO
3	DG/W	Vehicle speed sensor positive	VSS +
4	DG/Y	Ignition diagnostic monitor	IDM
6	O/Y	Vehicle speed sensor negative	VSS −
7	LG/Y	Engine coolant temperature sensor	ECT
8	O/LB	Fuel pump monitor	FPM
10	BK/Y	A/C compressor clutch	ACC
11	W/BK	Air management solenoid 2	AM2
16	BK/O	Ignition ground	IGN GND
17	T/R	Self-test output and "Check Engine"	STO/MIL
20	BK	Case ground	CSE GND
21	GY/W	Idle speed control (bypass air)	ISC/BPA
22	T/LG	Fuel pump	FP
25	Y/R	Air charge temperature	ACT
26	O/W	Reference voltage	VREF
27	BR/LG	EGR valve position sensor	EVP
29	DG/P	Heated exhaust gas oxygen sensor	HEGO
30	BR/W	Neutral drive switch (automatic)	NDS
	LB/W	Neutral gear switch, clutch engage switch	NGS CES
31	GY/Y	Canister purge solenoid	CANP
32	LG/W	Overdrive cancel indicator light (E4OD)	OCIL
33	DG	EGR valve regulator	EVR

Pin Number	Color	Use	Abbreviation
36	Y/LG	Spark out (timing control)	SPOUT
37	R	Vehicle power	VPWR
38	LB/Y	Electronic pressure control solenoid (E4OD)	EPC
40	BK/LG	Power ground	PWR GND
41	T/LB	Overdrive cancel switch (E4OD only)	OCS
42	O/BK	Transmission oil temperature sensor	TOT
45	DB/LG	Manifold absolute pressure	MAP
46	BK/W	Signal return	SIG RTN
47	DG/LG	Throttle position sensor	TP
48	W/R	Self-test input	STI
49	O	Heated exhaust gas oxygen sensor ground	HEGOG
51	W/R	Air management solenoid 1	AM1
52	O/Y	Shift solenoid 3/4	SS 3/4
53	P/Y	Converter clutch control	CCC
55	BR	Coast clutch solenoid (E4OD)	CCS
56	DB	Profile ignition pickup	PIP
57	R	Vehicle power	VPWR
58	T/O	Injector bank 1	INJ 1
59	T/R	Injector bank 2	INJ 2
60	BK/LG	Power ground	PWR GND

7.5-Liter F-Series

Pin Number	Color	Use	Abbreviation
1	Y	Keep-alive power	KAPWR
2	LG	Brake on-off	BOO
3	DG/W	Vehicle speed sensor positive	VSS +
4	DG/Y	Ignition diagnostic monitor	IDM
6	BK	Vehicle speed sensor negative	VSS −
7	LG/Y	Engine coolant temperature sensor	ECT
8	BK	Fuel pump monitor	FPM
10	BK/Y	A/C compressor clutch	ACC
12	LB/BK	4x4 switch (E4OD only)	4x4L
16	BK/O	Ignition ground	IGN GND
17	PK/LG	Self-test output and shift indicator light	STO/SIL

Pin Number	Color	Use	Abbreviation
20	BK	Case ground	CSE GND
21	GY/W	Idle speed control (bypass air)	ISC/BPA
22	T/LG	Fuel pump	FP
25	Y/R	Air charge temperature	ACT
26	O/W	Reference voltage	VREF
27	BR/LG	EGR valve position sensor	EVP
29	DG/P	Heated exhaust gas oxygen sensor	HEGO
30	GY/Y	Neutral drive switch (automatic)	NDS
	LB/W	Neutral gear switch, clutch engage switch	NGS CES
31	GY/Y	Canister purge solenoid	CANP
32	LG/W	Overdrive cancel indicator light (E4OD)	OCIL
33	DG	EGR vacuum regulator	EVR
36	Y/LG	Spark out (timing control)	SPOUT
37	R	Vehicle power	VPWR
38	LB/Y	Electronic pressure control solenoid (E4OD)	EPC
40	BK/LG	Power ground	PWR GND
41	T/LB	Overdrive cancel switch (E4OD only)	OCS
42	O/BK	Transmission oil temperature sensor	TOT
45	DB/LG	Manifold absolute pressure	MAP
46	BK/W	Signal return	SIG RTN
47	DG/LG	Throttle position sensor	TP
48	W/R	Self-test input	STI
49	O	Heated exhaust gas oxygen sensor ground	HEGOG
51	W/R	Air management solenoid 1	AM1
52	O/Y	Shift solenoid 3/4	SS 3/4
53	P/Y	Converter clutch override	CCO
56	DB	Profile ignition pickup	PIP
57	R	Vehicle power	VPWR
58	T/O	Injector bank 1	INJ 1
59	T/R	Injector bank 2	INJ 2
60	BK/LG	Power ground	PWR GND

7.5-Liter E-Series, E4OD only

Pin Number	Color	Use	Abbreviation
1	BK/O	Keep-alive power	KAPWR
2	LG	Brake on-off	BOO
3	DG/W	Vehicle speed sensor positive	VSS +
4	DG/Y	Ignition diagnostic monitor	IDM
6	O/Y	Vehicle speed sensor negative	VSS –
7	LG/Y	Engine coolant temperature sensor	ECT
8	O/LB	Fuel pump monitor	FPM
10	BK/Y	A/C compressor clutch	ACC
16	BK/O	Ignition ground	IGN GND
17	T/R	Self-test output and "Check Engine"	STO/MIL
19	DG/P	Shift solenoid 2	SS2
20	BK	Case ground	CSE GND
21	GY/W	Idle speed control (bypass air)	ISC/BPA
22	T/LG	Fuel pump	FP
25	Y/R	Air charge temperature	ACT
26	O/W	Reference voltage	VREF
27	BR/LG	EGR valve position sensor	EVP
29	DG/P	Heated exhaust gas oxygen sensor	HEGO
30	LB/W	Manual lever position sensor	MLP
31	GY/Y	Canister purge solenoid	CANP
32	LG/W	Overdrive cancel indicator light (E4OD)	OCIL
33	DG	EGR valve regulator	EVR
36	Y/LG	Spark out (timing control)	SPOUT
37	R	Vehicle power	VPWR
38	LB/Y	Electronic pressure control solenoid (E4OD)	EPC
40	BK/LG	Power ground	PWR GND
41	T/LB	Overdrive cancel switch (E4OD only)	OCS
42	O/BK	Transmission oil temperature sensor	TOT
45	DB/LG	Manifold absolute pressure	MAP
46	BK/W	Signal return	SIG RTN
47	DG/LG	Throttle position sensor	TP

Pin Number	Color	Use	Abbreviation
48	W/R	Self-test input	STI
49	O	Heated exhaust gas oxygen sensor ground	HEGOG
51	W/R	Air management solenoid 1	AM1
52	O/Y	Shift solenoid 3/4	SS3/4
53	P/Y	Converter clutch control	CCC
55	BR	Coast clutch solenoid (E4OD)	CCS
56	DB	Profile ignition pickup	PIP
57	R	Vehicle power	VPWR
58	T/O	Injector bank 1	INJ 1
59	T/R	Injector bank 2	INJ 2
60	BK/LG	Power ground	PWR GND

2.5-Liter CLC CFI ICM

Pin Number	Color	Use	Abbreviation
1	BR/O	Electro-drive cooling fan power into controller	Batt +
2	BR/O	EDF power into controller	Batt +
3	BR/Y	High-speed electro-drive cooling fan power to fan	PTF
4	BR/Y	H/EDF power to fan	PTF
5	PK/BK	Power to pump	PTP
6	BK/O	HEDF power into controller	Batt +
7	BK/O	HEDF power into controller	Batt +
8	Y	Battery voltage	VBAT
12	BK/O	Power to wide-open-throttle air conditioner cutoff	PT/WAC
13	R/LG	Key power	KPWR
14	T/O	EDF circuit	EDF
15	BK/LG	Power ground	PWR GND
16	BK	A/C ground	A/C GND
17	PK	HEDF Circuit	HEDF
18	T/LG	Fuel pump circuit	FP
21	PK/LB	A/C Power	ACCS
22	R	Wide-open-throttle A/C cutoff	WAC
23	BK/Y	A/C power to clutch coil	PTAC
24	R	Vehicle power	VPWR

2.5-Liter MTX CFI

Pin Number	Color	Use	Abbreviation
1	BR/O	Electro-drive fan power into controller	Batt +
2	BR/O	EDF power into controller	Batt +
3	BR/Y	High-speed electro-drive fan power to fan	PTF
4	BR/Y	H/EDF power to fan	PTF
5	PK/BK	Power to pump	PTP
8	Y	Battery voltage	VBAT
12	BK/O	Power to wide-open-throttle air conditioner cutoff	PT/WAC
13	R/LG	Key power	KPWR
14	T/O	EDF circuit	EDF
15	BK/LG	Power ground	PWR GND
16	BK	A/C ground	A/C GND
18	T/LG	Fuel pump circuit	FP
21	PK/LB	A/C power	ACCS
22	R	Wide-open-throttle A/C cutoff	WAC
23	BK/Y	A/C power to clutch coil	PTAC
24	R	Vehicle power	VPWR

3.0-Liter EFI

Pin Number	Color	Use	Abbreviation
1	BR/O	EDF power into controller	Batt +
2	BR/O	EDF power into controller	Batt +
3	BR/Y	H/EDF power to fan	PTF
4	BR/Y	H/EDF power to fan	PTF
5	PK/BK	Power to pump	PTP
6	BK/O	HEDF power into controller	Batt +
7	BK/O	HEDF power into controller	Batt +
8	Y	Battery voltage	VBAT
12	BK/O	Power to wide-open-throttle air conditioner cutoff	PT/WAC
13	R/LG	Key power	KPWR
14	T/O	EDF circuit	EDF
15	BK/LG	Power ground	PWR GND
16	BK	A/C ground	A/C GND
17	PK	HEDF circuit	HEDF
18	T/LG	Fuel pump circuit	FP
21	PK/LB	A/C power	ACCS

22	R	WOT A/C cutoff	WAC
23	BK/Y	A/C power to clutch coil	PTAC
24	R	Vehicle power	VPWR

3.0-Liter SHO SEFI

Pin Number	Color	Use	Abbreviation
1	BR/O	EDF power into controller	Batt +
2	BR/O	EDF power into controller	Batt +
3	BR/Y	H/EDF power to fan	PTF
4	BR/Y	H/EDF power to fan	PTF
5	PK/BK	Power to pump	PTP
8	Y	Battery voltage	VBAT
11	LB/O	High fuel pump	H/FP
12	BK/O	Power to wide-open-throttle air conditioner cutoff	PT/WAC
13	R/LG	Key power	KPWR
14	T/O	EDF circuit	EDF
15	BK	Power ground	PWR GND
16	BK	A/C ground	A/C GND
18	T/LG	Fuel pump circuit	FP
21	PK/LB	A/C power	ACCS
22	R	WOT A/C cutoff	WAC
23	BK/Y	A/C power to clutch coil	PTAC
24	R	Vehicle power	VPWR

3.8-Liter AXOD SEFI

Pin Number	Color	Use	Abbreviation
1	BR/O	EDF power into controller	Batt +
2	BR/O	EDF power into controller	Batt +
3	BR/Y	H/EDF power to fan	PTF
4	BR/Y	H/EDF power to fan	PTF
5	PK/BK	Power to pump	PTP
6	BK/O	HEDF power into controller	Batt +
7	BK/O	HEDF power into controller	Batt +
8	Y	Battery voltage	VBAT
12	BK/O	Power to wide-open-throttle air conditioner cutoff	PT/WAC
13	R/LG	Key power	KPWR
14	T/O	EDF circuit	EDF
15	BK/LG	Power ground	PWR GND

16	BK	A/C ground	A/C GND
17	PK	HEDF circuit	HEDF
18	T/LG	Fuel pump circuit	FP
21	PK/LB	A/C power	ACCS
22	R	WOT A/C cutoff	WAC
23	BK/Y	A/C power to clutch coil	PTAC
24	R	Vehicle power	VPWR

3.8-Liter SC SEFI

Pin Number	Color	Use	Abbreviation
1	BR/O	EDF power into controller	Batt +
2	BR/O	EDF power into controller	Batt +
3	BR/Y	H/EDF power to fan	PTF
4	BR/Y	H/EDF power to fan	PTF
5	PK/BK	Power to pump	PTP
6	BK/O	HEDF power into controller	Batt +
7	BK/O	HEDF power into controller	Batt +
8	Y	Battery voltage	VBAT
12	BK/O	Power to wide-open-throttle air conditioner cutoff	PT/WAC
13	R/LG	Key power	KPWR
14	T/O	EDF circuit	EDF
15	BK/LG	Power ground	PWR GND
16	BK	A/C ground	A/C GND
17	PK	HEDF circuit	HEDF
21	PK/LB	A/C power	ACCS
22	R	WOT A/C cutoff	WAC
23	BK/Y	A/C power to clutch coil	PTAC
24	R	Vehicle power	VPWR

Wire Color Codes

Wire Color Abbreviations	Wire Colors
BK	Black
BR	Brown
DB	Dark blue
DG	Dark green
GY	Gray
LB	Light blue
LG	Light green
O	Orange
P	Purple
PK	Pink
R	Red
T	Tan
W	White
Y	Yellow

10

Performance Modifications

Although stock performance has been a joke since the mid-1970s, Ford introduced a new generation of performance engines in the late 1980s. The SHO engine is a dual ohc V-6 mounted in the Taurus. With 24 valves, this engine begins to rival those of the 1960s in terms of performance. In fact, cubic inch for cubic inch, it far exceeds some of the iron boat anchors of the "good old days."

Nearly twenty years have passed since the golden age of the Detroit performance car. For nearly two decades, concerns about emissions, fuel economy, and safety have condemned the enthusiast to either running late-model slug bait or rebuilding wrecking yard refugees. However, in the late 1980s and early 1990s, the late-model sleeper was again a realistic possibility. The manufacturers themselves had shown a renewed interest in performance, starting with the 5.0-liter Mustang. Companies that were performance names in the 1960s, along with many new companies, were hitting the market with performance parts.

One major difference exists between modifying engines back in the 1960s and modifying engines in the 1990s: emission laws! Different jurisdictions will have different mandates concerning emission control systems and what modifications are legal. Throughout the United States, it is illegal to remove or modify any emission control device on a car that will be licensed for street use. A small amount of latitude is,

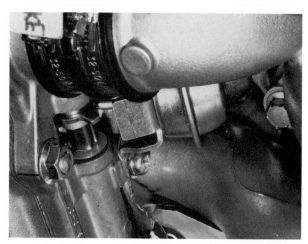

The manifold has two runners for each cylinder. A long set of runners provides good torque for acceleration off the line. At about 2200rpm, the ECA switches the manifold from the long runners to a short set of runners. The short set of runners provides high-end horsepower. The use of

this type of intake manifold configuration eliminates the compromise between torque and horsepower found in most engines. This vacuum valve controls which set of intake runners is used.

however, permitted in some states for the replacement of some components like intake manifolds, throttle bodies, and camshafts with specific tested and approved parts.

This chapter will therefore be divided into two major categories: street modifications and racing modifications. Please keep in mind that regulations and approvals change frequently when it comes to emission controls, so ask your parts supplier if a given modification is street legal in your jurisdiction. Do not accept what this book describes as a legal modification to be legal in your jurisdiction.

Street Performance

Any real increase in performance has to begin with an improvement in the engine's ability to breathe. The improvement of engine breathing can be divided into six categories:
Intake
Camshaft
Cylinder heads
Valve action
Exhaust
Fuel injection system

Intake

For street use, many of the modifications to the intake system that were traditional in the 1960s have already been done by the manufacturer when today's engine was designed. Any meaningful modification is going to be found either in the air cleaner and ducting to the throttle body or in the complete rethinking and reworking of the intake side of the engine, including throttle body, intake manifold, and valvetrain.

Let's begin by looking at what you already have on the car and what can be done to improve it. The example we are going to be looking at is the 5.0-liter Mustang.

Air Cleaner
The air cleaner for the Ford fuel injection systems is just one component in the total air induction system. Let's begin with a little mathematics relating to the air requirements of the engine. The air demands of the stock 5.0-liter Ford 302 engine can be estimated with the following formula:

$$\frac{\text{Cid}}{1,728} = \frac{302}{1,728} = 0.1748\text{cfd}$$

This formula converts cubic inches of displacement (cid) into cubic feet of displacement (cfd). It changes the standard measurement for engine size (cubic inches) into the standard measurement for airflow (cubic feet). The result of 0.1748cfd describes the volumetric change of all the cylinders as the pistons move through one complete engine cycle. Since all the engines that Ford uses are four-stroke engines, one engine cycle is represented by two revolutions of the crankshaft.

From this figure of cubic feet of displacement we can derive the cubic feet per minute (cfm) of air inhaled by the engine by multiplying the cubic feet of displacement by the maximum engine rpm we plan to run. We will then divide this number by 2, since each cylinder inhales air only on every other crankshaft rotation. For the purpose of discussing airflow, we will limit the rpm to 5250. Here is the formula:

$$\frac{\text{Cfd} \times \text{rpm}}{2} = \frac{0.1748 \times 5250}{2} = 459\text{cfm}$$

At 5250rpm, the maximum amount of air that can be pumped through the 302 is 459cfm. This figure is not realistic, however, because it assumes 100 percent volumetric efficiency. Thus, it assumes that each cylinder at this speed is capable of being completely filled with air up to atmospheric pressure each time the intake valve opens. As we work to improve the performance of the engine, we will be working to increase the volumetric efficiency ever closer to 100 percent. Keep in mind, however, that in spite of product claims of power increase and bolt-on horsepower, it is a violation of some of the basic laws of physics to expect more than 100 percent volumetric efficiency without pressurizing the combustion chamber with a supercharger or turbocharger. This limits the ability to increase performance simply by improving the intake system.

For a stock 302, it would be fair to assume an 80 percent volumetric efficiency. This means that the actual cubic feet per minute inhaled by our example engine will be lower than 459:

$$\text{Ideal cfm} \times 80\% = 459 \times 80\% = 367\text{cfm estimated actual}$$

Since the expected airflow through the engine is 367cfm stock, we must be able to flow at least this much through all the intake components just to avoid reducing power.

This beautifully chromed and virtually stock 5.0-liter Mustang engine has found itself in a performance role sitting in a 1940 Ford business coupe.

Air Cleaner Cover

The air cleaner on most cars is capable of flowing more than the actual airflow of the engine on which it is installed during normal operation. If the car is to be used under circumstances where maximum performance is required, such as racing or trailer towing, then the air cleaner assembly can become a restriction to airflow and therefore performance.

In the old days, people would flip the air cleaner lid upside down. Although the effects were largely psychological, doing so did bypass the snorkel tube of the air cleaner and increase the potential airflow. The design of fuel injection air cleaners does not make inverting the lid practical or desirable.

When the throttle plates are opened, the first thing that occurs is a sudden increase in the mass velocity of the air entering the intake manifold. Cruising at 2000rpm, our sample 302 is swallowing only about 140 cfm. When the throttle is matted, the demand suddenly jumps to a potential of 400cfm, and as the rpm climb, so will the demand. The more open and free flowing the intake system is ahead of the throttle plates, the faster the air mass will build and therefore the faster the torque will build.

A crude but effective method of increasing the airflow through the air cleaner is to trim the air filter lid so all the air filter is exposed and the airflow through the filter is unrestricted by the cover itself.

Air Filter

How do performance air filters differ from a standard air filter to the extent that power is noticeably improved? We need to begin with the premise that a stock air filter is designed to be easy and inexpensive to produce. The consumer who is not looking for performance is interested in reducing the cost of maintenance, and these "stock"-style air filters are designed to meet that need. A performance air filter sacrifices low price for airflow.

High-performance air filters are available through a number of sources. Technicians at Honest Performance like this unit from Hypertech. These filters provide excellent filtration and far better performance than the standard filter.

The high-performance air filter consists of multiple layers of cotton "gauze" that has been treated with a light oil. The oil attracts the dirt and dust particles, allowing the gauze element to have a more open weave and still have good filtering capability. Typically, the filtering element will be layered across a metal grid that holds the gauze in an accordion shape. As this accordion shape weaves its way back and forth, the frontal area for the passing of air into the engine is greatly increased. High-performance filters can result in a 25 percent increase in cfm through the filter. Keep in mind that a filter capable of flowing 500cfm will not increase performance significantly if it is mounted in an air cleaner assembly that will flow only 200cfm.

Some of the sales literature concerning performance air filters states that they are not legal for use on California pollution-controlled cars. The 1990 Bureau of Auto Repair (BAR) *Smog Check* manual states in appendix K that the air filter is a category 1 component. Category 1 replacement parts are not considered to be "of concern" as long as none of the emission control devices themselves are tampered with during the installation. Check with the shop that does your smog check about its interpretation of this rule, or contact your local BAR field office for a ruling.

These $50 filters are designed to be a lifetime replacement. They do need to be serviced regularly. A special solvent or cleaner that is sold removes road oil and dirt. You will find recommendations on the correct cleaners to use in the literature that comes with your new air filter. After cleaning, the oil barrier must be replaced. Using the wrong oil—penetrating oil and so forth—even though it looks right can reduce the efficiency of the air filter to the point where you would be better off with a stock filter. Again, follow the recommendations of the filter manufacturer. Plan on cleaning the air filter every time you change the oil. This may be a little more frequently than is really required, but it can't hurt.

Mass Airflow Sensor

Ford uses a Japanese-designed MAF sensor. In this Hitachi design, the "hot wire" sensing element is located in a bypass tube outside the main channel of airflow. Unlike most other MAF sensors, the one that Ford uses eliminates not only the airflow restriction created by the cooling fins but also the restriction of the sensing element itself—leaving, in effect, a big hollow tube for the air to pass through.

Throttle Body Assembly

The throttle body assembly holds possibly the most important potential for bolt-on improvement short of the intake manifold itself. Again, Ford spent much time and effort creating the tuned port system to be a good performer right off the showroom floor. As a result, any improvement in performance afforded by any of the techniques discussed here—including replacement of the throttle body—may be less likely to show up in the seat of the pants than it is on the quarter-mile. Even quarter-mile results might be disappointing to all but the most die-hard racer.

Big-bore kits are available from Air Sensors and others. These consist of a complete throttle body assembly that replaces the stock assembly. The Air Sensors version features a single large throttle plate replacing the small throttle plate pair in the stock unit.

Holley markets a wide range of CFI replacement units. These fall into two general categories: stock emission legal–street performance and street competition–nonemission.

Intake Manifolds

The stock "tuned" manifold is designed for peak performance; however, production tolerances are not such that perfection is always achieved. The tuned port manifold consists of a large central plenum box connected to the intake manifold base by individual tubes called runners. Some improvement in cfm can be achieved by matching the sizes and alignment of the plenum, runners, and manifold base. Matching the alignment of the plenums can be achieved by applying a light film of Prussian Blue to each end of the runner, installing the runner, and torquing the runner down. Removing the runner and inspecting the Prussian Blue contact point will show where the runners are misaligned. A more careful inspection will reveal where the runners are undersized or oversized compared with either the intake or central plenum. A die grinder and an ample supply of patience will enlarge the undersized orifices to match the larger. Do not get carried away; the sizes and shapes of the plenum, runners, and manifold are all basically correct.

After painstaking hours of work, you have gained only about 2hp or 3hp. You might say that it is hard to improve on what is basically a good design.

High-performance manifolds are available for the 5.0-liter engine from Edelbrock and others. These offer a rethinking of the basic Ford design as well as larger porting, improved runner matching, and improved runner flow angles. Overall improvement in performance may be disappointing, however, unless these manifolds are installed as a part of a complete performance upgrade.

Intake System Summary

Back in the 1960s, massive and noticeable improvements in performance could be effected through relatively minor and often inexpensive modifications. In those days, Ford's large brute engines had tremendous unlocked potential. The 429 had a flow rate potential of 521cfm although factory equipped with about a 650cfm carburetor (depending on the year and exact application, this varied). Installation of a carburetor with a greater flow rate would instantly unlock horsepower and torque hidden by the inability of the stock carburetor to fill the manifold with air quickly enough when the throttle was matted.

Today's cars have evolved from the 1960s through a period in the 1970s where anything and everything was done to maintain an acceptable level of performance while maintaining a legal emission level. During the late 1970s and early 1980s, the manufacturers began a quiet mutual challenge back toward performance. This time they did not have the luxury of simply bolting on a larger carburetor and dumping gallons of gas through the engine. As a result, today's intake systems are highly refined when they roll off the assembly line. A lot of work on the manifold without considering other engine, computer, and sensor modifications may yield disappointing results. Again, it's hard to improve on a good design.

Camshaft

The basic function of the camshaft is to open the intake valve as quickly, as smoothly, and as far as possible. The cam then leaves it open as long as possible to allow atmospheric pressure to push air and fuel into the combustion chamber. The camshaft —along with the assistance of the valve spring— must then begin to allow the intake valve to close in enough time for the combustion chamber to be sealed as the piston begins to move up on the compression stroke. Actually, the intake valve remains open for a short time as the piston begins to move upward on the compression stroke. Leaving the intake valve open briefly allows the velocity of the air traveling through the intake system to continue to cram air into the cylinder even as the piston begins to

Probably the single most effective performance modification is still the performance camshaft. The installation of the camshaft is more difficult, costly, and time-consuming than many people want to be involved with. In addition, the installation of performance-grind camshafts may violate local or federal law for street use. High-performance rocker arms and lifters, in conjunction with a performance camshaft, offer additional strength and performance.

move upward. This effect is even more pronounced on engines equipped with high-rise intake manifolds, such as on the MPI applications. This is why increasing the airflow potential beyond the capability of the engine's volumetric displacement will result in improved performance. Less restriction in the intake system will increase the cylinder charging capability.

The camshaft must also open the exhaust valve as far, as fast, and as smoothly as possible. The opening of the exhaust valve begins as the piston nears bottom dead center on the crank power stroke. This ensures that the exhaust valve will be completely open when the piston begins to move upward on the exhaust stroke. The camshaft begins to close the exhaust valve near top dead center; however, the exhaust valve remains open for a short time and the piston begins its downward travel. This does two things:

It takes advantage of the velocity of the exhaust gases exiting the combustion chamber to accelerate the incoming air-fuel charge. This increases the volumetric efficiency of the engine.

As the incoming charge is accelerated, some of the outgoing exhaust gases will be slowed, causing the exhaust gases to be left in the combustion chamber. From the perspective of performance, this is neither desirable nor efficient. It does, however, produce an EGR effect, causing combustion temperature to be lower and reducing the output of oxides of nitrogen.

Like the intake manifold, the 5.0-liter camshaft was designed by Ford with performance in mind. MPI minimizes the emission considerations in camshaft design, limiting them to performance and driving comfort. As a result, a significant performance improvement will come at a cost of low-speed–low-load drivability.

Several companies offer off-the-shelf camshafts for performance and economy. For obvious reasons, these performance cams are limited to the 5.0-liter. Designing a performance cam that will effectively increase torque and horsepower for an EFI engine is not a job for mere mortals. Changes in lift, duration, center line, and timing that have been infallible in the past can cause a loss of power, underfueling, and overfueling today. The reason is that changing the camshaft will change intake manifold vacuum (pressure) and airflow rates. These changes will affect the readings of the MAP and MAF sensors. Changes in the MAP or MAF sensor readings at a given rpm or engine load may cause undesired changes in air-fuel ratio and ignition timing. Crane Cams and others have lines of camshafts that have been designed specifically for use with EFI. Because of the research and development that has gone into these cams, it is unlikely that a custom-ground camshaft, unless it is ground by the best of the best, would work as well.

If you decide to perform a camshaft transplant, check with your supplier about how it will affect the street legality of your car. At the very least, consider that the increased valve overlap of a performance camshaft will tend to increase hydrocarbon emissions at idle. Since many states test emissions only at idle, installation may lead to emission test failure. The California BAR considers camshaft replacement—other than with a stock grind—to be an unacceptable modification.

Cylinder Heads

The stock 302 cylinder head may well be your single biggest candidate for improvement. The basic design of the 5.0-liter head dates back to the 1960s, and although improvements and upgrades have been made along the way, it remains a rather old piece of technology when compared with the cylinder head of an SHO or late-model Japanese engine.

To improve the cylinder head of the 5.0-liter engine, you have two good ways to go. Many aftermarket companies make performance cylinder heads ready to be bolted on and driven away. These heads sell for $500 to $1,000 but can provide the most noticeable change in performance of anything yet discussed. In most jurisdictions, these cylinder heads meet emission requirements with ease.

The second option is to modify the existing cylinder heads. You may prefer to have a machinist do this, for it requires a minimum of manual skill but a maximum of knowing what to do. Let's take a look at some of the basics.

Most people who get involved in a port-and-polish job do not have a good understanding of flow dynamics. The result is that many performance modifiers end up paying a lot of money or spending a lot of time to accomplish very little or even to decrease performance. The typical port-and-polish job consists of enlarging the intake and exhaust ports of the cylinder head and then polishing the enlarged surface to a high gloss. Although this may look impressive, the ports are basically large enough for the camshaft applications found in common street use and often the high-gloss shine reduces turbulence, which can actually decrease the ability of the fuel to remain atomized in the air-fuel charge and therefore reduce performance. By the same token, for most street applications, big valves can have an adverse effect on airflow in and out of the combustion chamber.

The area that needs the most work or concentration is the valve pocket. This is the area just in front of the valve in the cylinder head. The valve guide boss can restrict airflow, and on the stock 350 head, this boss is much larger than it needs to be. In addition, the casting ridges can be removed. Flatten and enlarge the radius where the air passage turns down toward the valve.

Shop around a little for a qualified performance machinist if you decide not to do the work yourself. As you look, remember that the best may not always have the biggest reputation in town, and who your buddy says is the best in town may not be. If performance is your goal, spend a couple of days at the local drag strip or circle track, and ask who has the most consistently fast car. Some of the fastest cars may not be consistent performers; inconsistency may be a clue that the performance comes from bells and whistles rather than quality workmanship. Once you have identified the consistent performers, find out who does their machine work. This is the person you want working for you.

Just pick up a copy of a popular hot rodding magazine and you will be bombarded with ads offering custom-built small-block Ford cylinder heads. These heads are just as valid for use on a 5.0-liter engine as they are for use on a carbureted engine. Most of them are well engineered and professionally done, making them well worth the money.

Valve Action

Remember, we are talking about street performance, and although we can do some tweaking such as to cylinder heads, camshafts, and intake systems, other performance parts do not justify their expense on street applications by improved torque or horsepower. One of these areas is in the valvetrain. Whereas valvetrain modifications can provide an all-out race car with a 0.1-second improvement in the quarter-mile, these improvements would only be seen between the ears on a street rod.

Valvetrain modifications include ratioed rocker arms, high-tech pushrods, performance lifters, and heavy-duty valve springs. Engine rebuilders disagree on the necessity of replacing these components when the camshaft is replaced. I feel that when a new piece of metal rubs with a force of up to 300,000psi against another piece of metal with only a thin film of oil in between and we are going to expect it to do this for 100,000 to 150,000 miles, I would prefer that the piece of metal the new piece is rubbing against also be new.

The bottom line is that if you decide to replace the camshaft, then spending a few extra dollars on high-performance valvetrain parts that should be replaced anyway makes good sense. Otherwise, put your money into areas where you can get more bang for the buck.

Exhaust

Back again in the 1960s, we saw a fascination among street enthusiasts with bigger pipes and freer exhaust flow. Today's stock exhaust systems are a far cry from the stock systems of those days. In spite of this, there is still room for improvement.

This improvement can begin with a set of headers bought over the counter with threads and fittings for the oxygen sensor and the air pump devices. Catalytic converters with high flow rates are also available. Be sure to check with local automotive emission officials concerning the legality of any exhaust modifications you are planning.

Past the catalytic converter, very few changes are not legal modifications in any state. Mufflers, connectors, and exhaust pipes are all fair game for the performance enthusiast. The only restrictions are related to noise.

Mufflers

Exhaust systems and their technology have come a long way since the muscle car days of the 1960s. Today's high-performance mufflers exceed the flow potential of even open headers.

Two things travel down the piping from the exhaust manifold: exhaust gases and sonic vibrations, or frequencies. The movement of the frequencies through the exhaust system tends to pull the exhaust gases along in much the same way that ocean waves pull a surfer to shore. The effect of the exhaust gases being pulled through the exhaust system helps to scavenge the cylinder, improving the breathing of the engine.

Back in the 1960s, several companies marketed the turbo muffler. This muffler was developed by Chevrolet to be used on the Corvair Turbo applications. It consisted of a hollow tube with fiberglass pressed against the sides to deaden sound. The problem with this was that as the sound frequencies entered the muffler, they were killed by the fiberglass packing, negating the "surfer" effect.

Today's high-tech performance mufflers are able to reduce sound without eliminating the surfer effect. Imagine for a moment that you are setting up a stereo in your living room. The only place you can find to put one of the speakers is in the center of the north wall. The only place you can find to put the other speaker is directly opposite the first on the south wall. The two speakers are facing each other squarely. The only place you can find to put your chair is exactly halfway between the two speakers. When the speakers are producing exactly the same sound, the frequencies being emitted will collide and cancel one another, creating a dead zone. Modern high-performance mufflers take advantage of this phenomenon. As the frequencies and exhaust gases enter the muffler, they are divided and sent in two different directions, only to be brought back together as they pass through the muffler. When they are brought back together, the identical frequencies that were split earlier collide and cancel each other, like those from the speakers. The end result is less sound without a loss of the surfer action.

Currently, mufflers such as these are being used on everything from road racers to sprint cars.

H-pipe Installation (on Custom Exhaust Systems)

Most exhaust systems have an area where the frequencies we have been discussing tend to build up and eddy the exhaust gases. To reduce this build-up on dual-exhaust systems, it helps to install an H-pipe between the two sides of the exhaust. Installing the

H-pipe in the wrong place, however, does more harm than not installing one at all.

To determine where an H-pipe is needed on your custom dual-pipe exhaust system, paint the area between the catalytic converters and the mufflers with black lacquer. Run the engine at 3200rpm for several minutes. Now inspect the painted area. Where the lacquer has begun to burn, or has burned the worst, indicates the place where the H-pipe needs to be installed. Install the pipe between the indicated hot spots in the two sides of the exhaust.

Fuel Injection System: Fuel Supply

Some of the easiest and least expensive performance modifications are those that can be made to the fuel supply system. Although the fuel pressure and injector flow rates are adequate under most driving conditions, significant horsepower and acceleration improvements can be gained. Again keep in mind that power comes from better handling of the air coming into the engine; it is easy to get more fuel into the engine.

Fuel Pressure

On the stock MPFI system, the fuel pressure is regulated at 35psi with no load on the engine. As the engine is put under a load, the fuel pressure increases in one step, jumping up to between 40psi and 45psi. Two types of fuel pressure regulators that are on the market can significantly improve power.

The first is an adjustable fuel pressure regulator. Dynamometer tests show that horsepower and acceleration improve with about a 20 to 25 percent increase in fuel pressure. While at the track with this unit installed, you will need to disconnect the oxygen sensor. When the ECA enters the closed-loop mode, the oxygen sensor would report the extra enrichment caused by the higher fuel pressure to the ECA. The injector pulse width would then be shortened, leaning the air-fuel ratio, defeating the benefits of the higher fuel pressure. Disconnecting the oxygen sensor will either keep the ECA from entering closed loop or deliver a neutral air-fuel ratio signal to the ECA if it does.

MicroDynamics of England builds a rising rate fuel pressure regulator. This unit is adjustable and accurately tracks manifold pressure to alter fuel pressure to meet engine demand precisely. Again, street legality is highly questionable, so you might want to save this modification for the track. The advantage of the rising rate regulator is gaining good top end performance without sacrificing a good idle. The U.S. price for the MicroDynamics rising rate regulator is about $300.

Other companies that market 45psi or adjustable regulators include Digital Fuel Injection of Farmington Hills, Michigan, and Hypertech of Memphis, Tennessee.

Changing fuel pressure is like changing a carburetor's float level: raising the float level a little can increase an engine's performance; raising it a lot can destroy an engine's performance. You will need to play around with it a little to determine the fuel pressure that is right for your engine.

So-called street-strip modifications give the best performance improvements when two or more are planned and executed together. Keep in mind that the power from an internal-combustion engine mostly comes from its ability to gulp, ignite, and expand air. Increasing the fuel pressure reaps its maximum reward when coupled with one of the engine breathing modifications mentioned earlier in this chapter. Again, it is easy to put in more fuel, but the power comes from more air, and more air is hard to put in.

Injectors

Different EFI applications use different injectors, and different injectors have different flow rates. The Chevy 350 uses an injector with a flow rate of about 22 pounds per hour (lb/hr). The 1989 Thunderbird SC 3.8-liter Super Coupe uses an injector that flows 32 lb/hr. At first glance, this might seem to be a favorable improvement, yet the end result of putting the Thunderbird injectors in the Corvette might well turn out to be the same as that of raising the float level too high on a carburetor. Injectors cost at least $30+; for a V-8, this means a minimum of $240 to replace the injectors, and a more realistic figure would be closer to $500. This investment would show almost no positive gain in performance and may cause drivability problems. Your money would be better spent in camshafts and recurving the distributor.

Required injector flow rates can be calculated using the following formula:

$$\text{Lb/hr} = \frac{\text{maximum hp} \times \text{brake specific fuel consumption}}{\text{number of injectors}}$$

The brake specific fuel consumption relates to the amount of fuel it takes to create 1hp. This figure is typically 0.45 on a normally aspirated engine and 0.55 on a turbocharged or supercharged engine.

Using a horsepower figure of 220 for a 3.0-liter SHO, the formula would look like this:

$$\frac{220 \times 0.45}{6} = \text{approximately } 16.5\text{lb/hr}$$

The formula for a highly modified turbocharged engine with a maximum horsepower of 500 would look like this:

$$\frac{500 \times 0.55}{8} = \text{approximately } 35\text{lb/hr}$$

An engine like this would require either an aftermarket fuel injection system or an alternative fuel source when operating under boost. To solve this problem, some performance modifiers have rigged the cold-start injector to energize when the turbo goes into boost. The problem with this is that the amount of additional fuel cannot be controlled accurately and not all applications you might be turbocharging have a cold-start injector.

MicroDynamics builds an electronically controlled auxiliary fuel injector for situations like this.

Fuel Injection System: Electronic Controls

The area with the greatest potential for cheap performance is the electronics of the injection system. Back in the old days—before 1980—any responsible performance specialist would accompany intake, engine, fuel, and exhaust modifications with changes in the timing advance curve as well as adjustments to the vacuum advance and power valve. Today, these adjustments are made by the computer as the car is being driven. The program in the computer does not determine initial timing; that is determined by the physical position of the distributor or by the crankshaft sensor. It does determine the amount of ignition advance based on coolant temperature, engine load, and rpm. In addition, the computer determines the amount of enrichment required by each of the above engine operating parameters as well as throttle position.

Since the computer plays such a dominant role in the control of two vital areas of engine performance—timing and load enrichment—any significant improvement in engine breathing must be accompanied by an improvement in the computer program. When Ford designed the computer program for the 5.0-liter EEC IV system, it had performance in mind, but it also had to deal with the Environmental Protection Agency (EPA). As a result, the program in the stock computer is a compromise between power, economy, and pollution. Compromises for the manufacturers are mandated to lean toward minimizing pollution and maximizing economy at the sacrifice of power.

Racing Performance

Three ways of overcoming the manufacturers' sacrifice of power are available when your car goes to the track:
Cheap tricks
Performance chips
Performance computers

Cheap Tricks

A lot of little racer's tricks have been rumored about since the late 1980s. Most of these involve dumping more fuel into the engine and are marginally effective at best. Here are several that show an appreciable improvement and are representative of the types of cheap tricks that are effective.

5,500-Ohm Coolant Sensor

Probably the least expensive and easiest performance modification is to replace the coolant tem-perature sensor with a 5,500-ohm resistor. Disconnect the ECT harness from the ECT sensor. Install the resistor across the terminals of the harness. The 5,500 ohms of resistance tells the computer that the engine is not quite warmed up yet. The computer will allow more advance, since it does not expect detonation when the perceived engine temperature is only about 150 to 160 degrees Fahrenheit. The net result is like that from recurving the distributor, rejetting the carburetor, and making power valve refinements. If you use this trick, its success will depend on the initial timing being adjusted properly and the fuel you are using being of good quality. If the car has poor-quality gas in it, the tendency for detonation increases. (Remember, the computer only believes that the engine is running cold; in reality, the engine is at operating temperature.)

Other systems may be affected by the installation of the 5,500-ohm resistor. For example, the torque converter clutch may be inhibited from operating with the resistor installed. On the 5.0-liter and other similar applications, torque converter lockup is inhibited at temperatures below 150 degrees Fahrenheit. Although this can improve performance by eliminating the bog inherent as the converter engages, prolonged operation without lockup can cause the internal temperatures of the transmission to increase, resulting in potential damage.

Some applications have no back-up coolant fan switch. As a result, the coolant sensor input is the only way the computer has of knowing when the radiator fan needs to be switched on. Leaving the 5,500-ohm resistor installed when you leave the track can result in severe engine overheating and damage.

This is an inexpensive but effective modification—about $0.19 will take care of two cars.

The power thermostat keeps the engine at 160 degrees Fahrenheit. The ECA sees the temperature of the engine at 160 degrees Fahrenheit and allows additional timing advance and a richer mixture. These performance improvements come at the cost of poorer fuel economy and higher emissions.

Power Thermostat

A double benefit for a power increase can come from installing a cold thermostat. A 160-degree-Fahrenheit thermostat will have an effect on the computer similar to that of the 5,500-ohm resistor, allowing additional advance and a richer mixture with the oxygen sensor disabled.

An added advantage is one that the resistor trick did not offer. The lower engine temperature results in less heat being transferred to the intake manifold. The lower intake manifold temperature causes the air in the intake to be heated less. The air remains denser and therefore capable of delivering more power. To a limited extent, you get some of the effect of a turbocharger without the expense.

The lower air charge temperature also serves to lower combustion chamber temperatures. This reduces detonation that would cause the TFI system to retard the timing, thereby reducing the power. The net result is more timing advance and therefore more power.

You might be wondering at this point why the manufacturers would not use a 160-degree-Fahrenheit thermostat as standard equipment if lower combustion temperatures would result. After all, lower combustion temperatures would result in a lower production of oxides of nitrogen. True as that may be, lower combustion temperatures result in a higher level of carbon monoxide and hydrocarbons being emitted. Again power is sacrificed to pollution.

Keep this in mind if you choose to install a cold thermostat. This simple operation may violate smog laws and may result in emission levels that are high enough to fail your smog test.

Remove the paper label over the end of the ECA and clip on electronic horsepower. This performance computer chip installs directly over the end of the ECA. When installed, a performance chips modifies the ECA program, allowing more timing advance and earlier enrichment during power demand.

Power Fan Switch

Along the same line of thinking and in conjunction with the colder thermostat is the low-temperature fan switch. The stock Ford radiator fan switch will turn the fan on at about 220 degrees Fahrenheit and off at around 180 degrees Fahrenheit. Intake manifold air density can be increased by installing a switch that turns the fan on at around 176 degrees Fahrenheit and off at around 166 degrees Fahrenheit.

On some applications, the cooling fan is controlled by the ECA. The only way to lower the fan cycling temperatures on these is to install one of the performance PROMs discussed under "Performance Chips" later in this section.

Manifold Absolute Pressure Sensor Delay Valve
(MAP Not Used on MAF Applications)

When the engine comes under a load, as happens when the car accelerates, manifold pressure increases (vacuum drops). The increasing manifold pressure signal from the MAP sensor causes the ECA to retard the timing to lower combustion temperatures, reducing detonation and the possibility of nitrous oxide.

Installing a short-delay vacuum delay device in the vacuum hose between the manifold and the MAP sensor can slow the increase in pressure to the MAP sensor and allow the timing to advance faster. The down side of this is that the MAP sensor also performs the power valve function for the ECA. If the car has too much delay, the air-fuel ratio will not enrich fast enough. The car will stumble or hesitate, defeating what you have tried to accomplish.

A good source for these delay valves is your local Ford dealer. Back in the late 1970s and early 1980s, these vacuum delays were a vital element in Ford's emission control program. A vacuum delay of about 1 second is about right. You may have to try several vacuum delays; for your car, slightly more or slightly less may do the trick. Basically, you want the delay to last no longer than the time it takes to move the throttle from the closed position to the wide-open-throttle position.

Sometimes, after going through the expense of trying several vacuum delays, you will find that none of them significantly increase power. It could be that to achieve what you are trying to accomplish, all that is needed is a restriction in the MAP sensor vacuum hose. Play around a little with vacuum line and electrical butt connectors.

Whether a butt connector or a vacuum delay is used, the beauty of them is that they can be installed and removed easily at the track.

Performance Chips

Imagine a day in the future when you can jump in your car, start the engine, back out of the driveway, and motor off quietly and smoothly to the racetrack. Once in the pits, you reach out to the instrument panel and throw a switch. The tame little kitten becomes a flame-breathing lion. Cam timing, lift, duration, and overlap have changed; the mixture has enriched to performance level and the distributor has been recurved. This is a picture of the future, all of which but the cam changes are here today.

Several companies make aftermarket computer calibration chips (or PROMs) for Fords. One of the most prominent is Hypertech.

These performance chips alter the event points of the ECA. They may do the following:

Alter the temperature at which the closed loop is entered (if at all)

Decrease the amount of manifold pressure required to enter the enrichment mode

Decrease the TP voltage needed to enter the enrichment mode

Accelerate the timing curve based on MAP and rpm increases

Recalibrate the activation of peripheral emission control devices such as the EGR, lockup converters, the CANP solenoid, and air pump switching

Where Ford leaned toward emissions and economy in its compromise with power, Hypertech and its competitors leaned toward performance.

These chips are probably the fastest and easiest route to a performance upgrade available for late-model Ford fuel-injected cars. To install an aftermarket performance chip, remove the ECA from the vehicle, remove the screws that hold the access cover on the side of the ECA, remove the ECA cover, and locate the calibration unit.

Note: Be careful of static discharge. Even a small zap can total the ECA.

Before removing the calibration unit, discharge any static electricity that may have built up in your body during the day. Radio Shack and similar stores sell grounding straps, which fit around the wrist and attach to a good ground. These wrist straps ground your body and prevent the build-up of static electricity. At an investment of less than $10, purchasing one of these is a good safety precaution.

After taking the appropriate precautions against static, carefully desolder the calibration unit.

Once the old chip is removed, inspect the socket on the mother board for damage and solder the new chip in place, being careful not to damage it.

Aftermarket chips come in three performance grades: street stock, performance modified, and competition. These chips are not California legal; they fall into category 3 of the BAR list of aftermarket parts. One company, Street Legal Performance, does market a California-legal performance-economy PROM.

Performance Computers

For total performance applications, companies like MicroDynamics, represented in the United States by Veloce Distributing of Seattle, offer custom-designed performance computers. These computers are available as either a replacement for the ECA or a piggyback add-on to the current ECA. These units offer little over the performance chip until major engine modifications such as turbocharging, high-compression pistons, and intake modifications demand it. On a standard street car where the owner is looking more for power improvements than for the ability to run the quarter-mile at warp speed, the performance chips are adequate.

Like a phoenix, a new breed of high-tech performance shops is rising from the performance ashes of the 1960s. Will the 1990s see the performance shop of that time, with coffee stains and beer bottles on the counter, replaced by a combination hot rod shop—latté bar?

11

Legalities of Engine Modification

Unlike most scientific regimens, the law has subtle twists, turns, and traps. This chapter is not intended to be legal advice; it is intended to point out some of the issues involved in the high-performance modification of late-model cars. The bulk of the information that follows came from California's BAR and the California Air Research Board (ARB). The laws on the books in many states are similar to those of California. California has the longest record of stringent enforcement, which is why I am using its information.

Three categories of replacement parts are recognized by the ARB.

Category 1

Category 1 items are not considered by the BAR or ARB to be of any concern as long as the required emission controls are not tampered with. Examples are as follows:

PCV air bleeds
Air cleaner modification
Air conditioner cutout systems
Antitheft systems
Blow-by oil separators and filters
Electronic ignition systems retrofitted to vehicles
    originally fitted with point-condenser systems, as
    long as the original advance controls are
    maintained
Engine shutoff systems
Ignition bridges and coil modifications
Throttle lockout systems
Intercoolers for original equipment of manufacturer
    (OEM) turbochargers
Undercarburetor screens
Vapor-steam-water injectors

Category 2

Category 2 addresses allowable replacement parts:

Headers on noncatalyst cars
Heat stoves for allowed headers
Intake manifolds for non-EGR vehicles that must
    allow for the installation and proper functioning
    of the OEM emission controls
Approved aftermarket catalytic converters
Carburetors marketed as emission replacements
Replacement fuel fill pipe restrictors
Replacement gas caps

You can see from this list that for catalyst-equipped fuel-injected cars, no performance replacements are allowable without type approval from the ARB. Today's cars are EPA inspected as an integrated system. Disturbing even the most minute portion of the emission control package would constitute a violation.

Category 3

Category 3 parts must have verification of acceptability. If you are replacing a part in category 3, ask for and retain a copy of the verification of acceptability for that product. It may prove handy later on, even if you live in an area that is not currently strictly controlled. Category 3 includes the following:

Carburetor conversions
Carburetors that replace OEM fuel injection
EGR system modifications
Replacement PROMs (computer chips)
Electronic ignition enhancements for computerized
    vehicles
Exhaust headers for catalyst vehicles
Fuel injection systems that replace OEM
    carburetors
Superchargers
Turbochargers

Resources

B&M Automotive Products
9152 Independence Ave.
Chatsworth, CA 91311

Competition Cams
3406 Democrat Rd.
Memphis, TN 38118

Edelbrock Corp.
2700 California St.
Torrance, CA 90503

Honest Performance
271 Ranier Ave. N.
Renton, WA 98055

Hypertech, Inc.
2104 Hillshire
Memphis, TN 38133

MSD/Autotronic Controls Corp.
1490 Henry Brennan Dr.
El Paso, TX 79936

OTC
655 Eisenhower Dr.
Owatonna, MN 55060

Veloce Distributing (MicroDynamics)
5003 S. Genesee St.
Seattle, WA 98118

Glossary

air mass—the body of air moving through the intake system

alternating current—a current whose magnitude and direction vary periodically

amp—basic unit of measurement for current flow

analog—relating to continuously variable voltages that change smoothly and without steps

BP—barometric pressure sensor

carbon dioxide—a gas resulting from complete combustion

carbon monoxide—a gas resulting from insufficient oxygen during combustion

CO—carbon monoxide

CO$_2$—carbon dioxide

digital—referring to electronic systems that operate by processing binary coded information

direct current—current that flows in a single direction and with a steady polarity

electrostatic discharge—the emission of high-voltage static electricity

ferrous—referring to metals with magnetic properties

frequency—the number of complete waveforms occurring during a given time, usually 1 second; commonly measured in hertz

Hall effect—the tendency of a magnetic field to alter or stop the flow of a current through a conductor

HC—hydrocarbons; unburned fuel resulting from the failure of the fuel in the combustion chamber to ignite

hydrocarbon—see HC

MAF—mass airflow sensor; used to measure the weight and volume of the air entering the intake system

MAP—manifold absolute pressure sensor; used to measure the pressure in the intake manifold

oxygen sensor—alternative term for the EGO or HEGO sensor

potentiometer—a resistor that varies output with mechanical movement

resistance—the tendency of a conductor to impede current flow; measured in ohms

self-induction—the tendency of a current to create a magnetic field to induce a voltage in itself when the current flow is cut off

sine wave—a waveform generated as a voltage slowly rises and falls

square wave—a waveform created as a voltage abruptly rises and falls

stoichiometric—the perfect mix of air and fuel

thermistor—a resistor that changes value as its temperature changes

volt—electrical pressure

Index

ACT sensor (Air Charge Temperature), 46, 84, 87, 122
Actuator circuits, 17
Air cleaner, 149-150
Air filter, 24, 64, 150
Air pump, 33
Air-fuel ratio, 23
Alcohol contamination, 25
Amps, 7
Analog voltmeter, 19

BAP (or BP) sensor (Barometric Absolute Pressure), 45

Carbon dioxide (CO_2), 30-31
Carbon monoxide (CO), 31
Catalytic convertor, 34
Combustion, 30
Compression, 23

Digital voltmeter, 18
Diode, 12
Distributor cap, 23, 24
Dwell meter, 20

ECA (Electronic Control Assembly), 8, 10-12, 14, 17, 25-27, 36-41, 43-58, 64-70, 156-157
ECA pin usage, 131-147
ECT sensor (Engine Coolant Temperature), 36-37, 46, 82, 120, 127
EEC (Electronic Engine Control system) I, 6
EEC (Electronic Engine Control system) II, 6
EEC (Electronic Engine Control system) III, 6, 36-42
EEC (Electronic Engine Control system) IV, 6, 43-71
EEC III quick test, 40
EEC III two-digit codes, 40-42
EEC IV STAR test (quick test), 71

EEC IV three-digit test codes, 110-112
EEC IV troubleshooting, 115-147
EEC IV two-digit test codes, 74-110
EGO sensor (Engine Gas Oxygen), 26 38-40, 43
EGR (Engine Gas Recycling) valve, 33, 56
EGR valve position sensor, 37-38, 51, 122
Emissions, 30-35

Fuel control assembly, 53
Fuel filters, 25, 59-60
Fuel lines, 67-68
Fuel pressure gauge, 20, 119, 154
Fuel pump, 59
Fuel tank, 58

HEGO sensor (Heated Exhaust Gas Oxygen), 44
Hydrocarbon (HC), 31

Ignition timing, 25
Ignition, distributor type, 28-29, 116-117
Ignition, distributorless, 29, 117-119
Injectors, 53-55, 61, 154

Kirchhoff's Laws, 8
Knock sensor, 50

MAF sensor (Mass Airflow), 50, 122, 150
MAP sensor (Manifold Absolute Pressure), 44, 122-123, 156
Microprocessors, 14
Multipoint injectors, 28

Nitrogen, oxides of, (NO), 31

Ohm's Law, 8
Ohmmeter, 19
Ohms, 7
Oscilloscope, low-voltage, 21

PCV (Positive Crankcase Ventilation) system, 33

PIP sensor (Profile Ignition Pickup), 48
Potentiometer, 11
Programmable Read-Only Memory (PROM), 14

Radio frequencies, 13
Random-Access Memory (RAM), 14
Read-Only Memory (ROM), 14
Resistor, 11
Road shock simulator, 21

Scanner, 21
Sensor circuits, 14-17
Sensors, 36-40, 43-52, 67-69
Sine wave, 9
Solenoids, 57-58
Spark plugs, 22-24
SPOUT connector, 25-26
Square wave, 9-10
Strain gauge, 12
Switches, 52-53, 63

Tachometer, 19
Test light, 19
Thermistor, 11
Throttle air bypass valve, 55
Throttle bore, 28
Tools, 18-21
TOT sensor (Transmission Oil Temperature), 86
TP sensor (Throttle Position), 37, 47, 121
Transistor, 12

Vacuum gauge, 21
Vacuum pump, hand-held, 20
VAF sensor (Vane Airflow), 49, 100-101, 121, 123
Volts, 7
VSS (Vehicle Speed sensor), 50

Watts, 7
Waveforms, 8